TO THE READER

You remember third grade vividly. You sit in a small circle. You are a member of one of the reading groups. The teacher sits with you as each of you in turn recites. You are a bit apprehensive as the teacher looks to you. She says "Next!" and it is your turn. You start a little shakey but gradually you gain confidence. At the end you are quite happy — even proud with your performance. You look to the teacher with anticipation.

"Next!"

You always felt a little uneasy about this experience. Somehow it left you feeling incomplete. And yet you remember it fondly because it was the end of the best of your learning years. Indeed, third grade marked the end of your positive learning curve. To be sure, you learned most of what you learned in school by the end of third grade. You wonder now.

"Why?"

Intervening in several third grade reading classes, we gave the teachers three cards. One said "happy," another, "sad," and the third, "angry." We asked only that the teacher use one of these three words in responding to the students. The students sat in their little reading groups. They gave forth their best efforts. The teachers responded in kind:

"You feel happy because you got all the words right."

The results were dramatic! Students given these simplest of responses made far greater gains in reading than students whose work effort was rewarded by the traditional, "Next!" And not all of the responses were "happy" responses. But all were tailored to the learner's unique experience.

"You feel sad because you still can't get those words."

Sometimes we feel sad because we can't always find the right words to communicate our understanding. Hopefully, these two images capture the findings of the National Consortium for Humanizing Education (NCHE). NCHE was comprised of a group of concerned people — teachers, administrators and parents — committed to transforming the public school classroom into a humane environment which promotes real student growth. Many children — especially minority children — go through an entire educational experience without ever having been responded to accurately! No one ever hooked them up with the teaching program. It is no wonder that they are unable to learn from people who are unable to communicate with them. The words of one of our forgotten children provide a capsule summary of one of our conclusions:

"Kids don't learn from people they don't like."

More than 500 teachers and administrators and 10,000 students in both urban and rural settings participated in the NCHE. Both teachers and administrators were trained in specific teaching discrimination skills (Flanders and Bloom scales) and specific interpersonal communication teaching skills (Carkhuff Model). Among other things, teachers learned how to respond to their students' experiences. The communication skills training paid off in high attendance, greater achievement and far fewer discipline problems. And that's what the results of the NCHE are really all about — teaching teachers to pay attention to kids, to understand them, to respond to them, to get through to them, to deliver their content. Giving people the skills they needed to communicate the liking they already felt for kids. And helping the kids to learn and grow.

Kids do learn from people they like.

KIDS

don't learn from people they don't like

David N. Aspy, Ed.D.
& Flora N. Roebuck, Ed.D.

Publishers of **Human Technology**

22 Amherst Road, Amherst, Massachusetts 01002
(413) 253-3488

International Standard Book Number: **0-914234-85-4**
Library of Congress Number: **77-71040**
First Printing — July, 1977
Second Printing — July, 1978
Third Printing — June, 1979
Fourth Printing — December, 1983

1.5, 1, 1.5

KIDS don't learn from people they don't like

TABLE OF CONTENTS

SECTION II LEARNING FROM RESEARCH

SECTION III LEARNING FROM PROGRAMS

SECTION IV REFERENCES

ABOUT THE AUTHORS

Dr. David N. Aspy is Executive Director, National Consortium for Humanizing Education. Formerly Distinguished Professor of Education at Texas Women's University. Dr. Aspy is the author of six books on education, including *"Toward a Technology for Humanizing Education,"* and more than 60 articles on teacher training and learner achievement.

Dr. Flora N. Roebuck is Assistant Professor of Medicine, Johns Hopkins University, Washington, D. C. and Associate Director, National Consortium for Humanizing Education. She has lectured extensively in the United States and Europe and has published more than thirty articles on humanizing education.

Almost from the beginning of any recorded writing, humans have searched for something greater than food, clothing, and shelter. To those diligent, few observers who took the time to reflect, and the effort to write and share with others, we are deeply indebted. They provided us with the prologue for a better tomorrow.

It is easy to forget that homosapiens are at best relatively new inhabitants on this planet. Their actions of the past can be studied to some degree through reading, visiting ruins, or uncovering relics of the past. This type of work is painstaking. One can devote all of a lifetime and only **hope** to add another insight to increase our knowledge.

Not too long ago, during the eleventh and twelfth centuries, some people began to question how they could live a better life. When this was put in the form of questions to several of the leading universities, the people got only one response: "Our concern is to study the hereafter, not what is happening now." Probably this was the first major effort toward humanizing living for more than the selected few of the ruling class.

Old values began to change and new values emerged. The movement was slow and did not happen everywhere at once. Many of the values were couched in the religions of the time and many wars were fought under the guise of these values.

By 1900, the industrial revolution began to have a major impact on how people viewed themselves. True, there was a lot of manual labor, but an increasing number of people in the United States now had more leisure time. In spite of two major world wars and two undeclared wars the search accelerated.

In the late fifties the Russians shocked the United States by launching a Sputnik into space. Suddenly everything we thought was good came under attack. Education did not escape. Indeed, it came under the heaviest attack because the schools were not producing either the caliber of scientists or a general population with science literacy. Absurd? Of course. How could such an illiterate group of citizens respond so nobly by having humans walking on the surface of the moon in only one decade?

During the 1960's and the early part of the 1970's, our country was almost ripped apart by two major crises: an increased fight for civil rights for humans, and a cancerous war in Vietnam. Little did we expect what was yet to come. Eventually the dam burst and we were emerged in Watergate, and now an energy crisis. Obviously it is much too soon to know what the real events were or are going to be. One thing did happen that was of major significance. Individuals began to examine their own being. Morals, values, ethics, and many "off-beat" types of "psychology" have erupted with the force of a volcano in the last ten years.

Personally, I can vividly recall the trauma of introducing humanizing learning as a major program component. We had been conducting a major field test using instructional materials designed to individualize learning in the elementary school. As the schools increased in number, it became apparent that we had to do more than the normal types of social science research. A team of researchers, using a modified Flanders system, went to work. Interactions were recorded among teachers and students in a variety of ways. All the measures used led us to believe that little or no transfer of learning was taking place. As teachers moved from the individualized setting to a conventional class, no skills of individualization were carried over.

Of course, this was frustrating, and being somewhat stubborn, our staff said, "Why don't we take a look at other measuring instruments?" We collected, synthesized, analyzed, and finally published a fifteen volume set called **Mirrors For Behavior**. Perhaps a quote from those works will serve to share with you our thoughts. "Interestingly enough, observation instruments may be gaining much slower acceptance in the public schools than in such diversified fields as medicine, business schools, large corporations, and theology."

Complexities that were present in 1967 became more complex in 1970. Then came the major breakthrough we were looking for. We had been questioning whether the processes used in observation instruments can themselves be used to form a new content for learners. The answer was yes, and humanizing learning was born. Paradoxically, the schools were under heavy attack for failing, but at the same time these schools were expected to solve the social problems of the day.

Asby and Roebuck know these experiences. They have walked the miles necessary by speaking and working with teachers and learners. They discovered that it is difficult to remain a stranger in a human research environment.

With overwhelming research data, the authors have clearly shown that **teacher's interpersonal skills do make a difference in student's learning**. Using a variety of recognized and accepted instruments, Aspy and Roebuck have conducted the most important research and demonstration study of the differential effects of teacher training programs generated by the work of Bloom, Flanders and Carkhuff. This book will be the cornerstone for tomorrow's educational systems.

Aspy and Roebuck have succeeded in maintaining the principles of scientific investigation under the most difficult conditions. They have seen the tragedy as well as the best of American education. One feels their struggle of trying to maintain the role of researcher without becoming too friendly with the subjects.

It is important to remember that any school will only be as good as the people of the community want it to be. If humanizing learning is going to succeed, the prerequisite skills must be taught. Every classroom should have genuine "homeric laughter" as a requirement.

April, 1977.

James W. Becker, Executive Director
National Foundation for the
Improvement of Education

PREFACE

Consider two images. In the first a very young boy and girl stand together, clutching each other with one hand and lunchboxes with the other. Eyes round and lips slightly parted, they look as though they were at the start of some impossibly long, impossibly exciting adventure. And so they are − for today is their first day of school.

Now the second image: the same two children some 10 or 12 years later. Long since grown beyond the stage where they thought of school as a source of wonder or excitement, their only concern now is to make the deadly hours pass as quickly as possible. The boy has traded his lunchbox for a modest supply of drugs and a hip sneer that lets the world know just what he thinks of it. The girl has exchanged her lunchbox for a dazzling variety of roles from "slinky sexpot" to "sincere scholar," any of which she can slip into as the need arises. Education, they have found, is not an adventure at all. Rather, it is a constant struggle between "them" and "me" to see who will give in first.

What has happened here? The transformation is as dramatic as it is depressing. What is going on in our schools today that might cause such a shift? And what if anything can we do to see that the positive energy, enthusiasm and capacity for growth that are manifested by the very young are not leeched from them by the very process of education itself?

The book which you are holding represents the culmination of more than 10 years of work to answer such questions on the part of concerned educators all across the country. The National Consortium for Humanizing Education (NCHE) was precisely that − a group of people committed to transforming the public school classroom into a humane environment which promoted real student growth and capability. The results of the National Consortium's research and training programs will be of significant interest to any individual − teacher-educators and administrators, teachers and counselors, parents and community leaders − whose concern for children in our schools goes beyond the merely theoretical to the truly practical.

It is our belief that, in establishing the critical importance of certain teaching skills, such as interpersonal skills, and the feasibility of training teachers in these skills, the results of the National Consortium may have a more profound effect on tomorrow's educational system than any development in recent history!

The text is presented in four sections. In Section I we give a narrative account of the background and development of the National Consortium, our summary of the literature, our own preliminary pilot studies using modifications of Flanders' Interaction Analysis, Bloom's Taxonomy of Educational Objectives and Carkhuff's Interpersonal Process Scales, the development and implementation of the National

Consortium's research and training programs, the results of these programs and the implications which these results have for education today. Each chapter in Section I is preceded by an overview of the information in that chapter. The basic conclusion of all this work is this: the systematic teacher training program in interpersonal skills (Carkhuff Model) is the most effective way to train teachers to facilitate student learning and reduce behavioral problems.

Section II presents a Research Summary — a hard-nosed look at the specific research studies which we undertook and the data which emerged from these studies. Anyone suspecting that the National Consortium was just another collection of nice-but-nebulous educators engaged in interesting-but-informal speculation may find the presentation of material in Section II particularly meaningful. The fact is that we felt our over-riding purpose to be far too important to risk by reaching for hasty generalizations or insufficiently-supported conclusions.

Section I, then, tells the story while Section II fills in the essential facts. Section III is where the reader will be able to look over the basic technological "tools" which we employed (e.g., the separate instruments developed by Flanders, Bloom and Carkhuff) as well as sample modules used to train teachers in the use of these "tools."

Section IV contains the references and bibliography for this research.

We were and are committed to moving education beyond where it has been rather than seeing it continue to pursue the same closed circle of fruitless activity which it has in the past. We were and are concerned with people — with their potential to grow and to help others to achieve similar growth. Perhaps for this reason our minds still retain a host of bright, sharp people-images:

Tom Shuler, shouting for joy when he received a letter verifying the **Times Picayune's** acceptance of his story about the Consortium;

Martha Willson, explaining the details of endless forms to the entire staff who listened only vaguely or not at all;

Linda Sadler, starting the metronome and saying, "Mark... ...mark..." as she trained the raters to score the audiotapes for Flanders' Interaction Analysis;

Shirley Lamm, counting and tabulating and inventorying myriad audiotapes, computer tapes and related forms;

Clara Smith, saying, "Good morning, this is the National Consortium" to dozens of phone callers and then returning to her typing without a break in her stride;

Drs. Dan Kratochvil and Hadley and Vicki Williams who doggedly trudged to the different school systems around the country in order to conduct teacher training programs.

Dr. David H. Berenson who served as educational consultant to the Consortium and helped us set up and apply many of the programs which we developed.

The patient, patient raters, putting on their headphones to listen to the mountain of audiotape recordings of teaching before scoring them for various research scales;

Teachers asking questions, making suggestions and working at the various training tasks;

O. B. Adams, smiling and shaking his head at the naive conversations around him yet letting everyone know in subtle ways that he would support the Consortium in ciritcal moments just because he believed it was generally right;

and, last in order but first in our minds, the students in the schools — fat kids and skinny kids, smiling and weeping, clamoring for attention and drifting off into private fantasies, kids who might someday make it on their own and kids who would never make it unless someone opened up their private sky and let a little sun shine in.

People. Those who worked with us and those others who always seemed to be working against us. Those whom we taught and those who taught us. From beginning to end, the National Consortium was a "people" project. We learned from each other as much as we learned from our work. This book presents the fruits of our learning.

For the support of much of our research efforts we are indebted to a grant from the National Institute of Mental Health, NIH Research Grant # PO 1MH19871, United States Department of Health, Education and Welfare.

In addition, we owe a special debt of gratitude to David V. Rowland and F. Jack Zigon for their extensive editing efforts in putting the final manuscript together.

With the learnings from the National Consortium's Studies, we can move beyond the destructive bickering over ideologies and approaches. We can deliver to teachers the specific interpersonal skills which make the difference between effectiveness and impotence. And in doing so, we can realize the aim which all of us have nourished for so long: to turn our schools into humane, decent places where children learn what they need to know in order to go beyond our own limitations and live fuller, richer and more constructive lives tomorrow.

March, 1977   DNA

Washington, D. C.   FNR

Dedication

To our students and our teachers —
may they one day be the same.

SECTION ONE

OVERVIEW

The National Consortium for Humanizing Education came into being through the efforts of a group of concerned educators from across the country — educators committed to the pursuit and development of specific ways in which individual teachers and administrators could transform the public school classroom into a humane environment which promoted real student growth.

CHAPTER ONE — Having selected Flanders' Interaction Analysis, Bloom's Taxonomy of Educational Objectives and Carkhuff's Interpersonal Process Scales as our basic "tools," **we conducted preliminary investigations which indicated that certain facilitative interpersonal skills used by teachers did facilitate student growth.**

Funded for a three-year period of study, the National Consortium worked to test two broadly-stated hypotheses: (1) that **teachers and administrators could be trained in large numbers to increase the levels of facilitative teaching skills** which they used in their schools; and (2) that **increases in such facilitative skills would be accompanied by positive pupil changes on indices of both mental health and cognitive growth.**

The subjects comprising the National Consortium's experimental and control groups included over 500 teachers and 10,000 students in both rural and urban school settings.

CHAPTER TWO — Following thorough pre-testing of all participants, **teachers and administrators were trained in specific verbal discrimination skills** (Flanders and Bloom) **and specific interpersonal communication skills** (Carkhuff). The effects of training were monitored in a variety of ways including audiotapes submitted regularly to trained raters.

The results which emerged from this three-year period of training and research were as hopeful as they were dramatic.

CHAPTER THREE — It was found that **educators could in fact be trained in large numbers in both discrimination and interpersonal communication skills**; and it was further found that **the interpersonal components of such training did result in positive and statistically significant changes in student attendance, student achievement and student self-concept.**

The National Consortium's findings have profound implications for all of us who are truly concerned with and committed to the individual and constructive growth of our students.

CHAPTER FOUR

For one thing, **there can be no separation of "humanistic" and "skills" concerns in education. Only those teachers trained in specific interpersonal communication skills can make good their delivery of specialty or subject skills to students. Teachers who cannot employ interpersonal skills will invariably have a retarding rather than a "neutral" effect upon their students.**

As outlined and documented here, the work of the National Consortium dispels any lingering doubts about the critical need for interpersonal skills in the public school classroom. Education today is still torn by theoretical conflicts between "values" and "skills," "learning" and "training." Education tomorrow must reconcile and synthesize these warring factions — for in the end there can be no values without the skills needed to live them, no learning without the effective teaching that makes such learning possible.

OVERVIEW

We begin this chapter by explaining the way in which our own past experiences prompted our concern with facilitative teaching skills - and the way in which our values served to focus this concern on the individual student. All that we had seen and done as professionals in the field of education seemed to indicate that some critical ingredient was missing from the overwhelming majority of public school classrooms.

We began our collective effort by conducting a thorough review of the relevant literature. Our aim in doing so was to find evidence which either supported or contradicted the contention that learning is enhanced when the teacher provides high levels of the interpersonal dimensions of empathy, congruence and positive regard. In essence, we wanted to know what happens in the classroom when the teacher is able to show the students that he or she really likes them, understands them and wants to help them.

Mapping our own campaign, we selected three "tools" for our use: Flanders' Interaction Analysis, Bloom's Taxonomy of Educational Objectives and Carkhuff's Interpersonal Process Scales. These tools were, to be sure, all designed to do different things in the classroom as their descriptions indicate. However, together these "tools," we felt sure, would enable us to determine some of the critical sources of teaching effectiveness in the classroom.

We conducted a number of small-scale preliminary studies over a period of several years. The net result was a good deal of initial evidence strongly suggesting that students experiencing high levels of facilitative interpersonal conditions did indeed fare better in our school systems than students experiencing low or retarding levels of these same conditions. More specifically, we were able to confirm in tentative fashion a positive and significant correlation between interpersonal skills used by the teacher and student attendance, I.Q. increases, cognitive growth and enhanced self-concept.

A related aspect of our preliminary work involved training small numbers of teachers in interpersonal skills. The results were most encouraging. We found strong initial support for the contention that teachers can be trained to provide higher levels of facilitative interpersonal conditions. We were ready to go ahead with plans to establish the National Consortium.

THE EFFECTIVE INGREDIENTS OF TEACHING

Linda was a beautiful child in my fourth grade class. Linda did not know that she was "retarded." She only knew that it took her longer than many of the other children to master a task. Possessed of a natural cheerfulness and a very real degree of self-confidence, her approach to any problem was to keep trying until she "had" it. Having struggled and succeeded at last, her marvelous smile invariably became a beam of pure joy.

I enjoyed working with Linda and her unfailing cheerfulness made her a favorite of the other children even though this was her first full year in the school. Her achievement tests, administered the year before shortly after she had transferred to the school, indicated that she was more than two years below grade level. We worked hard to "catch her up;" and Linda's joy in each new skill she mastered was beautiful to see and share. When the achievement results from her latest tests came back in early May, I was pleased to find that she had made one-and-a-half years of progress during that school year.

My pleasure was short-lived, however. Only two days after the tests came back, the principal called me to his office. He told me that he had arranged a conference with Linda's parents and that he would like me to help him explain to them why Linda was going to be retained in the fourth grade.

My mouth fell open in astonishment. "But I'm not going to fail her! She's done well this year — made more than a year's progress. I plan to pass her to the fifth grade!"

The principal calmly explained that it was the school system's policy to retain any child who scored below grade level for two years in a row. No exception would be made for Linda. Eventually realizing that none of my protests were having the slightest effect, I consoled myself with the thought that things might still turn out all right. But they did not.

The next Fall I saw Linda occasionally in the halls, in the lunchroom and on the playground. As hard as I tried to pretend that everything was all right, I could not escape the plain and observable fact of her deterioration. As the year wore on, Linda became increasingly silent and withdrawn, her smile coming less and less often. Eventually Linda's teacher for this second year in fourth grade confided her worries to me:

"Linda's always been slow. But now she's slowing down even more! She doesn't seem to have any enthusiasm left for school. And she doesn't seem willing any more to try to do anything new!"

The system had won its point — but at the expense of the individual. In losing her self-confidence, her ability to see herself as a capable person, Linda had been deprived of her single greatest asset.

3   The lesson for all of us was clear: any system which cannot or will not adjust to and meet the needs of every individual becomes a destructive system. Somehow a way had to be found to create a system which gave the Lindas the time they needed to do their own growing at their own pace.

Not all of our experiences were negative or depressing ones by any means. As a matter of fact, we found that if joy and real growth abound anywhere it is in those places where children live and work. This was particularly true of a nursery school in Florida which we visited one beautiful spring day. We watched a group of some 20 children move eagerly and easily through their day. They seemed to find two specific activities to be sources of tremendous pleasure.

At one point the teacher asked, "How many would like to paint?" Twenty small artists donned big shirts and started painting with gusto. After a few minutes, each child showed her or his picture to the class and said whatever he or she wanted to say about it. A little later the same teacher asked if anyone wished to dance to some music. The 20 small artists quickly turned themselves into dancers. It was almost overwhelming to see their ecstasy as they danced "big," "ugly," "strong" and "pretty."

Twenty children — each unique in the way he or she danced and painted yet all made one by their common joy at simply being alive and having a chance to grow. The sounds of this joy rang in our ears and minds long after we returned from Florida. One day during an in-service meeting of about 20 elementary school teachers, I talked about our experience in the Florida school. Then, without having planned to do so, I asked the teachers how many of them would like to paint or dance. Not surprisingly, no one wanted to do either — not even the art and music teachers in the group. The contrast with the children in Florida was clear. Something had been lost in growing up or getting educated — and I couldn't help feeling that this "something" had to be very important to all of us who wished to become full human beings.

Two experiences — one almost wholly negative, the other a study in contrasts. Two experiences out of many hundreds shared not only by those of us involved in developing the National Consortium for Humanizing Education but by all people professionally involved with children as learners. Needless to say, we do not relate these experiences here in any effort to pinpoint sources of difficulty in our school systems. Rather, we begin by sharing the experiences in order to indicate in the most general terms the direction taken by our initial concern. We were — and are — committed to the individual growth of individual people. We were — and are — convinced that many "systems" of education have the potential to facilitate such individual growth yet all too often function in such a way as to profoundly retard the individual child's ability to realize and sustain such growth. In short, our experiences helped us to catalyze and express those values which informed our initial work in developing the Consortium.

Life is, for most of us, an unending series of choices between various alternatives. Thus we are invariably most effective when we are able to decide prior to any period of action how each alternative may be affected by – and may in turn affect – our own personal values. In other words, we must be able to decide what we want out of life in general and each situation in particular if we are to make the most of those opportunities presented to us. Our experiences helped us to focus our energies in terms of the Consortium by making it possible for us to formulate our values in clear and positive terms. From the outset we were able to state the following values in unequivocal terms:

1. People are the most important part of our existence.
2. Each individual human life is important.
3. The joy of challenge supercedes the agony of struggle.
4. Optimism is a necessary if not a sufficient condition for success.
5. Both internal and external data are important.

In retrospect, we can see now that each of these values made a specific contribution to our thrust in creating the Consortium. The first two ensured that our commitment to the individual, whether alone or in a group, would never be sacrificed in the name of some elusive, unyielding "system." The third value made it possible for us to risk a great deal in the face of quite considerable discouragement. The fourth value affected our selection of people with whom to work and theories to consider. And the fifth value, mandating the treatment of both science (external facts) and phenomenology (internal experience) as significant sources of data, enabled us to avoid the pitfalls of orthodoxy, whether of the "let 'em hang loose" or the "train 'em up tight" school of thought.

From the beginning, then, our efforts were motivated by a wealth of common experiences and given direction and focus by a number of specific and shared values. Beyond this, we were agreed that, while some individuals and systems could and did facilitate the meaningful growth of children, far more seemed caught up in activities which resulted in the retardation of just such growth. As we saw things, each teacher and administrator was faced with the choice between accepting a random cycle of positive and negative outcomes or intervening effectively in order to increase the probability that their schools would facilitate student growth more frequently than retard this growth.

Growth: the term suggests so many directions and dimensions that the incautious person may get bogged down before he or she is hardly started. As educators, we were able to focus our initial concern on those two areas traditionally associated with student growth: the domains of affective and cognitive development. Children grow emotionally and they grow intellectually. Needless to say, these two areas have long been recognized as inter-dependent rather than discrete or isolated from one another. Our future work, we knew, could not focus on one at the expense of the other. Yet our experience and values together predisposed us to look initially to the areas of affective growth. Far less work had been done in promoting students' affective development than in codifying and promoting their cognitive achievement. Here, we decided, was a starting point.

The next thing we had to do was begin to gather some facts by undertaking a careful review of the pertinent literature. The facts we were looking for would have to provide us with some answers, however tentative, to the most basic question of all: what is really important in promoting students' individual growth?

THE TEACHING INGREDIENTS

Like all investigators of educational materials, we began with an initial "set." In our case, the set had been provided some time earlier by Carl Rogers. While Rogers is most widely recognized as the founder of client-centered counseling, it may well be that his most important contribution from a research point of view has been his delineation of three factors which he thought were related to all human learning situations. Specifically, Rogers contended that learning is enhanced when the counselor (teacher) provides high levels of empathy (E), congruence (C) and positive regard (PR) (Rogers, 1957). Paraphrased in terms more immediately appropriate to an educational setting, Rogers' formulation becomes "The higher the levels of understanding, genuineness and respect a teacher gives to students, the more the students will learn." Thus Rogers provided us with exactly what we were looking for: a testable hypothesis concerning the specific ways in which affective and cognitive development were linked. We set out to learn what the literature had to say about the role of empathy, congruence and positive regard in the contemporary classroom.

Empathy

In the simplest terms, empathy involves one individual's ability to perceive and understand another person's inner world of private and personal meaning. Our review of the literature pertaining to empathy indicated that there was a consensus among many writers. More specifically, there was general agreement on the need for some measure of empathy as an ongoing and dynamic force; on the difference between cognitive (predictive) understanding and communicative (interactional) empathy; on the positive relationship between teacher levels of empathy and student attitude; and on the need for further investigation of empathy within the classroom situation. In short, we found neither startling support for nor damning denial of Rogers' link between empathy and learner achievement. Instead, we found just enough to make us want to learn more. We next turned to the literature congruence.

Congruence

As indicated above, congruence really means geniuneness: the degree to which an individual's words and actions accurately reflect her or his real feelings and attitudes. Unfortunately, we found that relatively little work had been done concerning the role and importance of congruence in the classroom.

Reviewing the literature concerning genuineness or congruence in the classroom, we were consistently struck by one fact: despite the feeling by most people that congruence is an important teacher characteristic, relatively little had been done to assess the real impact of such congruence — or the lack of it — on student performance. Once again, little or no hard data could be brought to bear upon the Rogerian hypothesis with which we had begun. Necessarily suspending judgment, we went on to review that body of literature related to the importance of positive regard.

Positive Regard

For the most part, positive regard is used as a construct in educational research only by those investigators specifically concerned with implementing the theoretical models developed by Rogers. As employed by Rogers, however, positive regard is closely allied to warmth — a term used quite widely by a number of investigators. Thus we broadened the scope of our own research to include studies dealing with warmth.

By now the pattern had become a familiar one. Our review of the literature concerning unconditional positive regard or warmth revealed a considerable degree of general agreement. The consensus seemed to be that warmth had yet to be defined in any satisfactorily precise manner, that students may respond differentially to warmth, that the impact of teacher warmth upon specific student achievement had not been adequately defined and that a need existed for closer examination of the role of warmth or positive regard in the classroom.

Quite clearly, our review of the pertinent literature did not provide instant and complete support for the Rogerian hypothesis with which we began. Nor did this review undermine the hypothesis. Instead, we were left with two simple and yet vastly exciting conclusions: most investigators seemed to feel that the affective dimensions of empathy, congruence and positive regard were potentially important; and no one had really initiated and carried out the type of research evaluation that we found ourselves planning.

OUR TOOLS

As indicated earlier, we had identified three key dimensions of interpersonal functioning that appeared to be critical. Now we needed tools which we could use in assessing the role of teacher interpersonal functioning in the classroom. The three most important such tools were Flanders' Interaction Analysis, which categorized classroom interactions between teachers and students; the Metfessel, Michael and Kirsner Instrumentation of Bloom's Taxonomy of Educational Objectives, which classified cognitive content; and Carkhuff's Interpersonal Process Scales for evaluating individual levels of teacher interpersonal functioning in relation to students. While these tools were intended for different purposes, we felt they were the best available tools for factoring out the dimensions of teaching effectiveness. We will preface our report on several prototypic investigations by reviewing only the essential elements of these three tools. A more detailed outline of the Flanders and Bloom instrumentation is presented in Section III, along with the most recent version of Carkhuff's Scale for assessing Interpersonal Skills.

The Flanders scale was employed in all those studies where we needed to keep close track of specific modes of interaction between teacher and students. As shown in Figure 1, this system allows the

TEACHER BEHAVIORS

INDIRECT	1.	Teacher accepts student's feelings.
	2.	Teacher praises student.
	3.	Teacher accepts or uses student's ideas.
	4.	Teacher asks question.
DIRECT	5.	Teacher lectures.
	6.	Teacher gives direction.
	7.	Teacher criticizes.

STUDENT BEHAVIORS

8. Predictable student response to teacher question.
9. Student-initiated response.

MISCELLANEOUS

10. Silence or confusion.

Figure 1. Flanders' Interaction Analysis showing
ten categories of teacher and student verbal behavior.
(See also Section III.)

investigator to discriminate between "indirect" and "direct" verbal behaviors on the part of teachers. Generally speaking, our use of the Flanders system involved training raters to evaluate audiotapes (in some cases supplemented by videotapes) of in-class interactions. Raters listened to three-second taped segments of interactions, decided which of the Flanders categories best described the interaction during that three-second period and recorded the appropriate number for this category. Thus we could quantify a full-length class in terms of precisely what was being said during any single three-second segment.

We were, of course, quite concerned with evaluating outcomes as well as processes — and particularly those outcomes related to levels of student cognitive development. One obvious way to measure such outcomes involved keeping track of student scores on standardized achievement tests. Such tests, however, frequently emphasize cognitive gain as a function of simple memory or recognition. The Metfessel, Michael and Kirsner Instrumentation of Bloom's Taxonomy allowed us to measure student attainment of levels of cognition beyond memory and recognition. Figure 2 provides an overview of the six categories and

1.00 KNOWLEDGE OF
- 1.10   Specifics
- 1.11   Terminology
- 1.12   Specific Facts
- 1.20   Ways and means of dealing with specifics
- 1.21   Conventions
- 1.22   Trends, sequences
- 1.23   Classifications and categories
- 1.24   Criteria
- 1.25   Methodology
- 1.30   Universals and abstractions
- 1.31   Principles and generalizations
- 1.32   Theories and structures

2.00 COMPREHENSION
- 2.10   Translation
- 2.20   Interpretation
- 2.30   Extrapolation

3.00 APPLICATION

4.00 ANALYSIS OF
- 4.10   Elements
- 4.20   Relationships
- 4.30   Organizational principles

5.00 SYNTHESIS
- 5.10   Production of a unique communication
- 5.20   Production of a plan or a proposed set of operations
- 5.30   Derivation of a set of abstract relations

6.00 EVALUATION
- 6.10   Judgment in terms of internal evidence
- 6.20   Judgment in terms of external criteria

Figure 2. Skeletal summary of the Metfessel, Michael and Kirsner Instrumentation of Bloom's Taxonomy of Educational Objectives. (See also Section III.)

many subcategories of cognitive functioning detailed by this Taxonomy. Here again we used trained raters to evaluate audio- or videotaped classroom interactions. In general, this procedure required three different raters to review the same four three-minute segments from one taped hour of classroom teaching. Each rater assigned a rating to each verbal expression during the selected segments. An inter-rater reliability of .85 was necessary for research purposes. Using the Bloom Taxonomy, we were thus able to study student cognitive functioning as a process variable (as opposed to achievement tests which focused on levels of cognition solely as product variables).

Finally, of course, we needed to know something of the quality of a given teachers' interpersonal functioning. A review of counseling, psychotherapy and psychology research literature revealed the work of Carkhuff as the most useful and most heavily validated. It seemed from ours and the field's perspective that Carkhuff was the most-cited authority in counseling psychology in general and on empathy and interpersonal skills in particular. Three scales developed by Carkhuff allowed us to translate the qualitative dimensions of empathy, congruence and respect into accurate quantitative terms.

As indicated in Figures 3, 4 and 5, the Carkhuff Interpersonal Process Scales assess a teacher's level of functioning using a five-point scale where 1.0 is low, 3.0 is minimally effective and 5.0 is considered high. A minimally effective empathic response includes a mention of both the student's feeling state and the reason for that 'feeling. For example, "You feel bad because the test was hard." Above this level the teacher helps the student by personalizing the student's experience and identifying deeper and unexpressed feelings. Below this level the teacher ignores the student's feelings or the reason for these feelings.

Level 1.0   The verbal and behavioral expressions of the teacher either do not attend to or significantly detract from the verbal and behavioral expressions of the student(s) in that they communicate significantly less of the student's feelings than the student has expressed himself or herself.

Level 2.0   While the teacher responds to the expressed feelings of the student(s), he or she does so in such a way as to subtract noticeable affect from the communications of the student.

Level 3.0   The expressions of the teacher in response to the expressed feelings of the student(s) are essentially interchangeable with the latter in that they express essentially the same affect and meaning. This is the minimal level of facilitative conditions.

Level 4.0   The responses of the teacher add noticeably to the expressions of the student(s) in such a way as to express feelings a level deeper than the student was able to express himself or herself.

Level 5.0   The responses of the teacher add significantly to the feeling and meaning of the expressions of the student(s) in such a way as to (a) accurately express levels of feeling below what the second person was able to express or (b) in the event of on-going deep self-exploration on the student's part, be fully with the student in his or her deepest moments.

Figure 3. Carkhuff Scale: Communication of
Empathy in Interpersonal Processes.

Level 1.0   The verbal and behavioral expressions of the teacher communicate a clear lack of respect (or negative regard) for the student(s).

Level 2.0   The teacher responds to the student in such a way as to communicate little respect for the feelings, experiences and potentials of the student.

Level 3.0   The teacher communicates an unconditional respect and concern for the student's feelings, experiences and potentials. This is the minimum level of facilitative conditions.

Level 4.0   The teacher clearly communicates a positive respect and concern for the student's experience.

Level 5.0   The teacher communicates the very deepest respect for the student's worth as a person and his or her potentials as a free individual.

Figure 4. Carkhuff Scale: Communication of
Respect in Interpersonal Processes.

Level 1.0   The teacher's verbalizations are clearly unrelated to what she is feeling at the moment, or her only genuine responses are negative in regard to the student(s) and appear to have a totally destructive effect upon the student.

Level 2.0   The teacher's verbalizations are slightly unrelated to what he is feeling and usually represent a prescribed role or professional manner. When he is genuine his responses are negative and he is unable to employ them as a basis for further inquiry into the relationship.

Level 3.0   The teacher provides no "negative" cues between what she says and what she feels but provides no positive cues to indicate a really genuine response to the student. This constitutes the minimal level of facilitative funcitoning.

Level 4.0 The teacher presents some positive cues indicating a genuine response (whether positive or negative) in a nondestructive manner to the student(s).

Level 5.0 The teacher is freely and deeply himself in a nonexploitative relationship with the student(s).

Figure 5. Carkhuff Scale: Communication of
Genuineness in Interpersonal Processes.

A minimally effective level of respect again responds to the student's feelings and experiences. The teacher says in effect, "I really care about you." While high levels of respect concentrate on communication of deep personal concern, low levels of this dimension show an obvious negative regard for the student as a person.

Finally, a minimally effective level of genuineness is communicated by a lack of discrepancy between the teacher's true feelings and non-verbal expressions. For example, the response, "I know I feel good when something like that is over," communicates a genuine response to the student's experience. In turn, high levels of genuineness focus on a free and open expression of feelings and experiences, while low levels contain obvious discrepancies between what the teacher says and how she feels at that moment. Once again we used trained raters to evaluate taped segments of classroom interactions. As with Bloom's Taxonomy, the usual procedure was to employ three raters, each of whom monitored and evaluated the same selected segments of taped activity. Since precision is a paramount concern of the Carkhuff Interpersonal Process Scales, both inter-rater and intra-rater reliability were of critical concern to us.

These, then, were three of the most important tools which we used in developing and carrying out our own initial studies. What follows is an overview of some of the more significant of these studies (Aspy, 1972) — an overview, as it were, of the preliminary work which was to lead to the development of the National Consortium for Humanizing Education.

INTERPERSONAL SKILLS AND STUDENT OUTCOMES

Student Attendance

One of the most fundamental facts-of-life related to education is student attendance. Attendance is a "rock bottom" factor in that a given student is either present or absent from a class at any given point. Since we were interested in gathering a wide range of basic data, we decided to investigate the effect which various levels of interpersonal functioning might have upon student attendance. We began this study by using the Carkhuff Interpersonal Process Scales to monitor and evaluate the interpersonal skills of a number of third grade teachers

in a public elementary school system. We were able to identify three
such teachers who, in terms of the Scales, were offering high levels of
interpersonal facilitation and three additional teachers who were
functioning at a low level in the same interpersonal areas. Going on, we
selected 60 third grade students who were getting the as-yet-unproven
benefits of a high level of skills and 60 others who were working with
teachers functioning at low skill-levels. Controls included matching all
students for sex, socio-economic level and I.Q. When the results
became apparent, they showed that students in "high" conditions had a
significantly lower rate of absenteeism ($p \leqslant .05$) than those working in
"low" conditions. In other words, the children missed fewer days of
school when their teachers offered higher levels of the facilitative
interpersonal conditions as measured by the Carkhuff Scales.

None of us were particularly surprised by these results. After all,
common sense alone reminds us that we are more likely to spend time
in places where we are treated decently. But anticipated or not, these
results provided some initial support for the hypotheses with which we
were concerned.

Student I.Q.

Another question which concerned us dealt with the possibility
that facilitative conditions (again as measured by the Carkhuff
Interpersonal Process Scales) might affect or be related in any way to
changes in student I.Q. We addressed ourselves to this question by
following roughly the same procedures as those used to assess the
inter-relationship of interpersonal skills and student attendance. Here
we began by using the Carkhuff Scales to evaluate the level of
interpersonal functioning of a number of first grade teachers. We then
randomly selected 25 first graders receiving "high" conditions and
matched them with a second group of 25 students receiving "low"
conditions. The Stanford-Binet Intelligence Test was administered to
students in both groups at the beginning of one academic year and
again at the end of the year. The results of these pre-and post-tests
indicated that students in "high" conditions had made an average gain
of **nine I.Q. points** while students in low conditions had experienced no
significant change. As with the results of our study of attendance, the
findings here certainly appeared to support the original hypothesis with
which our work had begun.

Student Cognitive Growth

One of our primary concerns, of course, was to assess the
relationship between teachers' level of affective or interpersonal skills
and the levels of cognitive growth achieved by students. A number of
separate studies were developed and carried out to evaluate this
relationship.

In one study, we examined the academic progress of 120 third
grade students. Using the Carkhuff Scales once again, we were able to

focus on three teachers at this grade level who were supplying high levels of interpersonal skills and three others who were supplying low levels of these same skills. Sixty students who were receiving high-level facilitative help were matched for sex, socio-economic status and I.Q. with 60 other third graders working in "low" conditions. Using standardized achievement tests, we pre- and post-tested all students across one academic year and found that those students receiving "high" conditions made significantly more gain (.01 level) on their achievement tests than did those working in "low" conditions. Again, the results appeared to support the contention that facilitative interpersonal conditions were significantly and positively related to cognitive growth of students.

A second study in this area focused on the instruction of reading groups by 40 elementary teachers. We began by asking each teacher to tape record one hour of instruction. These tapes were then evaluated by trained raters. The raters first conducted a blind assessment of the teachers' levels of interpersonal functioning using the Carkhuff Scales. The same segments of each tape were then evaluated by the raters according to Flanders' Interaction Analysis. Finally, raters employed a procedure for obtaining levels of cognitive functioning adapted from Metfessel, Michael and Kersner's Instrumentation of Bloom's Taxonomy of Educational Objectives. Here each segment of tape was given a rating based upon the highest levels of cognitive functioning achieved by students with significant frequency during the segment. The ratings which emerged from this procedure were collapsed into two categories: Group I students who achieved Level 1 of Bloom's Taxonomy ("memory"); and Group II students who achieved Levels 2-6 of the Taxonomy ("thinking"). Thus we were ultimately able to investigate the differential interpersonal functioning of teachers whose students attained only Level 1 and of others whose students attained Levels 2-6. The results showed that teachers whose students achieved Levels 2-6 were providing significantly higher levels of positive regard. Stated simply, there seemed to be evidence of a significant and positive relationship between teachers' levels of positive regard and students' levels of cognitive growth.

A third study in this area dealt with the relationship between teacher empathy and student cognitive gains. Six third grade teachers tape recorded their interactions with reading groups during one week in March and one week in May of the same academic year. The recordings were done as randomly as possible to neutralize such variables as time of day and day of the week. Twenty subjects were selected from each teacher's class as follows: (a) the five boys with the highest I.Q.'s; (b) the five girls with the highest I.Q.'s; (c) the five boys with the lowest I.Q.'s; and (d) the five girls with the lowest I.Q.'s. The differences between mean I.Q.'s for each of the six low groups were nonsignificant, and the same was true for the six high groups. All subjects were given five subtests of the Stanford Achievement Test during September and again during May of the year in question. Differences between test scores were used as a measure of individual students' academic gain. The subtests — Word Meaning, Paragraph Meaning, Spelling, Word Study Skills and Language — were all related to verbal quantities. The teachers' tape-recorded classes were evaluated by trained raters and each teacher was given a rating where 1.0 indicated the lowest level of expressed empathy and 5.0 indicated the highest level of empathy. The results of this study clearly showed that a positive and significant relationship existed between teachers' levels of empathy and student cognitive gains. This positive relationship was reflected in student performance on all of the subtests except the Spelling test and was evident as well in the total gain. Results were statistically significant at or above the .05 level of confidence. Once again, we seemed to have found evidence supporting the contention concerning the positive relationship between empathy and cognitive growth.

TRAINING TEACHERS IN INTERPERSONAL SKILLS

As we studied students' levels of performance and their relationship to teachers' levels of interpersonal functioning, we gradually built up a wealth of significant data concerning the latter area. Since our earliest evidence was all from pilot studies, we decided to collect larger samples systematically from a broader geographical area. This was accomplished by conducting a series of workshops for teachers throughout the country and collecting pre- and post-workshop data from each participant. In this way we were able to get large samples from Massachusetts, Maryland, Florida, Louisiana, Kansas, Kentucky, Michigan, Minnesota, Texas and North Carolina. The results of our assessments showed that geographical distribution was **not** a source of variance in teachers' levels of interpersonal functioning. The data also showed that most teachers were providing levels of interpersonal skills which tended to **retard** rather than facilitate learning by their students! Hardly an encouraging situation. Far more encouraging, however, were the results of our initial forays into teacher training.

One pilot training program involved 32 secondary English teachers enrolled in a six-week summer workshop designed to help them become more student-centered in their classroom practices. Two hours of audiotape recordings were made of the teachers' classroom teaching during the first and last weeks of the training session. These recordings were evaluated by raters using both Flanders' Interaction Analysis and Carkhuff's Interpersonal Process Scales. For the actual training, the 32 teachers were divided into two groups that were matched in terms of sex and years of experience. The trainer who worked with the first group (Trainer A) was capable of functioning above the minimal level of facilitative conditions (3.0) according to the Carkhuff Scales while the trainer working with the second group (Trainer B) functioned well

15 below this level. The data obtained from pre- and post-program evaluations of the tapes showed that the teachers working with the "high" level Trainer A made significant changes ($p \leqslant .05$) in four of the Flanders Interaction Analysis categories while teachers working with Trainer B did not achieve significant changes in any of the categories. Thus the study indicated that teachers can indeed be trained in modes of "indirect" teaching — and that a necessary condition of such training is that the trainer himself or herself be capable of exercising high levels of interpersonal skills.

A second study of teacher training made use of training procedures developed by Carkhuff for working with counselors. The program involved a 15-hour didactic-experiential model of training with five hours of didactic instruction about the key conditions (empathy, congruence and positive regard), five hours of rating standard audiotape recordings of classroom instruction and five hours of role-playing in groups to promote minimally facilitative levels of interpersonal functioning. (Note: The most recent version of this training method is presented in Section III.) This training procedure was employed with three groups of elementary teachers (N = 200) and two groups of secondary teachers (N = 150) in two different settings. Pre- and post-training assessments revealed that the majority of teachers entered at levels below minimally facilitative conditions and, during training, moved upward to achieve facilitative levels. Again, we had found much to encourage us in the possibility of delivering substantive interpersonal skills to teachers.

A SUMMARY OF PRELIMINARY RESEARCH

These and other related studies occupied several years and took place in a wide range of geographical settings (Aspy, 1972). At the end of our preliminary investigations we found that we had generated a substantial data base which supported the following contentions:

1. Teachers' levels of Empathy, Congruence and Positive Regard are positively and significantly related to:
   a. Students' cognitive growth
   b. Students' I.Q. gains
   c. Students' attendance
2. Teachers' present levels of interpersonal functioning (E, C and PR) are generally below those required for minimal facilitation of student growth.
3. Teachers' levels of interpersonal functioning (E, C and PR) can be enhanced and promoted by systematic skills training as developed by Carkhuff.
4. Teachers' gains in the interpersonal dimensions (E, C and PR) are translated into positive gains by their students.

5. Geographical setting is not a significant source of variance in the levels of interpersonal functioning evidenced by teachers. That is, the problem is a national rather than a local one.

6. Teachers demonstrate approximately the same levels of interpersonal functioning as the general population. That is, the problem is cultural rather than career-specific.

As an indirect by-product of our preliminary work, we had generated a series of technologies by which it was possible to (1) diagnose levels of teacher interpersonal functioning, (2) train teachers for improvement of interpersonal skills and (3) assess the effects of such training in terms of both teacher and student behaviors. In addition, we now knew that the training and feedback system could be used with large populations as well as with individual teachers.

I thought back then, as I do now, to our meeting and conversation with Colonel Al Worden at the Houston Space Center. One of the high points in our conversation with Colonel Worden occurred when the Colonel spoke about the one person in his life who had done the most to promote his real growth as an individual – his high school principal! The astronaut's face fairly glowed with intense feeling as he said, "You know, he wasn't a big guy, but boy did he have an impact on people! He knew every kid in the school by his first name, and not by accident. He was really concerned and everybody felt it. He knew what you were planning to do in life and how to help you get there. The real test is that I still talk with him regularly – at least once a month."

I thought, too, of the other individuals who might be able to point to one or two educators who had made a profound difference for the better in their lives. Finally, I thought of all the many, many people – students past and present – who had never experienced what it was like to work with a truly facilitative, truly skilled teacher. Up to now such students had been condemned to an academic career which bred despair rather than hope, anguish rather than joy, repeated failures rather than cumulative successes. They had been the unwitting victims of our own collective failure to isolate and promote those skills which could really make a difference in their lives – a difference for the better rather than the worse.

Colonel Worden had travelled to the moon and thus shared in that great technological thrust reflected in the statement "One small step for man, one giant leap for mankind." Now we found ourselves taking the first steps on a journey which might prove even more momentous. Inspired by Colonel Worden and all those who testified to the value of skilled teachers, galvanized into action by the mute pleas of all those others who could only testify to the numbing, deteriorative effects of unskilled teachers, we were breaking new ground. Our research had confirmed our belief that interpersonal skills really did make the difference between student growth and student deterioration – and that the necessary technologies existed to train teachers in the requisite dimensions of interpersonal functioning.

We thought of the implications of our "three card" responding exercise. Teachers in several elementary reading classes had been given three cards, each bearing a single word: one "happy," the second "sad" and the third "angry." We asked each teacher to incorporate one of these words in her or his response to each student's handling of a brief reading assignment: perhaps "You feel happy because you got all the words right;" or, "You feel sad because you missed some words;" or even, "You feel angry because you still can't get the hang of it." Our thought had been to force each teacher to understand his or her feelings in the most general sense. We had hoped that such simple responses might make a difference to the students. But we were completely unprepared for the dramatic increases in reading skills which such responses seemed to prompt in the children! The teacher really saw them! The teacher really understood them! The teacher actually seemed to like them! This in itself was enough to prompt new efforts, new energy, new achievement!

We began with the individual. We learned, in the words of one of the kids, that kids do not learn from people they don't like. In this respect students are no different from anyone else. We all defend ourselves against people who do not seem to appreciate us as individuals —and we all work a little harder for the one or two people who really seem to understand our own worth. Throughout our acquisition and development of technological tools and our preliminary work, our commitment to children and our belief in the importance of liking the people you want to help never wavered. We ourselves were people attempting to understand and meet the real needs of other people. No work, we were convinced, could be more worthwhile.

And no results, we are now convinced, could have been more promising!

The implications were profound indeed. We could not turn back. The challenge was too great, the promise too profound for us to do anything but move ahead. We would do our best in the arena which we had chosen, just as Colonel Worden had done his best in his own arena of choice. And just as he had shared in a far larger thrust, so we might share in something that went far beyond ourselves. One small step for a single group of educators might, through the National Consortium, be transformed into one giant leap for education in this country.

CHAPTER TWO

OVERVIEW

This chapter will outline the data collection and training procedures used by the National Consortium.

We began by outlining the three hypotheses which we sought to test in establishing the Consortium:

1. Teachers can be trained to increase the levels of facilitative interpersonal conditions which they offer to their students.

2. It is feasible to provide Interpersonal Skills Training to large number of teachers at one time.

3. Increases in the levels of facilitative interpersonal conditions provided by teachers will be accompanied by pupil gains on indices of both mental health and cognitive development.

Our major work during the three-year period for which the National Consortium was funded involved over 500 teachers and 10,000 students in both rural and urban school settings. Our first task was to select those teachers who could be trained to serve as in-service trainers for other teachers in their own schools. Second, we had to make sure that our entire training program was organized into a skills-oriented, step-by-step series of individual modules, each designed to deliver to teachers a specific capability or set of techniques. Third, we had to make sure that our teacher-trainers did in fact deliver the requisite skills to the other participating teachers. Fourth, we had to ensure the continued reliability of our audiotape monitoring and rating procedures.

In essence, the training program made a delivery in two broad areas of concern. By learning how to use the Flanders and Bloom instruments themselves, participating teachers developed the capacity to monitor and discriminate the types of verbal activity in their own classrooms. By receiving training in interpersonal skills like attending and responding using modules designed by Carkhuff, teachers learned to raise the levels of facilitative interpersonal conditions which they provided for their students.

THE EFFECTIVE INGREDIENTS OF TEACHER TRAINING

The chair in the last row was empty. I had gotten to know Jimmy in my in-service teacher training capacity. I asked the teachers where Jimmy was. They didn't know. The kids didn't know either. The class moved on with their normal classroom procedures. In retrospect, it was not surprising that none of the others knew where Jimmy was. He seemed a quiet, lonely boy who tended to become embarrassed rather easily. For some reason his frequent embarrassment always seemed to anger him; it was almost as though he blamed himself for whatever it was that was causing him to be vulnerable to others.

Later that week, over a cup of coffee in the faculty lounge I happened to ask one of the other teachers about Jimmy's absence.

"Oh," she said, looking at me rather strangely. "You mean the counselor didn't tell anyone?"

"Uh...no," I answered, wondering what this was all about.

The other teacher met my gaze, then looked away uncomfortably. "Jimmy — hung himself," she said. In her voice was all the hollowness of impotent grief that we, the living, feel for those who have moved beyond our care or our control.

I said nothing. At first I could think only of Jimmy's sad eyes, his perpetual self-aimed anger. Gradually I began to wonder what those of us at the school might have done to help him deal with the causes of his inner pain. Would he have been able to like himself more if we had shown we liked him? Only later did I learn that suicide is the second leading cause of death among young adults.

I mention this infinitely sorrowful experience because it may serve to show one aspect of the "root system" out of which grew the National Consortium for Humanizing Education. Yes, our orthodox roots could be found in the 10 years of individual and collective investigation in which we had engaged. Yet beneath and beyond all such formal and rigorous activities, each of us drew strength and motivation from innumerable private experiences like my own sad encounter with Jimmy. Working together, we had found our common belief in the efficacy of interpersonal skills supported by the results of preliminary studies. We had begun to develop an integrated technology which would allow us to test certain fundamental hypotheses related to training large numbers of teachers in interpersonal skills. At the same time, however, we knew we could never afford to forget that the living heart of our project, our concern, our joint commitment, was the individual student — the one person whose pattern of growth or deterioration would be determined by the people working in the classroom.

Our own chance to grow was given to us by the National Institute of Mental Health which, by funding us for a three-year program of training and research, transformed the National Consortium from a theoretical project into a practical reality.

"Good morning, this is the National Consortium..."

After months and years of planning and waiting and struggling, we were on our way!

In essence, the aim of the National Consortium was to test a relatively straightforward "input/process/output" model. Input was to be provided by administrators, classroom teachers and students from several parts of the country. Process variables would consist of the training which we gave individuals in specific interpersonal skills. And output would be measured in terms of discernible changes in the behaviors of these same administrators, teachers and students.

In order to accomplish our purposes, of course, we needed systematic modes of gathering information. First, we needed to know where administrators, teachers and students were functioning on some specific measures. Second, we needed to conduct training in order to increase the frequency of constructive behavior in the classroom. Third, we needed to measure the performance of all subjects after training in order to assess changes. And fourth, we needed to compare the before and after performances of each group to see what patterns of change had emerged. In the pages that follow, we will focus our concern on the first category of information — the "input" aspect of our basic research model.

GATHERING INITIAL DATA

We have already mentioned the informal hypothesis which gave rise to the National Consortium: that interpersonal skills make an important difference in the classroom. This broad contention evolved into three closely related formal hypotheses:

1. Teachers can be trained to increase the levels of facilitative interpersonal conditions which they offer to their students.

2. It is feasible to provide Interpersonal Skills Training for large numbers of teachers at one time.

3. Increases in the levels of facilitative interpersonal conditions provided by teachers will be accompanied by pupil gains on indices of both mental health and cognitive development.

As indicated earlier, the National Consortium was funded for a three-year period of study. The actual time-span was from 1971 to 1974. A total of over 500 teachers and 10,000 students were involved during this time. Participants were drawn from elementary, junior high and senior high schools in urban and rural areas. The populations were analyzed extensively for the effects of age, sex, grade level and teaching experience (see Section II).

Since it was imperative that we learn whether differences in teacher and student behavior at the end of the period of study were directly related to our training, we established two different groups. The first was our **experimental group** involving those teachers who would receive intensive Interpersonal Skills Training. The second was the **control group** whose progress would be monitored without benefit of any other intervention or training.

One question of paramount importance, of course, dealt with the manner in which we on the staff of the National Consortium would gather the necessary data. Continual on-site observing would clearly have been impossible because of the tremendous investment of money and personnel required. Fortunately, our preliminary studies had already shown us that audiotapes of classroom interactions were desirable for a number of reasons: (a) fewer personnel were required; (b) there was less intrusion into the classroom; (c) interactions could be "frozen" for repeated scoring; and (d) audiotape ratings concurred at a high level with both on-site observations and videotape ratings.

The basic data-gathering technique which emerged involved getting a one-hour audiotape once a month from each teacher. Principals submitted one-hour tapes of faculty meetings and/or other interactions with teachers at the beginning, middle and end of the school year. All tapes were forwarded to the central Consortium office where trained raters evaluated each one in terms of specific scales and modes of measurement. Knowing that the research depended heavily upon the accuracy of our raters, we were more than pleased to find that these raters developed fine levels of both inter- and intra-rater reliability (correlations above .90).

In assessing the audiotapes, raters selected four 3-minute segments from each tape. The first segment was taken from the beginning of the hour, the second from about 20 minutes into the hour, the third from about 40 minutes into the hour and the fourth from near the end of the hour. Raters then coded their evaluations of each segment.

While the audiotapes submitted by teachers and principals were certainly a key source of data, they were by no means the only such source. From participating students we gathered the results of How-I-See-Myself Tests and Achievement Tests as well as regular attendance and socio-demographic data. While school principals only submitted audio recordings, teachers underwent pre- and post-testing on both the Minnesota Teacher Attitude Inventory and the Classroom Climate Semantic Differential tests.

What emerged from all of our gathering and collecting activities, of course, was a veritable mountain of raw data dealing with both instrumental scores and behavioral indices. We adopted some fairly rigorous statistical procedures in order to transform this raw information into more meaningful form (see Section II).

These, then, were the specific people and proceudres with which we were concerned as the National Consortium began its three-year journey of discovery. We had come a long way to get to this, our real starting point. Some readers may find it jarring to confront our attempt to integrate real human concern and a complex technology. Yet if we had learned anything up to this point, it was that only such an integration of the human and the technological could allow us to make a real difference in the lives of the people we cared about — the teachers and students for whom our public school system was a full-time commitment. We would have to work for three years to get the final results of our control and experimental groups. And the first step involved training.

THE TRAINING INGREDIENTS

Someone says to you, "I have a headache."

What do you say?

We gave this same test question to some 10,000 teachers of all descriptions and backgrounds across the country. And all but 100 of these teachers responded to the question in ways which our preliminary (and subsequent) research indicated was at best irrelevant and at worst downright harmful! Many of these responses were all too familiar.

The Stoic's Response: "Stop thinking about it and it'll probably go away." (**Sufferer's private reaction:**"Yeah?; I'd like to see you handle it that way...")

The Sympathizer's Response: "A headache? Gee, that's a shame." (**Sufferer's private reaction:** "Damn right it is!")

The Advisor's Response: "Why don't you take some aspirin or something?" (**Sufferer's private reaction:** "Now there's a hot tip! Too bad I already tried it...")

What was universally missing from the 9,900 non-helpful responses was any sign that the responder understood or could enter the original speaker's own frame of reference. In sharp contrast, the 100 teachers who managed to respond effectively knew that the important thing was the actual feeling (lousy) and the reason for that feeling (the speaker's head was probably pounding). Given this knowledge, the constructive responses invariably sounded something like the following:

"You feel really lousy because the old head is pounding." (**Sufferer's private reaction:** "Hey, this person knows what's going on with me!")

Our preliminary work had shown us that only responses which indicated the teacher's ability to enter and understand the student's own frame of reference were truly helpful. Moreover, the work had made it clear that such responsiveness was not a matter of luck or inherent ability but a matter of skills. Teachers could be trained on an individual basis to respond effectively to their students. Now our concern was to make such training work with a far larger group of teachers than any with which we had worked before.

There were, in essence, three major phases in our overall approach to training. We had to select and train the teacher- trainers who would subsequently work with the teachers. We had to train teachers to make discriminations concerning their own and others' use of interpersonal skills. And finally, we had to train the teachers in our experimental group to use interpersonal skills themselves.

TRAINING THE TRAINERS

The trainers were selected from among the larger group of teachers with whom we would be working. We began by deciding that each individual selected to serve as a trainer would need a high level of physical health and energy. People with low levels of physical energy simply could not contribute a great deal to others.

Those individuals who met the initial physical criteria for trainers were subsequently taken through each of the following levels.

1. They were trained in each of the previously-developed training modules.
2. They successfully trained a "student" group in each of the training modules.
3. They demonstrated their proficiency in actually using the interpersonal skills developed through their own training (e.g., by responding to trainees' feelings).
4. They demonstrated their ability to design and construct an appropriate training module.
5. They trained other trainers to use the new module which they had developed.
6. They were trained in the use of other new modules developed by other trainees. (In-service training was built into the staff program.)

The marked growth of the trainers themselves would make an interesting study. For now, it may be sufficient to note that they probably made the largest gains on the various interpersonal skills measures. We may be tempted to shrug and say, "Of course." Yet this informal finding has profound implications for almost every type of in-service training. All of us have said for a long time that "the best way to learn something is to have to teach it." Perhaps the target population in any such training program should always be used as trainers.

Once our training staff was complete, we were ready to get down to the basic work for which the National Consortium had been developed: training teachers. By this time we had developed a series of training modules, each systematic in its presentation of specific skills as a sequence of levels and steps. The aim of each module was to make a clear and substantive delivery to each teacher of something which she or he could put to immediate use in the classroom. Each training module was designed to have the following characteristics:

1. Modules were **self-testing** on a pre-program and post-program basis. In other words, teachers used self-administered and self-scored tests before and after their training in each module to assess their own gains.

2. Each skill was presented within the **frame of reference** of the teachers involved. That is, each skill was related to daily tasks and goals and, wherever possible, to teachers' own experiences and class materials.

3. Each module emphasized the **successful completion of a series of substeps.** Larger skills were always presented as a sequence of separate skills or components which could be mastered within the training session and put to immediate use in class.

4. Trainees **participated** in the training process. In other words, each module focused on experiential as well as didactic learning.

5. The emphasis throughout training was on **practical applications.** In particular, each module included a "practical application" section which provided teachers with specific suggestions of ways in which particular skills could be used in class.

Armed with effective trainers and a sequential series of individual training modules, we were ready to work with the teachers who comprised our experimental group.

TRAINING IN DISCRIMINATION SKILLS

The technology for training teachers and principals for more effective interaction with people focused first upon giving them insight into their current modes of functioning. Therefore, we introduced Flanders' Interaction Analysis as the first assessment instrument because it yielded descriptive rather than evaluative feedback. This approach was designed to reduce the trainees' anxiety and resistance to the interpersonal skills program in general.

The training program for Flanders' Interaction Analysis proceeded through sequential levels of difficulty and applicability. These levels and sequences are as follows:

LEVEL I: Didactic presentation of Flanders' Interaction Analysis (FIA).

LEVEL II: Application of FIA to a written transcription of a classroom interaction.

LEVEL III: Use of FIA to achieve a 4 - 8 interaction (see page 12) in the group for one minute. The trainers ask questions and the trainees answer them.

LEVEL IV: Use of FIA to achieve a 3 - 9 interaction (see page 12) in the group for one minute. The trainees ask questions and the trainer answers them.

LEVEL V: Application of FIA to an audiotape recording of classroom interaction. The trainees scored a one-minute segment and results were discussed.

LEVEL VI: Trainees scored one-minute segments of audiotape recordings of classroom interaction until they attained 90 percent agreement with a trained rater.

This sequence continued until the trainee could use FIA to assess some of his or her own classroom teaching. At this point the trainee submitted an audiotape recording of one hour of classroom teaching to be scored by the trained raters of the NCHE. These ratings were returned to the teacher so that he or she could see his or her modes of functioning and alter them systematically if desired.

In like manner, the teachers were taught to use an adaptation of Bloom's Taxonomy to discriminate modes of cognitive behavior in their classrooms. That is, the identical levels and sequences as used for FIA were followed. The object was to give teachers feedback concerning the cognitive dimension of their actual classroom teaching.

As we had anticipated, there was little if any significant change in teachers' classroom behaviors immediately after the discrimination training and feedback with Flanders' Interaction Analysis and Bloom's Taxonomy of Educational Objectives. The real value of this preliminary training in discrimination skills was that it provided accurate and nonthreatening feedback which told the individual teacher (and us) about the specific interpersonal areas in which she or he lacked skills. This brings us to the fourth and most crucial phase of the National Consortium's program: training teachers in particular interpersonal skills.

TRAINING IN INTERPERSONAL SKILLS

Each of the skills-training modules was designed to be self-contained. That is, each module presented and trained teachers in a particular skill. The following is a list of separate modules which were developed and used based upon the Carkhuff models for interpersonal as well as living and learning skills development (Carkhuff, 1972, 1973, 1974). While the titles for elementary school and secondary school modules were the same, the substance of many of these modules was modified to reflect the unique needs of teachers working with either the former or the latter student populations.

Accepting Feelings
Increasing Praise
Accepting Student Ideas
Questioning Skills, I
Questioning Skills, II
Increasing Student Involvement
Problem Solving
Program Development
Planning for Learning
Organizing for Learning I: Teacher/Pupil Interaction
Organizing for Learning II: Physical Environment of Classroom
Organizing for Learning III: Curriculum/Pupil Interaction
Organizing for Learning IV: Pupil/Task Interaction
Working with Small Groups
Consumatory Experience

What we had, then, was a sequence of skills-modules which could be "plugged in" to meet the real and perceived needs of individual teachers in our experimental training group. As noted, most of these modules could be used in isolation if needed. There were, however, exceptions to this, In particular, the four "Organizing for Learning" modules were originally designed to be used in sequence; however, by omitting one portion of the Overview section of each of these modules, they could be and were used at times in an independent fashion.

All of the interpersonal skills training was done within a format of Overview, Training, Review and Practical Application. The Overview served to acquaint the teachers with the module's purpose, goal and activities. The Training section was used to give the teachers an opportunity to learn these new skills in a safe and structured manner. The Review gave the teachers a chance to summarize their learnings just before trying them out in their own classrooms as outlined in the final Practical Applications section.

The Training sequence was the heart of the program. Here the trainer explained the skill in detail and in terms that the teachers could understand. Uses for the skill were discussed followed by a thorough description of the steps and behaviors involved.

Following this explanation, the skill was demonstrated by the trainer to allow the teachers to see a concrete example in action. What was just words a few minutes before became living actions. Next the teachers were given opportunities to learn and practice these skills in a sequence of exercises that became progressively more realistic. Initially the entire group might practice responding in writing to a student's expression role-played by the trainer. Next they form smaller groups with pairs of teachers responding to each other in a live interaction under the supervision and guidance of the trainer while the rest of the group observes and writes their own responses. Then they began more extensive practice using triads by rotating through the roles of teacher, student and coach.

When the teachers had acquired the skills at a minimally helpful level, the process of actually using the skills in the classroom was begun. To insure success, the teachers were encouraged to apply the skills slowly, beginning with a student with whom they already had a good rapport and then expanding to other students. By gradually increasing the length of the interactions and the number of students involved over a four-week period, the teacher was given time to build a base of success that would help her continue to respond accurately when she later began to deal with those students with whom she had had little rapport up to this time.

While initially teacners caught themselves talking to the class while writing and facing the blackboard, now after training they would make it a point to face each child squarely and watch each of their expressions while speaking.

Following a reading assignment in the past, a teacher might have only said, "Next." Now after training in responding skills she might say, "You feel good because you did well" or "You feel bad because it was too hard."

Statements of "Don't worry, the test won't be too hard" were replaced with "When I start to pass out a test you get tense inside."

The initial group of skills and the modules used to present them have evolved into more effective and useable forms. The best and most recent version of the interpersonal skills for teachers can be found in **The Skills of Teaching: Interpersonal Skills** (Carkhuff, Berenson & Pierce, 1977). Each of the skills is presented in a module format that includes pre- and post-training self-assessments for each of the skills to allow the teacher to gauge her own progress.

An example of a more recent training module for teaching groups is presented in Section III of this book. This module along with the content presented in the **Teachers Guide for The Skills of Teaching: Interpersonal Skills** outline the essential content and an effective delivery method that can be used for teacher training.

MOTIVATING THE TEACHERS

This review of the training program would be incomplete without some mention of the subject of motivation for training. We conducted studies of a wide range of groups receiving various kinds of rewards for participation in different aspects of the program. Some received money for each step, others got days off; some got release time for training, others got additional hours of teacher aide help; still others were given relief from playground duties; and some received nothing. Such rewards served a double purpose — they were good to receive in themselves but they also demonstrated to the teachers in a very material and forceful way that their local administrators thought the training was worthwhile. **There is no doubt at all that immediate, tangible reward is a** *sine qua non* **of an effective interpersonal skills program.**

Effect of Rewards on Participation in Training

Reward	% Attendance
Stipends	91%
Teacher Aides	89%
Relief from Duties	88%
No Rewards	78%*

*Significantly different (p $\leq$ .05) from others.

To illustrate this anecdotally, it was nearly stupifying to see experienced teachers push and shove each other to get in line for a $15.00 check for participating in an in-service training program. Maybe we are just like most other people after all. The data from our project made it clear to us that any interpersonal skills program geared to a large segment of the teaching staff would succeed to the degree that it differentially reinforced all the participants at each step of the program.

This, then, was the nature of the training program on which the National Consortium for Humanizing Education embarked. We selected and trained teachers to serve as trainers. We trained teachers in appropriate discrimination skills so they could accurately identify just what they were doing in the classroom. And finally, we trained the teachers in those interpersonal skills which they needed to acquire.

A SUMMARY OF TEACHER TRAINING

What it all came down to, of course, was training people to show the kids that they really liked them. By learning the skills they needed to attend and respond to their students in terms of the students' own frames of reference, the teachers could promote far more constructive activity on the part of these same students. And with more constructive activity — better attendance, greater achievement and effort, less "goofing off" — would come the teachers' own reward. For after all, were these not the things that teachers themselves were most committed to?

The overall process which has been collapsed into a single chapter here took three full years to complete. Needless to say, we continued to gather feedback in the form of hard data and audiotapes reflecting the day-to-day progress of teachers in both the experimental and control groups. We had to wait the full three-year period before we could really assess our findings. But again, this does not mean that the training-and-research process did not entail any learning for us. Quite the contrary!

One of our earliest and most dramatic learnings was that **we** **ourselves were students in that we had to deal on a daily basis with the facilitative and retarding effects of other people's words and** actions. These other people were, quite literally, our teachers, promoting or obstructing our real growth through their efforts. Now we moved beyond this point and came to understand something equally dramatic and significant: **we ourselves were the teachers on whom the growth or deterioration of individual pupils depended!**

Consider the way in which most skills-training programs work — say a program designed to teach people how to perform basic repairs on their own automobiles. The instructor must, to be sure, be an experienced mechanic himself or herself. Given such a level of experience, the instructor invariably follows a simple tell/show/do format (Carkhuff, Berenson and Berenson, 1977): **telling** students how to perform a particular repair job, **showing** them how to do this through personal demonstration and then having them actually **do** the job while he or she oversees the work. In such a program, attention is focused on the object of concern: the car.

Our own experience was quite different. We quickly realized that a tell/show/do format focusing on the "pupil" as the sole object of concern was ineffective. Rather, we had to begin our own efforts by focusing on the teachers, whether as trainers or as trainees. Simply stated, **we found that our presentation of skills could never exceed the quality of our instructional use of these same skills.** We had to function as effective teachers ourselves by employing those same interpersonal skills that we wished to promote in other teachers.

Our trainees' ability to acquire attending skills was enhanced when we ourselves attended to them in physical and psychological ways.

Our trainees' ability to acquire responding skills was enhanced when we ourselves responded to them in an accurate and empathic manner.

Our trainees' ability to learn those skills needed to increase the amount of praise given to students was enhanced when we ourselves increased the praise given the trainees.

And so it went, all down the line. We found that there was a clear correlation between our own ability to use interpersonal skills with our trainees and their ability to acquire these same skills. **We were the teachers!** When we were off or down, our "students" reflected our low condition. When we were on or up, our "students" were able to accomplish far more. In a sense, we had come full circle. We began by recognizing that we in the NCHE were students in that we had to deal with both facilitators and retarders on a daily basis. Now we came to understand that we ourselves could not escape from the responsibility for our own facilitative and retarding activities. The very nature of the National Consortium's program meant that what we taught was inextricably bound up with the way in which we taught it. For us there could never again be the kind of Olympian objectivity with which a set of self-proclaimed "experts" often seeks to inculcate others with their own expertise. Rather, there had to be an unfailing recognition of our own obligation as teachers to use the very skills that we were seeking to teach.

One educator may have stated the substance of our learning most succinctly. Refuting the old saw that "those who can, do; those who can't, teach," she said quite simply: "You teach what you do, no more and no less."

OVERVIEW

In this chapter we present the results of both major and related studies undertaken or supported by the National Consortium. In summary form, these results indicated positive and statistically significant relationships between:

1. teachers' gains in levels of functioning on interpersonal process scales and their participation in training programs designed to enhance these skills;

2. teachers' levels of interpersonal functioning and student gains as measured by attendance, achievement test scores and enhanced self-concept;

3. the focus of training upon a particular interpersonal skill and the probability that the skill will be incorporated into a teacher's normal classroom functioning;

4. principal's levels of interpersonal functioning and teachers' tendency to employ the same interpersonal skills in the classroom;

5. the skills of the teacher-trainer and the success of the training program itself.

In other words, the results of our work confirmed our original hypotheses and established once and for all the critical importance of interpersonal skills in the classroom. "Kids don't learn from people they don't like;" but they do learn from people they do like, and people can learn to show kids they like them. Instead of a series of catch-phrases, these were now demonstrable facts! All the evidence pointed to interpersonal skills as a missing ingredient in the classroom — and to the feasibility of training teachers in these skills so that they could achieve their aim: the promotion of students' real growth!

THE RESEARCH OUTCOMES OF TEACHER TRAINING

Bruce was an elementary school principal in Shreveport, Louisiana. He and his staff got together to improve their delivery to students. In order to accomplish this during the academic year of 1972-73, they decided to adopt an organized approach to their work. They used programs in the discrimination skills training of Flanders' Interaction Analysis and Bloom's Taxonomy of Behavioral Objectives. In addition, using Carkhuff's **The Art of Helping,** Bruce trained the staff in interpersonal communication skills. In short, they began to attempt to systematize the teaching delivery of their school.

A contributory (or perhaps causative) factor in the program was Bruce's level of functioning as the principal who led the delivery effort. He "had it together" physically, intellectually and emotionally. He was ready to be a real educational leader.

The results of this program were truly amazing in terms of student outcomes as well as staff indices. The staff acquired high-level proficiency with (1) Flanders' Interaction Analysis, (2) Bloom's Taxonomy of Educational Objectives and (3) Carkhuff's Interpersonal Skills as well as the ability to develop skills specific to their own school setting.

The proof of the pudding was whether or not all of these positive factors could produce a significant, positive change in this school which served a predominantly (98%) black student population in a very low income neighborhood. The following are the results from the first year of the study (1971-72):

1. The school had the highest attendance rate in its 45 years of existence (91.2%).

2. Vandalism decreased significantly (from a serious problem to none).

3. Teacher turnover was reduced from 80% to 0%.

4. Teachers from other schools began requesting assignments to this school.

5. All teachers increased the frequency of their responsive class-room behaviors (significantly more responses to students' feelings).

6. The school increased its rank nine places within the system for its average reading score (the school has the highest concentration of disadvantaged students in the system).

7. The students in grades 2, 3, 4 and 5 progressed through a mean of more math levels than the mean for the entire system (math curriculum in this system is a continuous program with an individualized approach).

8. The number of student fights decreased significantly.

These results held up in succeeding years. They made the teachers very happy with their deliveries. They made the students very full with their learning. They made Bruce very proud of his educational family.

Our excitement in reporting the sample results noted above clearly indicates that, while doing everything necessary to maintain the requisite degree of cool objectivity, our collective hopes were riding on our experimental groups of teachers and principals. These were the people with whom we had intervened. These were the people for whom our entire training program in interpersonal skills had been designed. And these were the people with whom the greater part of this text has so far been concerned.

But what of the control group which received no special training? It might be a good idea to pause for a moment here and focus our attention on this group of teachers and administrators. We have noted that they represented the traditional public school classroom — what might be termed the "business as usual" approach to education. But just what was — or is — this approach?

Perhaps a conversation I had with one elementary school principal will serve to cast some light on the "business as usual" approach. George Gamble was nothing if not dedicated. Indeed, before I had even met him I had heard him spoken of as a person who put his school "first, last and in between." His interest, energy and quite considerable authority were all evident as he sat and talked with me in his office one late spring afternoon. Our talk eventually came around to the subject of new faculty. George had spent several hours that morning interviewing candidates for a third-grade teaching spot that would be open in the fall.

"Well, there's at least one good thing about the teacher market today," I commented. "With so much competition for so few jobs, you must be able to really pick and choose your new people."

George nodded glumly. "Oh, sure, I can do that, all right," he agreed. "Take this job, for example. I advertised one third grade opening for the fall. And within two weeks I had well over 150 separate applications. People all the way from kids just getting through with college to Ph.D's with years of experience."

Despite his words, George didn't seem overjoyed by the situation. "You feel frustrated because you aren't able to select the best people out of all the applications you get," I offered.

Instead of responding right away, George looked at me for a moment. Then he sighed. "Look, maybe it'll help if I tell you about the experience we've had this year. It began last year, actually. Then we were looking for someone to fill a one-year vacancy in the fourth grade. Our regular teacher was going to take a leave of absence to have a baby. So we advertised. And we were flooded with candidates. And like always, a lot of them looked good.

"Our fourth grade for this year was shaping up to be a real

challenge. 32 kids and not enough money to hire an extra teacher and split the class in two. In the end I decided to go with a full-time teacher and a full-time aide."

"As I said, a lot of the applicants looked great on paper. And a lot of them came across well in interviews. I finally settled on two that I would recommend to the School Board. One was a woman in her early thirties. She had back-to-back M.A.'s in regular elementary and special education. She'd also spent several years as a regular fourth grade teacher. And best of all, she'd had experience working with schizophrenic kids. A number of the students entering fourth grade had exhibited behavioral disorders of one sort or another. This woman seemed perfect for the full-time teaching job."

"The second person I chose was a young woman just out of college to serve as the aide. She had a good degree from a good school. She'd also had a year of experience in between her sophomore and junior years of college as an aide in a fine independent elementary school. Most of all, she came across in the interview as someone with a total, enthusiastic commitment to helping kids grow. Although she already had her teaching certificate and was really hoping for a full teaching job, she knew the score so far as the job market was concerned and was more than ready to work as an aide."

"Well, the Board looked these two women's credentials over and approved my recommendations on the spot. We thought we were all set. Only — only — " George shrugged and sighed again.

"You seem pretty disappointed. I guess things didn't work out the way you hoped," I said.

"They sure didn't! It turned out that our wonderful new full-time teacher was just about burnt out. She didn't like the kids. She didn't like the school's policies. She couldn't make any of her fancy approaches work. Inside of a month she must have been in here to see me eight or ten times, moaning and complaining about how nothing was going right. I eventually found out that she hadn't wanted to work this year but her husband had gone back to graduate school and she was stuck. And so were we. She wasn't malicious or anything — she was actually a really nice person when you could get her to relax. But she was doing terrible things to our morale around here. And the kids — God, they were going wild!"

"And they're what it's all about," I offered.

"Well, fortunately she decided around Thanksgiving time that she really couldn't hack it. One morning she just up and quit."

For the first time George smiled. "Then I decided to go for broke! Instead of looking around for another teacher with lots of experience and impressive degrees, I turned the class over to the woman who'd been working as the aide. By then she knew the class. And she thought she could handle it. I made her teacher and got her an aide of her own. And it was the best move I could have made. She had those kids shaped up before Christmas. You'd never have recognized it as the same class!

"The whole point is," he went on, leaning forward for emphasis, "There are a lot of teachers who look and sound just great until you get them into a classroom. But looking and sounding great isn't always enough. You can't tell how someone'll be until they've gone to work in the classroom. And that means that no matter how much you want to choose the best person for the kids, in the end you just have to close your eyes and take a chance!"

"Close your eyes and take a chance." George was not a person who took his responsibilities as principal lightly. Yet in the end, he saw no choice but to leave the quality of his teaching staff up to chance. In practical terms, of course, this meant that the children in George's school would have a chance to grow — and an equal chance to go nowhere at all!

"Chance" may serve as well as any term to characterize our control group of teachers and principals. Left alone, there was a chance that they would facilitate the real growth of their students. But there was the same chance that their efforts would do nothing but retard this same growth. Our own efforts at the NCHE, then, were aimed at ridding the educational system of this element of chance. We sought to demonstrate that interpersonal skills made the difference between chance effects and certain growth. If we were right, principals like George would have a whole new set of criteria on which to base their teacher-related decisions. If we were right, one of the most fundamental characteristics of effective teaching would be revealed as concrete, measurable and substantive interpersonal skills.

If we were right! This brings us back to the matter at hand — the results of NCHE's three-year program of research and training.

The first concern of the NCHE had been the development of a technology which could train teachers to behave more humanely in their normal classrooms. Given this concern, the first problem to be solved was whether or not the logistics developed for small studies could be applied to a larger one (over 10,000 students and 500 teachers and administrators). Solving this problem meant determining whether or not it was possible to get a large staff to accept human relations training from an outside agency. Remember, the procedure was: (1) tape-recording actual classroom teaching; (2) sending the tapes to the NCHE office for evaluation; (3) receiving assessments of classroom performance from the NCHE; and (4) attending training sessions after receiving this feedback. This procedure was repeated several times each year.

The data indicated clearly that it was possible to develop and implement such a technology. Specifically, 85 percent of the local staff participated voluntarily in this kind of process during the first year of the NCHE. If nothing else had been accomplished throughout the entire project, achieving this cooperation would have been a miracle! The

NCHE staff and the local teachers were able to establish and maintain a
trusting relationship of a sufficiently high order to continue to share
sensitive information across an extended period. This was indeed a
significant accomplishment. Anyone who doubts this can go into ten
classrooms and ask the teachers if he or she can tape-record their
teaching for later study. If one teacher volunteers, the researcher is very
fortunate. Imagine, then, what it was like for relative strangers to begin
this kind of cooperative thrust!

Our preliminary findings, then, showed that our technology was
amply validated by the data reflecting cooperation on the part of
individuals in our experimental group. These preliminary findings laid
an essential base for treating the results of our major effort in teacher
training (see Section II, Learning from Research, for a detailed
explanation of the major findings).

MAJOR FINDINGS

Throughout our three-year period of study our fundamental
concern focused equally on teachers, principals and students — with
student outcomes as the inescapable "bottom line." In the secitons that
follow we will present those findings that related specifically to the
skills of facilitation (the teachers), the **skills of leadership** (the
principals) and **learning outcomes** (the students).

The Teachers: Skills of Facilitation

Needless to say, we were vitally concerned with the efficacy of our
training procedures. The question which we sought to answer was a
fundamental one: would our training programs result in higher levels of
facilitative interpersonal conditions in the classroom? Could we, in other
words, help teachers move toward those behaviors generally thought of
as helpful or decent?

Since we had used three kinds of instruments — Interaction
Analysis, Cognitive Functioning Categories and Interpersonal Process
Scales — we were able to describe not only changes on one of the scales
but also the interaction between them. In terms of movement on the
separate scales, **we found that the training groups made more significant
movements toward the facilitative conditions than did the control
groups who did not receive the training!** Table 1 shows the clearest
differences between the trained and untrained teachers on the Carkhuff
Interpersonal Process Scales. Table 2 shows similar, if less dramatic,
differences between the trained and untrained teachers on the Flanders
Interaction Analysis and Bloom's cognitive categories.

The data indicated that, in general, **the training did result in
teachers' movement toward more facilitative classroom behavior.** That
is, there was significant change in the expected direction. The major
effect of the training was a change in the quality of the interactions
between student and teacher with a supporting change in the

Table 1

Pre- and Post- Change in Elementary Teacher
Levels of Functioning on Interpersonal Process Scales

Scale	Experimental Teachers Pre-Test X̄	Change X̄	Control Teachers Pre-Test X̄	Change X̄
Empathy	2.47	0.68	2.55	0.13
Genuineness	2.47	0.65	2.54	-0.09
Respect	2.66	0.63	2.65	-0.14

proportions of teacher/student verbal interaction.

Further examination of the data was helpful in delineating some additional supportive findings. For example, in the first year the training focused upon the Flanders' Interaction Analysis and the Interpersonal Process Scales. During that year, teacher-changes as registered on those instruments was greater than for the cognitive scales. However, in the second year the training shifted to the Cognitive Scale and specific components of the other scales – e.g., Category 2 (Teacher Praise) of the Flanders' Interaction Analysis. As expected, the changes in the second years were greatest in the categories for which the specific training was carried out.

As we read the data, the general rule which emerged was that **the closer the training was to the specific desired behavior, the greater was the probability that it would be used in the classroom.** It may be that if we want teachers to generalize, we must teach them the skill of doing so. Conversely, it is possible that teacher-training must focus on the nitty-gritty behaviors we wish teachers to use and that the attitudes and/or generalizations will emerge naturally.

A second feature of the research was the relationship between the process variables themselves. For a long time researchers had apparently assumed that interpersonal skills operated in linear relationships with learning. In practice, this means that if a little of a certain quality or behavior (e.g., empathy) increases learning a little, then a lot of that quality will cause it to soar. We investigated this assumption and found that "it ain't necessarily so."

We used a response surface analysis procedure for this study. In this way we could examine three quantities to see how they changed together. The process is something like a mechanical toy in which pulling on one side causes the other sides to shift accordingly. That is, all sides have to accommodate each other's movement. One three-dimensional graph (or response surface) showed that the relationship between Flanders' Category 6 (teacher gives direction), and the teacher's use of facts is **not** one in which an increase in one necessarily results in a corresponding increase in the other(s). The same effect was

TABLE 2

Comparison of Third Year Experiemental Teacher Mean Exiting Levels (After NCHE Training) With Control Teacher Normative Data Across a Three Year Period

Instrument	Classroom Functioning Variable	Elementary Teachers		Secondary Teachers	
		Experimental Teachers' Exiting Levels	Control Teachers' Means	Experimental Teachers' Exiting Levels	Control Teachers' Means
Flanders' Interaction Analysis Categories	Teacher Accepts Feelings of Student	1.5%	0.0%	0.8%	0.0%
	Teacher Praises or Encourages Student	2.6	0.6	1.0	0.3
	Teacher Accepts Ideas of Student	2.0	0.3	1.9	0.1
	Teacher Asks Questions	10.0	8.7	8.3	2.9
	Teacher Lectures	29.1	36.5	42.5	47.5
	Teacher Gives Directions or Commands	3.3	3.3	1.8	2.4
	Teacher Criticizes or Justifies Authority	0.2	1.0	0.4	1.2
	Student Responds	36.2	30.2	31.6	25.1
	Student Initiates	7.9	4.5	6.6	5.8
	Silence or Confusion	7.3	15.0	5.8	13.9
Cognitive Functioning Categories	Teacher Recalls Facts	30.1%	38.3%	44.2%	48.1%
	Teacher Asks for Facts	7.9	21.3	6.5	5.9
	Teacher Thinks	1.0	0.0	5.5	0.2
	Teacher Asks for Thinking	2.5	0.3	1.8	0.5
	Student Recalls Facts	39.4	33.7	32.9	28.3
	Student Asks for Facts	2.4	0.6	1.8	1.8
	Student Thinks	2.4	0.8	2.7	0.7
	Student Asks for Thinking	1.0	0.0	0.2	0.1
	Non-Cognitive Behavior	5.0	2.2	1.2	0.8
	Silence or Chaos	8.3	15.4	4.6	12.9

% = Percent of Class Time in Category

observed in a separate graph where the inter-relationships of four variables were considered.

The importance of this kind of procedure is that for the first time we may be able to tell which specific interpersonal behavior, and under what circumstances, may result in a given outcome. For example, a great deal of empathy may actually be the least desirable in a given situation. This is a very unusual finding for people who set out to demonstrate the importance of interpersonal skills. Lest we miscommunicate, it should be "perfectly clear" that we **are not** saying that Empathy is Bad. We **are** saying that our research finding showed effective interpersonal skills to require very complex orchestrational processes.

Our research results, then, showed quite clearly that our training had meant movement by teachers in the experimental groups toward more facilitative conditions. But what of the principals? At the end of our three-year study we had generated a great deal of data specifically related to the critically important role played by these individuals in their respective schools.

THE LEADERSHIP OF PRINCIPALS

The data from the NCHE supported the hypothesis that the principal is pivotal in a school's program. We supplemented our statistical analyses of large-group data by in-depth naturalistic investigations aimed at detecting the specific behaviors which were instrumental in the principal's influence on teacher or student functioning in the school.

Teachers whose principals demonstrated high levels of interpersonal functioning reported more favorable perceptions of their school environment and their teaching tasks than did teachers whose principals were functioning at low levels. These differences reached statistical significance ($p \leqslant .05$) for those aspects of the school environment (such as services requested from the central office and public relations in school/community affairs) which were most directly affected by the principal. The four aspects of the principal's behavior which were highly related to teacher/student behavior were: (1) his/her levels of respect for the teacher or student; (2) his/her level of empathy in dealing with the teacher or student; (3) his/her use of praise; and (4) his/her acceptance of the ideas proposed by the teacher or student.

As indicated by the data, the principal's behavior appeared to set a pattern for the school. It would seem that the principal models the kinds of behavior he or she expects in classrooms, and teachers tend to use these behaviors in their teaching. In this way, the principal teaches teachers how to conduct a class in his or her school and thus fosters better (or worse) human communications.

Our naturalistic investigations indicated that the central role of the principal in the local school seemed to revolve around her or his control and use of real rewards. Principals are frequently able to give teachers some of the "goodies" (tangible and interpersonal) that make their daily teaching situation either more or less livable. This may be what teachers and principals are speaking about when they talk about the "real" world.

Of course, the "goodies system" is a two-edged sword in that it can be used for either constructive or destructive ends. Our studies indicated that most potent administrators understood the power of the reward system they controlled. On the other hand, ineffectual principals tended either not to comprehend the power of positive reinforcement or to be unable to control a significant portion of it. Thus we found three general types of principals: (1) potent constructive; (2) potent destructive; and (3) impotent in terms of means and ends. And, again, the teachers generally reflected or acted out many of the same tendencies as the principal of their school demonstrated.

Thus far our research findings demonstrated the importance of a principal's skilled leadership and indicated that large groups of teachers could indeed be trained in interpersonal skills. But what of the most important group of all — the students? What had been the impact of our training of teachers in terms of specific student outcomes?

THE LEARNING OUTCOMES OF STUDENTS

One of the most important variables in the NCHE program was that of increasing **student achievement** in terms of test scores. We used a pre- and post-testing procedure for data collection. The data were treated by analysis of covariance with I.Q. and pre-test scores used as co-variates to adjust for entering differences. The results are displayed in Table 3.

Again, **the findings supported the position that the teachers' facilitative conditions were positively and significantly related to student achievement!** The relationship was stronger at the elementary level than at the secondary level which is consistent with earlier studies suggesting differential effects upon these populations.

The circle of impact expanded from the staff of the NCHE to the teaching staff in the schools and finally to their students. The interpersonal skills training had been translated into better student performance on these very important dimensions of cognitive (intellectual) gain.

When we speak of the "bottom line" in this research, we can appropriately say that such a line is represented by **student attendance.** There is no gray area: either the student is present or he/she is not. Student attendance is particularly important to those schools which get reimbursed financially on a per-pupil daily attendance basis. This means that if we can do something to increase student attendance, we can also increase the money coming to a school system. That is really the practical side of research outcomes for some people!

Table 3

Mean Differences (Between Experimental and Control Students)
in Adjusted Achievement Gains

Grade Level	Reading Achievement	Math Achievement	English Achievement
1-3	+10.88***	No Test	No Test
4-6	+ 3.66**	+15.44***	+18.66****
7-9	+ 1.96**	+ 4.10**	+11.75***
10-12	+ 1.56*	+ 1.94*	+ 0.96 NS

* p $<$.05
** p $<$.01
*** p $<$.001

+ = In favor of Experimental (training) Group
- = In favor of Control (no training) Group
NS = Not Significant

The evidence from the NCHE study of the relationship between facilitative conditions and student attendance is presented in Table 4. The data strongly support the contention that teachers' **facilitative conditions are positively and significantly related to student attendance.** This finding is consistent with several of the small studies completed prior to the NCHE and indicates a possible relationship between low levels of facilitative conditions and school phobia.

The above hypothesis is further supported by the data from **self concept** testing using the "How I See Myself" Test (see Table 5). Here the data indicates **positive and statistically significant relationships between teacher levels of interpersonal functioning and almost all aspects of student self-concept.** In general, students' concepts of their own worth and capability seem to be enhanced by the facilitative conditions provided by their teachers.

SERENDIPITOUS FINDINGS

As we studied the data and our theoretical models, it became obvious that we had missed a very basic variable: physical health. Although suspecting its importance, we had looked only at emotional and intellectual indices and virtually ignored physical measures. We decided to conduct a more formal study along these lines.

We administered the Harvard Step Test to several female elementary teachers, all of whom were below 30 years of age. We randomly selected five "very fit" teachers and five "very unfit" and tape recorded their teaching all day long for all five days of the same week. We then assessed the audiotape recordings with Flanders' Interaction Analysis, Bloom's Taxonomy of Educational Objectives and Carkhuff's Interpersonal Process Scale. The results indicated that the 10 teachers began the week (Monday, 8:00 a.m.) at about the same levels on all the scales; but as the week progressed, the groups diverged. The "high" physical fitness group improved and reached some high activity peaks by Friday afternoon. On the other hand, the "low" fitness group moved in one of two directions: (1) they became very permissive or (2) they became very oppressive (i.e., a lot of criticism registered on Flanders' Interaction Analysis). The latter groups seemed to indicate that tired teachers either give up or retreat to the last barricade, cruelty. This naturalistic study indicated that the entire skills repertoire in the physical, intellectual and emotional areas must be considered in order to predict who could implement any one type of skills training. Again, it was a matter of "having it together" in order to be a teacher.

A subsequent study with 150 teachers bore out this hypothesis. Very simply, we found that the teachers' level of physical fitness on entering the training program was the single most frequent predictor of the degree to which she/he would subsequently use her/his new skills in the classroom. Interestingly enough, the physical fitness of the teacher was the **only** predictor of the size of the increase in student-initiated

Table 4

Comparisons of Mean Total Days Absent Per Student by Grade Level

Grade Level	Experimental Means	Control Means	Significance of the Difference p $<$	Mean Additional Days Absent for Control Groups Per Student	Per Class
1-3	6.44	8.94	.05	2.50	62.50
4-6	4.98	8.35	.001	3.37	84.25
7-9	7.15	10.11	.05	2.96	74.00
10-12	8.30	12.13	.01	3.83	95.75

Table 5

Results of Comparisons of Adjusted Treatment Means From
How I See Myself Test Scores

HISM* Factor	Grades 3-6 Experimental $\bar{X}$	Grades 3-6 Control $\bar{X}$	Sig. of Diff. $p <$	Grades 7-12 Experimental $\bar{X}$	Grades 7-12 Control $\bar{X}$	B.A.T.M.** $p <$
Teacher-School	2.56	1.61	.05	1.52	0.53	NS
Physical Appearance	1.45	-0.96	.01	1.81	0.01	.05
Interpersonal Adequacy	2.87	2.20	.05	1.99	-0.28	.01
Autonomy	0.96	-1.89	.01	2.19	0.89	.01
Academic Adequacy	1.25	0.02	.05	0.86	0.30	.05
Total Score	8.61	1.08	.001	6.85	0.92	.001

*HISM = How I See Myself
**BATM = Between Adjusted Treatment Means

behavior which would follow training aimed towards that. That is, the higher the teachers' level of fitness, the greater the increase in student-initiated behavior occurring in her or his classroom subsequent to the training program. To us, the obvious interpretation seemed to be that tired teachers are afraid to let students get out of the well-trodden ruts because they might not be able to handle what might come up.

The initial study was repeated with a group of 25 student teachers at Southern University in Baton Rouge, Louisiana. The subjects had received interpersonal skills training and could all make interchangeable responses. In order to explore the effect of various levels of physical fitness in the helping relationship, each of the subjects was first administered a Harvard Step Test to determine his or her level of performance. They were then assigned five clients whom they saw at one-hour intervals throughout the day, thus simulating a normal work-day for a tutor and/or counselor. Each session was audio recorded and assessed for the number of interchangeable responses during the entire day. The results showed that the "high" fitness subjects mainained their level of performance while the "low" fitness group deteriorated significantly during the last three interviews. That is, both groups began at about the same rate of interchangeable responses and the "high" fitness group continued that rate while the "low" fitness group decreased steadily to none in the last hour. In fact, most of their conversations in the final hour dealt with their concern about whether or not it was time to quit!

Of course, this stirred our attention considerably, and we looked for trends in our larger data which might support these small studies. We found such a tendency in the pattern of the levels of facilitative conditions provided by classroom teachers throughout the year. Generally, the levels are highest at the beginning of the year and lowest at the end. This was supportive of the interaction of physical and emotional skills, but a second aspect made the case even stronger. The levels of conditions deteriorated between September and December; but they rose during January. This rise came after the Christmas vacation. We could only conjecture that teachers had caught their physical breath which was translated into higher interpersonal conditions.

These, then, were our findings. Our in-service training technology had worked as we had hoped it would. To say that we were pleased would be to understate the obvious. Perhaps the word which best captures our collective reaction to the results of our work is "awed." We had begun our study in order to find answers to some basic questions concerning the role of interpersonal skills. The answers were clearly presented in our data. A summary of our most significant findings would have to include all of the following.

FINDING 1: There is a positive and significant relationship between teachers' gains in levels of functioning on interpersonal process scales and their participation in training programs designed to enhance these skills.

FINDING 2: There is a positive and significant relationship between teachers' levels of interpersonal functioning and students' gains on achievement test scores.

FINDING 3: There is a positive and significant relationship between teachers' levels of interpersonal functioning and student attendance.

FINDING 4: There is a positive and significant relationship between teachers' levels of interpersonal functioning and enhanced student self-concept.

FINDING 5: The more focused the training in a specific interpersonal skill, the greater the probability that the skill will be incorporated into the teachers' normal classroom behavior.

FINDING 6: There is a positive and significant relationship between principals' levels of interpersonal functioning and the tendency on the part of their teachers to employ the same interpersonal skills in the classroom.

FINDING 7: The skills of the trainer appear to be critical variables in determining the success of an interpersonal skills training program.

FINDING 8: Teachers' levels of physical fitness are positively and significantly related to their ability to employ interpersonal skills in a sustained manner.

In the broadest and most general sense, of course, these findings showed that interpersonal skills training could be successfully undertaken with both large and small school populations – and that such training would indeed make a difference in promoting the facilitative conditions which teachers afforded to their students. We had learned a great deal from our study — including one crucial piece of information which was not clear until all the results were in.

As indicated throughout, the technology which we employed was based upon three primary instruments: Flanders' Interaction Analysis, an adaptation of Bloom's Taxonomy of Educational Objectives and Carkhuff's Interpersonal Process Scales. We trained teachers in the use of all three of these instruments. But only one seemed to make any substantive difference in terms of their teaching behaviors.

Learning to use the Flanders and Bloom scales enabled teachers in our experimental groups to understand just what they and their students were doing in class. But it was the mastery of the Carkhuff Interpresonal Skills alone which made it possible for the teachers to translate such understanding into new and more effective modes of action. These scales and the training modules based upon them turned out to be the greatest promoters of teachers' interpersonal skills — the skills which enabled each teacher to begin dealing with her or his students in the best and most constructive manner possible.

Inevitably, perhaps, I could not help imagining the effect which our findings might have upon the educational community. Which meant, of course, the impact on individual people who make up that community. People like "George Gamble," for instance. In a moment of happy relaxation, I tried to imagine how a new conversation with this earnest principal might go...

"Hey, George, you still look worried. Listen! I've got great news for you about the problems you've had selecting the best possible teachers."

"Yeah? I thought I already told you it was all a matter of chance. You look them over, you weigh all the factors which need weighing, you check things out and try to ask all the right questions. But in the end you just have to close your eyes and take a chance."

"Not so, George. Yesterday, maybe, but not anymore. Your kids here need more than a 'chance' — a random opportunity to be either helped or hurt — and I know how you can give it to them."

"Oh yeah? How's that?"

"Interpersonal skills, George," I tell him. "Select and train your teachers in interpersonal skills. It makes the difference, believe me!"

He looks at me skeptically. "I'd like nothing better than to believe you. But I've been around too long to put my faith in every pre-service or in-service training program that comes along. I'm afraid I'd need something a lot more convincing than your word to get involved in — what was it? Interpersonal skills training?"

"You're still pretty skeptical, George. It'll take something more convincing. Like the data collected over a 13-year period from a whole range of studies — including the results of a three-year research and training program conducted by the National Consortium for Humanizing Education. Data like these — "

I show him statistical evidence related to teachers' skills and student achievement, student attendance, student self- concept. I show him reports from other schools all across the country which have begun to experience the first real fruits of systematic skills-training programs. Head down, eyes flicking rapidly from one page to the next, George struggles to take it all in.

"I'm not a salesman, George," I tell him. "I'm not in here as front man for some outfit that wants to sell you a bill of goods. I'm not even here in my usual role of educator/researcher. I'm here as a representative of your students.

"Your students, George. The kids who fill this building every day. The kids who will either learn to grow or learn to fail right here in your school. I'm here because I'm like you. I want to give those kids more than a chance. It's taken me a long time to learn how to do that — a long time to understand exactly why three kids may eventually fall apart for every one who gets it together. But now I know. The only reason I'm talking to you about interpersonal skills is that I know they work. George, **we've proved it!**"

George looks across the desk at me, then down at the papers in front of him, then back up at me. He's a thoughtful, honest person. His mind is open. And he wants the best for each and every student in his school.

"It sounds good," he says at last. Then, shrugging and indicating the papers I have strewn before him, "I'll have to take some time, you know. Nothing happens overnight in a school system."

I nod. "Of course. I know that." I look across the desk at him and our eyes meet and hold. "But not too much time, huh George? For a kid in school, a lot can happen in a very short period of time — for better or for worse! And I've got a feeling you and I just ran out of excuses. It's one thing to take a chance because you don't know what's really going on. But once you learn the truth, there's really only two choices."

George nods. "Yeah. You either reach up and grab the truth and make it yours — or you try to pretend you never saw it." He sighs and his face relaxes into a smile. "Well, I guess I've got to be ready to grow myself if I want my teachers and my kids to grow. Interpersonal skills, huh?"

"That's it, George," I answer. Then I look at him. "What it really comes down to is very simple. Like the kid said, 'Kids don't learn from people they don't like.' If a teacher wants students to learn and grow, that teacher must begin by showing the students that she or he likes them. And that 'showing,' that communication, cannot be left to blind luck or chance! The teacher must use skills to show the kids how he or she feels — and how he or she recognizes the students' own feelings! Interpersonal skills! Check the data out and you'll see you don't need to take any more chances."

49   George grins. "Sounds good. Maybe all I'll have to worry about is changing my last name..."

OVERVIEW

In this concluding chapter in Section I, we outline some of the profound implications of the National Consortium's findings — and the direction which education can and must take tomorrow.

Perhaps most importantly, we can no longer afford to indulge ourselves in the traditional arguments over "humanistic" as opposed to "skills" concerns, "learning" as opposed to "training" procedures. If we want our children to recognize and accept basic human values, we must give them the skills they need to implement these values in their own lives. And if we want learning to be more than a vague and nebulous process which is only dimly understood, we must accept that systematic organization which is the basis of all teaching.

We can and must develop teachers to serve in turn as in-service trainers for their colleagues. We can and must recognize that specialty-area skills are worthless without the interpersonal skills needed to deliver them. We can and must ensure that students acquire learning skills as well as subject-area skills. We can and must recognize the inter-dependency of physical, emotional and intellectual levels of capability in principals, teachers and students.

Finally, we can and must recognize where education needs to go from here. The direction for tomorrow is perhaps best reflected in Carkhuff's model delineating the phases of student learning:

EXPLORATION ▶ UNDERSTANDING ▶ ACTION

and the inter-relationship of these learning phases with teacher interpersonal skills:

ATTENDING ▶ RESPONDING ▶ PERSONALIZING ▶ INITIATING

and teaching skills:

CONTENT DEVELOPMENT ▶ DIAGNOSING ▶ GOAL SETTING ▶ TEACHING DELIVERY

which facilitate student learning. In short, we must develop and implement a human technology of human effectiveness in our schools based upon real interpersonal and teaching skills.

THE FUTURE OF TEACHER TRAINING

"Away from Earth, it was impossible not to regard the planet's sheer size and beauty with something approaching reverence. It was equally impossible not to think of Earth as one entity — whole, unified and indivisible. Yet as human beings, we knew all too well that any such thought was sadly mistaken..."

These words were spoken by one of our astronauts shortly after his return from space. The vision of Earth which he had is one which many of us have undoubtedly summoned up in our own wistful imaginations. And his realization that life on our planet is far from whole, unified, indivisible is one in which we all must sadly share. The same realization is perhaps reflected in the familiar statement, "Humanity is great; it's people I can't stand." In this statement, as in the astronaut's perceptive vision, we can find echoes of that great gulf which seems to separate theory and practice.

In theory, our planet is indeed unified. In practice, however, it is a sprawling collection of separate nations and states, each often aggressively at odds with others.

In theory, humanity is a single, unified species. In practice, however, the species has broken down into a rag-tag host of warring factions, each sure of its right to supremacy.

In theory, our own nation is committed to the actual and democratic equality of all its citizens. In practice, however, "equality" often becomes the privilege of a few rather than the right of all.

And in theory, our system of public education is dedicated to the creation of an intelligent, capable and enlightened citizenry. But in practice, alas, we all too often thwart intelligence, deny capability and treat enlightenment as a foolish, unattainable ideal.

"Humanity is great; it's people I can't stand." This profoundly cynical statement is echoed in turn by the teacher who, surveying a school's sparkling halls and pristine classrooms on the final day of vacation, turns to a friend and remarks wistfully, "This is such a great place. If only the students didn't have to come back..."

If only the students didn't have to come back. If only the astronaut could spend his life in orbit, circling the planet and musing upon its unified majesty and grace. If only we could keep the soothing, even inspiring theoretical visions and forget the eternally frustrating, nitty-gritty world of actual practice. If only...

Yes, if only. Those of us who were involved in the National Consortium were no different from anyone else. We, too, had our dreams, our visions, our collections of wistful, unspoken "if onlys..." At the same time, we knew that to reject the real world in order to pursue our visions would be more than simply foolhardy — it would ultimately be self-destructive. And in the end such futile pursuit would do nothing to help the people who were the focus of our collective concern: the students in our schools. Jane, Tom, Janet, Dick, Juanita and Harry: each face was the face of ten thousand children who entered Kindergarten with little more than a lunch box and an apparently inexhaustible supply of curiosity and enthusiasm; each face, too, was the face of countless other children who, curiosity stifled and enthusiasm subverted, took far less from the educational experience than they had brought with them.

In developing and carrying out the programs of the National Consortium, we did not abandon our vision of theoretical unity, intelligence, capability, enlightenment. But neither did we allow ourselves to forget the troubled reality of our schools, the actual practices of our educational system. Rather, our goal throughout was to learn whether it was possible to reconcile theory and practice, ideal and actuality. In pursuing this aim, we focused our attention and our research on what seemed to us to be an area of significant concern: the lack of interpersonal skills which would allow educators to transform schools into truly humane, truly decent environments fostering the real growth of students.

In the real world, of course, no one every fully attains her or his idealized goal. Perhaps this is as it should be — for we are always left with more to do, more to be, more to grow toward. Nevertheless, the work of the National Consortium did achieve much that it set out to achieve. And the results of the Consortium's work have the most profound implications within and even beyond the world of educational systems. In this concluding chapter we will explore some of these implications.

HUMAN VALUES AND HUMAN SKILLS

Implication 1: Humanistic values and technology are interdependent rather than mutually exclusive concerns. Broadly speaking, we can discern what may seem at first to be two separate features of individual growth. On the one hand, we say that a person is growing or maturing when he/she shows signs of an increasing ability to deal constructively with other people in a wider range of situations. As the current idiom would have it, the individual who grows in this way is "getting it all together." He or she is developing human values which embrace other people and a set of functional human responses which allow him or her to deal positively and effectively with these people. Thus the child whose early adolescent selfishness gradually gives way to mutual concern is said to have grown; so, too, has the individual who takes increasing control of her or his life and begins to set and work toward goals which are both personally and socially constructive.

If the movement by the individual toward more effective human interactions represents one type of growth, a second type is reflected in the individual's acquisition of certain fundamental and specific skills.

Indeed, this may be the more commonly understood mode of growth in that it is both recognizable and easily measurable. Such growth may be seen in the child's development of basic physical skills like walking, running and talking; in educationally-related skills like reading a book, writing a composition, developing an algebraic equation or learning to operate a machine of one sort or another; and in later work skills like managing a business, working in an office, driving a truck or teaching a class.

Educators, of course, have always been aware of these two modes of growth — the first "humanistic" and the second "technological." And their awareness has invariably manifested itself in round after round of argument over the type of growth which education ought to focus upon.

For example: "The primary aim of education must be to teach students how to be better and more constructive people — how to develop their resources and make the most of their lives."

"Not at all. The primary aim of education must always be to teach students the basic technical skills they need to get along in modern society — the '3 R's,' for instance."

Both sides have summoned up effective arguments and the battle has swung in one direction and then the other over the years. Yet neither side has ever scored a conclusive victory. Nor is any such one-sided victory possible. The NCHE study showed once and for all that "humanistic" and "technological" concerns in education must always be inter-dependent!

Yes, individual growth is only meaningful when it entails that individual's increasing ability to relate to other people and the world in general in constructive terms. And yes, individual growth can and should be measured in terms of that individual's acquisition of basic skills like reading, writing and arithmetic. Yet neither of these two modes of growth can be promoted without the other! The teacher who possesses none of those "humanistic" interpersonal skills with which the NCHE study was concerned will be sorely limited in his/her ability to deliver basic reading or writing skills to learners. By the same token, the student who develops superior skills in, say, accounting will find it hard to get or hold a job without having developed the interpersonal capabilities which allow him or her to relate effectively with others.

Values education with all its humanistic concern and technical education with all its mechanistic proficiency are still two sides of a single coin — and common sense alone tells us that we need a whole coin to buy anthing in this world. The common denominator which ties together these two modes of growth is **skills**. For as the work of the National Consortium showed, skills are the means whereby teachers can transform classrooms into decent and humane places no less than they are the means whereby substantive student capabilities can be developed. Just as the individual must possess skills in order to be a good doctor or typist or long-haul truck driver, so he or she must possess skills in order to be a fully effective, truly constructive human being.

TEACHER TRAINING SKILLS

Implication 2: Educators can be taught to serve as trainers for their colleagues. As indicated earlier, one of our concerns in pursuing the aims of the National Consortium was to determine whether it was possible to train large numbers of teachers in interpersonal skills. The results clearly indicated that this was indeed possible. The key to our approach involved training selected teachers and other educators to serve themselves as trainers for groups at their respective schools. And the key to this initial training-of-trainers involved the development and delivery of effective content modules, each concerned with a specific interpersonal skill and all arranged in a sequential, systematic fashion.

Here again we found that skills are the primary concern. For a very long time indeed, people have sought to promote the decent and constructive behavior of others through well-intentioned but vague advice: "Always go out of your way to help someone," "Try to see his side of things," "Be more considerate of her needs" and so on. Alas, it is quite clear that advice of this sort is largely powerless. Recognizing this, we in the NCHE began by seeking to define and operationalize the particular behaviors and capabilities entailed by human understanding, genuineness and respect. We found that we could develop sequential, step-by-step modules for use in training educators to serve as trainers in their own turn for larger populations within their own school systems. There now seems little doubt that this same approach could be used to develop a training capability – and, eventually, truly facilitative conditions – within every public school in this country.

Two related points need to be made here. Many people may react negatively to the notion that human decency can be reduced to a set of specific, observable behaviors. The same people may also have an adverse reaction to the work "training" as applied to educators. 'We're not machines," they may argue. "As human beings, we're far more than the sum of our visible behaviors." Such an argument, of course, is completely valid – and also completely irrelevant. Of course we're not machines! We are complex beings, each capable of deep thought, equally deep feelings and profound insights. Student or teacher or administrator, each of us is unique in many ways. Yet since we must live and function together in the world, we must somehow come to terms with each other's unique feelings and thoughts – and then have effective ways in which to communicate our understanding. We can only achieve such communication through our words and behaviors. And it is a demonstrable fact that some expressions or actions promote such communication while others obscure or hinder it.

The teacher who leans back in his chair, arms behind his head and feet on this desk, may believe that he is genuinely concerned with the students in his classroom. Yet the majority of students will see his behavior as reflecting only minimal concern and interest.

The teacher who leans forward toward the students, listening carefully and making frequent eye contact with each individual, may also feel that she is fully involved with, fully committed to her class. And in her case, her involvement and commitment are communicated in clearly visible terms to the students.

To sum up on the first point, then, decency is never reduced to behaviors. Rather, words and behaviors are the only ways in which such decency can be communicated to and shared with the people who really count — the students in the classroom.

As for the second point, what does "training" really mean? As we have used the term here, it refers to nothing more or less than a careful, step-by-step manner of teaching someone certain specific skills. Thus we have all experienced any amount of training already in our individual lives. A good English teacher trains us to write effectively. A good coach trains us to compete effectively. A good theatrical director trains us to act effectively. Training is simply a systematic approach to teaching — an approach which says, in effect, "Here are the things you must know and understand and do in order to practice this skill — and here is the best order in which to approach the task."

In the end, then, we can reject the behaviors associated with decency only if we wish to keep our own decency to ourselves. And we can likewise reject the necessity of training only if we are content to think of growth as random rather than systematic, chaotic rather than coherent.

LEADERSHIP SKILLS

Implication 3: The importance of skilled leadership in the individual school cannot be over-emphasized. The results of the three-year study undertaken by the National Consortium served to underline the vitally important role of the principal in each school. The principal is, in many ways, a "model" figure in that she or he models roles and behaviors which teachers in the school tend to adopt. Here again, we found that skills are the key ingredients. The principal who employs interpersonal skills in order to understand a teacher from that teacher's own unique frame of reference, for example, will learn a great deal about that teacher's capabilities; at the same time, the principal will promote the teacher's own development and subsequent use in the classroom of similar "understanding" skills.

Assuming the development of an in-service training program within a school, the trainer and the principal will tend to serve as co-equal promoters of teacher effectiveness and facilitation. The trainer's role is to deliver to each teacher a fundamental and practical grasp of each skill. The principal's role is to model and reinforce the specific ways in which each skill can and should be used in real-life situations long after the training program itself has been completed. In the end, the principal must recognize the truth in the axiomatic statement that "no school can be better than the person heading it up" — and must live accordingly!

TEACHING SKILLS

Implication 4: Teachers must possess both interpersonal and specialty skills in order to facilitate rather than retard student growth. As has been indicated frequently, the primary thrust of the National Consortium's training program was to deliver to teachers the interpersonal skills they needed to deomonstrate understanding, genuineness and respect in the classroom. At the most basic level, these skills involved two related capabilities. In the first place, the individual teacher needed to develop an awareness of each student's unique frame of reference. And in the second place, the teacher needed to develop methods of communicating this awareness to the student.

Awareness and communication — two fundamental concerns which are, alas, all too often overlooked in the rush to develop a wide range of impressive specialty area skills. Consider the teacher who begins her class in Social Studies one morning by saying to her 28 students, "All right, today we're going to learn about the Bill of Rights."

Does she know that Henry, slumped in the back row, is tired and in a foul mood because he just flunked a Math test? Or that Sharon is full of energy and ready to take on the world?

Does she understand that Margaret is glaring at her desk in anger because she feels the teacher never calls on her? Or that Jim is really miles away, drifting happily in the never-never-land of daydreams?

Does she have the skills she needs to really see each student as a unique individual, possessed each day of an energy level and degree of interest and capability which will largely determine what he or she actually learns? Or does the teacher simply go on with her prepared lesson, her lack of skills serving to transform her collection of unique individuals into a faceless, homogeneous mass?

And if the teacher does possess the skills needed to enter and understand each student's own frame of reference, is she then capable of communicating this understanding to the students? Recognizing that Bill's sullen "I dunno" in answer to her question really means "I don't care" while Belinda's wistful "I don't know" translates as "I wish I did," can the teacher respond in such a way as to generate true concern in Bill and new confidence in Belinda? Or will her lack of responsive skills force her to deal with the two students in an indentical manner, thus indicating to them that she really cannot tell them apart?

Awareness and communication of awareness. Without the specific interpersonal skills needed in these basic areas, the classroom teacher will find himself or herself largely impotent. With such skills, the same teacher can breathe real life and meaning into her or his specialty subject area. For these skills enable the teacher to experience things fully at any given moment — and by sharing this experience, this awareness, to open the student to the possibilities of real growth within the subject area.

A knowledge of one's subject is obviously essential for the development of effective content. As the National Consortium's study has made clear, fundamental interpersonal skills are equally essential to the delivery of this content to students in the classroom.

This is by no means a "pie in the sky" situation. As we have stressed, interpersonal skills training of teachers will result in substantive student benefits. But schools can go beyond this and use the methodologies developed and/or implemented by the National Consortium to select new personnel. While resumes, interviews and application forms are all helpful, a critically important addition to the selection process might involve a one-hour tape of an interaction by the prospective teacher. This taped interaction could then be rated in terms of Carkhuff's instruments to determine the level of facilitative conditions being provided.

LEARNING SKILLS

Implication 5: The individual growth of each student can only be promoted and sustained if the student develops real learning skills as well as subject-area skills. In recent years there has been a great deal of concern in the educational community about students' decreasing command of basic subject-area skills. Many teachers feel that students enter their particular classes with little or no real preparation. They argue that today's student cannot write clearly and succinctly, cannot add a simple column of figures, cannot develop and follow a simple procedure in a basic science class. And there are many indications that these teachers are quite right.

Why?

We may be able to understand what is happening in many of our schools if we take a look at a hypothetical learning situation. Let us suppose that an English teacher in a given school has a masterful command of the language and of the techniques of writing — and nothing else. He delivers effective writing skills — and nothing else — to his students. Among these students is a girl who goes on to become an English teacher in her own right. She in turn delivers what she has learned to her own class. The lesson has inevitably lost something in translation since this new teacher has nothing to go on besides what she was told some years before by her original mentor. Her own students can write fairly well but not quite as well as she can. One of these students goes on to become an English teacher in turn. Since he, too, lacks the skills to develop the original lesson to meet his own and his students' unique needs, he can only deliver a still-more-diluted version of the original lesson. His students learn to write with only minimal competency.

So it goes. The process is reminiscent of that old children's game where one child makes up a message and whispers it to the child sitting next to him or her in a circle. By the time the whispered message has gone all the way around the circle, it is all but unrecognizable.

The point is clear. Teachers must deliver more than the content of their subject-areas to their students. They must deliver a command of the process which alone can bring the subject to life for the student. In short, teachers must deliver to their students the learning skills which constitute the "how" of the educational process and not just the "what." Unless this is done, each student will inevitably take from a class slightly less than the teacher brought in.

In relation to the interpersonal skills that we have researched, there are several applications in learning skills. At the most basic level, we can teach students the same interpersonal skills that we have taught the teachers. For example, the students can learn to attend to the teacher and to the content. In this manner, they can pay attention most fully. They can observe and listen to what is going on, a necessary although not sufficient condition of learning. There are many other learning skills and they remain to be more fully detailed elsewhere (Carkhuff and Berenson, 1976).

The difference between teaching a student only about a subject and teaching the same student both the subject and the process whereby he or she can keep learning is profound. It is the difference between leaving a person in a heated house in the dead of winter with no instructions about how to start the furnace and leaving the same person in the same house with a full set of instructions. Every furnace will malfunction sooner or later. When it does, the first person will feel the increasing cold as the last vestiges of heat seep out around doors and windows. The second person, having learned the appropriate procedures, will have no trouble taking over control of the heating plant and generating a continuing supply of warm air.

As indicated, interpersonal and specialty skills function interdependently in determining how well a teacher can facilitate real student growth. In the same way, learning and subject-area skills function interdependently in determining how well the student can take control of and sustain such growth.

HUMAN GROWTH AND DEVELOPMENT

Implication 6: Growth and facilitation are always dependent upon the individual's level of physical, emotional and intellectual capability. Those of us involved in education have always assumed the importance of individual intellectual capability: if we cannot think clearly ourselves, we can never hope to teach our students to think clearly. Indeed, at times we have been guilty of believing that intellect and cognition alone are the concerns of education. As the National Consortium's study has shown, this is far from the case. The inter-relationship of cognitive and affective processes, of thinking and feeling, can no longer be in doubt. As teachers, our ability to understand and deal effectively with our own unique feelings and the unique feelings of each student is no less important than our ability to come to intellectual terms with a complex subject.

Perhaps the least expected finding which emerged from the National Consortium's work related to the critical role played by an individual's level of physical energy and fitness. For years we have gone along assuming that no one besides athletes and a few cultists need be particularly concerned with physical fitness. Caught up in a life-style and career which is often sedentary, we have completely overlooked the way in which our physical health allows us to teach effectively – or keeps us from doing just that. Yet just as there can no longer be any doubt about the interdependency of cognitive and affective processes, so there can no longer be any doubt that physical energy and fitness constitute a third element closely related to the other two.

The whole teacher must be just that: not a walking, talking brain nor even an animated brain possessed of a responsive heart; but a whole person comprising brain, heart and energy, an individual whose physical, emotional and intellectual capabilities have been developed and integrated in order to allow him or her to teach others effectively. And if this is true for the classroom teacher, it is equally true for the principal and for the pre-service or in-service trainer.

If we want our students to become whole people, we must begin by making sure that we ourselves are whole.

Six implications for today: implications for training, for teaching, for learning. These implications represent, in a very real sense, the meaning which we found in the results of the three-year program undertaken by the National Consortium. And this meaning, this significance, points far beyond itself. If we are truly to learn from the results of the National Consortium's work, we must understand what significance this work has for our lives tomorrow – and for the lives of our students.

THE DIRECTIONS FOR TOMORROW

In the preceding section we indicated that a teacher must teach her or his students "how" as well as "what" to learn. This may represent the best starting point for us in considering the directions in which education must move.

How does a student learn? For that matter, how do any of us learn? There are clearly any number of approaches to this simply-stated yet profoundly complex question. Yet the approach which is at once most direct and most functional may be that taken by Dr. Robert R. Carkhuff in his pioneering work in the area of human resource development.

A Learning Model

According to the models which Carkhuff has developed, all learning involves a similar pattern (Carkhuff and Berenson, 1976). The individual begins by **exploring** a new area of concern. This initial exploratory phase is characterized by an expanding awareness of facts, concepts, principles, possibilities, implications and the like. From exploration, the individual moves on to develop an accurate **understanding** of the area being investigated. Such understanding is reflected in the individual's elimination of irrelevant data, in the focusing of attention and concern and in the developing of an awareness of what this subject matter means to him or her in terms of personal goals and values. Finally, exploration and understanding give way to **action** as the individual confirms and demonstrates mastery of the content which she or he has learned by putting it to practical use.

Exploration must precede understanding; and exploration and understanding together are the prerequisites for effective action. Or, as Carkhuff outlines in his model:

EXPLORATION ▶ UNDERSTANDING ▶ ACTION
(E)   **(U)**   **(A)**

There seems little doubt that this E-U-A process accurately reflects the phases of individual learning. We have only to watch a very young child dealing with a new toy — or an experienced professional approaching yet another assignment—to see the process in action.

Turning to our students, then, we can say that they will learn how to learn once they have mastered the techniques or skills entailed in this E-U-A process. A few of the specific skills involved during each phase of the learning process are given below in Figure 6.

Exploring	Understanding	Acting
Analysis	Generalization	Evaluation
Manipulating	Categorization	Application
Listening	Classification	Acquisition
Observing	Comparing & Contrasting	Program Implementation
Attending	Associating	Program Development

Figure 6. The phases of learning.

A Human Teaching Model

If the skills involved in exploration, understanding and action represent the goal of the teacher who is committed to helping students learn how to learn, what are the skills which the teacher herself or himself must use to attain this goal? We have already documented part of the answer through the work of the National Consortium. The teacher must begin by developing the skills needed to become aware of each student's unique frame of reference and to then communicate this awareness in accurate terms to the student. The terms "awareness" and "communication" here correspond to Carkhuff's skills of **attending** and

1977; Carkhuff and Pierce, 1975). For as Carkhuff has found, the effective teacher can promote student exploration — and learn from this same exploration — by attending to the student in both physical and psychological terms. Going on, the teacher can reflect the awareness gained through attending by responding to the student's situation and feelings at the level at which the student expresses them.

A student appears at a teacher's desk and announces, "I can't do this assignment." **Attending**, the teacher faces the student and notes the student's unhappy expression, his dishevelled appearance, his ink-smudged fingers, the crumpled paper in his hand. She tries to see "where he's coming from." At the same time, her physically attentive posture and behavior reflect her real concern. The student sees that she is neither mad nor pleased but simply concerned and attentive.

"You've really tried but it's just too hard," the teacher says, **responding** to the student's apparent situation. Encouraged, the student **explores** his own situation.

"Yeah — it's that business about topic sentences. That's really confusing me."

The teacher **responds interchangeably** again, continuing to show understanding for both the student's feelings and the reason for those feelings: "You feel pretty lost because the requirements for a topic sentence aren't clear."

As shown here, albeit in highly abbreviated form, a teacher's attending and responding skills can promote student exploration. To these basic skills, Carkhuff adds two others of equal importance: **personalizing** and **initiating**. A teacher uses personalizing skills to promote student understanding of the way in which the student, himself or herself, is involved in a particular problem or situation. By personalizing responses, the teacher can transform the student's "It's-me-against-them" attitude into the "It's-partly-on-account-of-my-own-actions" attitude essential for constructive action.

"You feel dumb because you can't figure out how to write a good topic sentence and you really want to do well on the assignment." After a prolonged exchange with the student, the teacher **personalizes** both the problem and the goal in terms which she feels the student is ready to accept. So long as the student felt the assignment was too hard, he himself was helpless. Now, however, he has a handle on the way in which a personal deficit of his own is contributing to the situation.

"You want to get at least a B on this assignment. That means you'll have to master the skills involved in writing a good topic sentence. Let's figure out all the different things you'll need to know to get where you want to go. You might begin by listing two characteristics of any good topic sentence." Here the teacher **initiates** with the student, helping him to develop a particular program of action which will take him to his goal.

Attending. Responding. Personalizing. Initiating. These are the four major interpersonal or helping skills which a teacher must use in order to promote student exploration, understanding and action. Returning to Carkhuff's model, we can outline these phases in the following way.

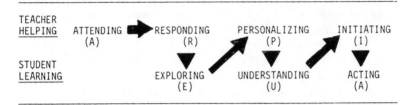

Figure 7. The phases of interpersonal helping as related to the phases of learning.

A Content Teaching Model

In addition to using interpersonal skills (A-R-P-I) to promote student exploration, understanding and action, of course, the teacher must also possess and be able to use those specialized skills peculiar to her or his profession. These skills, too, may be seen to promote the student E-U-A learning process (Carkhuff and Berenson, 1976).

The teacher **attends** by **developing content** which is uniquely suited to the needs of her or his particular students. The teacher **responds** to the students' exploration of this new content by **diagnosing** the students' individual levels of competency. The teacher **personalizes** the material for the students by working with each student to **set individualized learning goals** based upon her or his diagnosis. Finally, the teacher initiates with the students by making a **teaching delivery** carefully designed to enable each student to achieve her or his new goal.

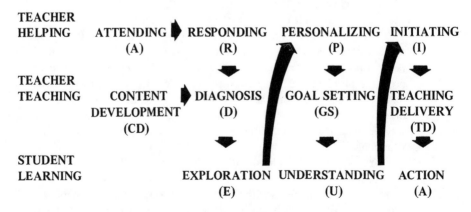

Figure 8. The phases of teaching and helping as related to the phases of learning.

We have, then, a model outlining the separate phases of teacher helping, teacher teaching and student learning. Each of these phases entails the development and use of specific skills. In the background stand two other figures: the teacher-trainer and the school principal. The trainer makes the initial delivery of necessary skills to individual teachers. The principal plays a vitally important support role in modeling and promoting the use of these same skills by the teachers in her or his own school. The effectiveness of every person functioning at every level in the model is characterized by her or his level of physical, emotional and intellectual capability.

Thanks to Carkhuff, we have a model on which to base our future educational efforts. Given Carkhuff's own research findings (Carkhuff and Berenson, 1976) and the clear results of the National Consortium's work, there can be little doubt that the processes reflected in the model we have outlined are real and essential — and that the skills which these processes require are concrete and functional.

We have a model. But we also have more, far more than that. For the direction in which this simple model points is all but infinite in its promise. By mastering the specific skills needed to teach our students both the "what" and "how" of the learning process, we can open their world up for them. For the E-U-A process of student learning is by no means a closed circle. Rather, it is an open spiral which leads onward and upward to new growth. Every action which the student takes, every goal which she or he achieves, provides a wealth of new experience. And this experience in turn becomes the focus for a new round of exploration, a new round of understanding, a new round of increasingly effective action.

We began this final chapter by sharing the vision of one of our astronauts — a vision which served to underline the vast gulf between theory and practice, ideal and reality. Perhaps we can now begin to understand that it is this very gulf in which we are in danger of dying.

Yes, dying. And the greatest mistake we can make is to shrug off such statements as pure exaggeration.

Children in this country as well as in many foreign lands have died this year from starvation, from malnutrition, from a lack of the simplest necessities of life itself. A part of us died with them, unable to make sense out of the needless gulf between a shrivelled infant and a Ronald McDonald.

Friends, relatives or strangers, thousands have died on our highways, consumed by their need to rush from one place to the next in the shortest possible time. A part of us died with them, unable to cope with the demands for human control exerted by a technology which, left to itself, is at best mindless and at worst brutalizing.

And students, too, have died. They have died through overdoses and crimes and senseless destruction. They have died through lack of concern, lack of care, lack of direction. Far more have learned to live a half-life, moving self-indulgently from one empty, inconsequential task to the next, keeping as much as they can and sharing only what they cannot conceal, left to their own devices and existing in such a way that their actual deaths may finally receive no attention at all. Yet part of us dies with each of them, unable to continue in a world where few have bothered to learn the simplest, most fundamental techniques for living constructively with other people.

The gulf between theory and practice is not a figurative but a real one. And all of this gloomy talk of death and dying points to an equally real fact of life: **we get back from this world exactly what we put into it.**

If we decide that our system of public education need do no more than provide interested students with a nodding acquaintance with the 3 R's, we'll turn the world over to a generation possessed of little more than precisely that: a nodding acquaintance with a minimal number of basic skills.

If we decide that our sole aim in education should be to inculcate our students with vague, platitudinous concepts dealing with the need for decency and human understanding, we'll trade our birthright and the birthright of our children for nothing more lasting or constructive than a mess of miscellaneous verbiage devoid of the capacity for action.

If we continue to try in our desperate manner to separate skills from learning, training from teaching, we'll have no cause to be surprised at the endless stream of unskilled, untrained and totally disaffected young people who turn their backs on the schools with a sigh of collective relief.

But if we ourselves are capable of learning — if we are capable of exploring, understanding and acting upon the implications of studies done by The National Consortium for Humanizing Education, by Carkhuff, by researchers of Flanders and Bloom and a host of others — we can still bridge the gulf between theory and practice, dream and reality. We can give our students the gift of real life — life lived on the most constructive, facilitative and fulfilling terms possible.

We can learn to like our students — and to **show** our liking, our concern, our understanding. We can recognize the fundamental, inescapable truth in the statement "Kids don't learn from people they don't like." And recognizing this truth, we will know what we have to do.

Archimedes said "Give me a lever long enough and I will move the world." For us, the world is bound up in the four walls of the public school classroom. The lever we need is the model of helping, teaching and learning skills we have outlined — a model which itself implies a vast and infinitely promising technology of human effectiveness. We have what we need. The question that remains is profound in its simplicity.

What will we do with what we have learned?

Statement of Problem

The goal of the applied research program conducted over a three year period by the National Consortium for Humanizing Education was to devise, demonstrate, and document (the effects of) Interpersonal Skills Training for Teachers. Hypotheses of the project were:

1. Teachers can be trained to increase the levels of facilitative interpersonal conditions which they offer to their students.
2. It is feasible to provide Interpersonal Skills Training for large numbers of teachers.
3. Increases in the levels of facilitative interpersonal conditions provided by teachers will be accompanied by changes in pupil outcomes indicative of gains in both (a) indices of mental health and (b) cognitive indices.

In carrying out the project to reach the above goal and test the hypotheses set forth, major activities of the NCHE were:

1. To devise a training program in Interpersonal Skills for teachers
2. To carry out the training program with a substantial number of teachers
3. To conduct research into the effects of the training program on (a) changes in teacher classroom functioning and (b) student outcomes.

Research Questions

As an applied research project, the primary goal of the NCHE was to seek answers to these six questions:

1. Did the experimental treatment (Interpersonal Skills Training for Teachers) make a difference in teacher behavior? (Study No. 10)*
2. Was the teachers' response to training affected by teacher characteristics of race, sex, or years of teaching experience? (Study No. 11).
3. Were revised training procedures more effective than the original procedures? (Study No. 12.)
4. Were training effects enhanced when the principal of the school had received prior training in Interpersonal Skills? (Study No. 13.)
5. Were teacher behavior study variables related to student outcomes on indices of mental health and cognition? (Study No. 14).
6. Did the experimental treatment (Interpersonal Skills Training

---

*The Study numbers in parentheses refer to the order in which the studies are presented in this section.

of Teachers) translate to differences in student outcomes on indices of mental health and cognition? (Study No. 15.) However, because this was action research in a natural (field) setting, there were additional questions of a basic research nature which needed to be answered in order to ensure proper consideration of confounding variables and to aid in the interpretation of results from the applied research studies. Accordingly, the following additional questions were posed:

7. Is there a relationship between the behavior of the school principal and the response on the study variables by the teachers in his/her school? (Study No. 1).

8. Is there a relationship between the school principal's over-all level of Interpersonal Functioning and the way in which the teachers in his/her school perceive their working environment and instructional tasks? (Study No. 2).

9. Are there grade level effects on the teacher behavior study variables? (Study No. 3 and 4).

10. Are there subject matter effects on the teacher behavior study variables? (Study No. 5).

11. Are the teacher behavior study variables affected by time of year? (Study No. 6).

12. Were initial levels of the teacher behavior study variables related to teacher characteristics of race, sex or years of teaching experience? (Study No. 7).

13. Is there a relationship between the level of physical functioning of the teacher and the teacher behavior study variables? (Study No. 8).

14. Are there relationships among the study variables of teacher and student classroom functioning? (Study No. 9).

Each of the above questions was formulated as a null hypothesis capable of being tested statistically within the design of the project. Later parts of this section present the results of the individual studies and summarize and integrate the findings.

DESIGN

Statistical Treatment

The research was conducted in what was essentially a two-group pretest-posttest design, although process measures of classroom functioning were taken periodically in both control and experimental groups. Illustration 1 displays the variations in design for the three year period.

Illustration 1: Design of Study

Project Year 01

	EXP	CON
Grades 7-12	2	2
Grades 1-6	4	4

Treatment: E-1

Sample:

  12 schools
  309 teachers
7,408 students

Project Year 02

	EXP		CON	
Grades 7-12	2		1	
	EE	CE*	CC	EC+
Grades 1-6	3	1	3	1

Treatments: E-2 and
             E-1 revised
Sample:

  11 schools
  230 teachers
4,200 students

Project Year 03

	EXP	CON
Grades 7-12	2	2
Grades 1-6	4	2

Treatment: E-2 Revised

Sample:

  10 schools
  136 teachers
2,922 students

Treatment E-1 - Process Skills training only
Treatment E-2 - Process & Application Skills training

*Control school rotated to Experimental condition; received Treatment E-1 revised.

+Experimental school rotated to No Training (Control) condition.

The data collected included both instrumental scores and
behavioral indices. (For specifics, see the discussion of study variables
below). The statistical procedures for treatment of the obtained data
included:

1. Sixth-Degree orthogonal polynomial multilinear regression analysis across time,
2. Backward elimination multilinear regression analysis with quadratic terms,
3. Stepwise multilinear regression analysis,
4. Analysis of co-variance of gains between groups,
5. Analysis of variance of group means,
6. Chi-Square analysis of contingency tables,
7. Kruskal-Wallis one-way analysis of variance by ranks.

Samples

The teachers involved in the Year 01 (1971-72 school year) and
Year 02 (1972-73) samples were "informed consent" participants from
eight elementary schools, two junior high schools, and two senior high
schools in a large city in north-central Texas. The schools represented
all socio-economic levels and racial distributions in the city. The
teachers in the Year 03 (1973-74) sample were "informed consent"
participants from ten schools in a rural and suburban parish in
northeastern Louisiana. They represented all but one of the schools in
the Parish.

The numbers in Illustration 1 represent the actual number of
individuals who participated to the extent of supplying one or more
items of data. After initial editing each year, the data base was reduced to
the levels displayed in Table 1. In this initial edit, adult participants
were retained if they had (1) submitted 3 or more tapes during the year
and (2) completed the Professional Information sheet supplying
socio-demographic data. Student data was edited on the basis of
mobility; i.e., students were retained who had taken both pre and post
tests on at least one index. Table 2 displays the distribution of the
teachers in the three samples by race, sex, school level, and years of
teaching experience. Tables 3, 4, and 5 present the distribution of the
students within treatment conditions by race, sex, and grade level.

Table 1: Data Base for Project
After Initial Editing

Participants	Year 01	Year 02	Year 03
Number of Schools	12	11	10
Number of Principals*	11	10	6
Number of Teachers	272	205	104
Number of Students	6,412	3,759	2,401

*There are fewer principals than schools because
not all principals submitted the three tapes
requested.

Table 2: Distribution of Teachers within Samples by
Race, Sex, Level of School, Years of
Teaching Experience, and Location

	Classification	Samples		
		Yr. 01	Yr. 02	Yr. 03
Race	Total Black American	66	48	38
	Total White American	203	154	65
	Total Other	3+	3+	1*
Sex	Total Male	40	21	15
	Total Female	232	184	89
Sex & Race	Black Males	13	7	6
	White Males	27	14	9
	Black Females	53	41	32
	White Females	176	140	56
	Other Females	3+	3+	1*
Level	Elementary (grades 1-6)	168	142	59
	Secondary (grades 7-12)	104	63	45
	Total (grades 1-12)	272	205	104
Teaching Experience	1 Yr. Experience	25	24	19
	2 Yrs. Experience	23	14	14
	3-7 Yrs. Experience	54	35	30
	8-15 Yrs. Experience	68	48	20
	16-25 Yrs. Experience	60	49	14
	Over 25 Yrs. Experience	42	35	7
	Location	Urban Texas	Urban Texas	Rural LA.

+Sample included 1 American Indian Female, 1
Mexican-American Female, and 1 Oriental Female.
*Sample included 1 Mexican-American Female.

Table 3: Distribution of Year 01 Students by Race, Sex, and Grade Level Within Treatment Conditions

Grade Levels	CONTROL SCHOOLS									EXPERIMENTAL SCHOOLS									ALL SCHOOLS									TOTAL		
	Black			White			Mex.Am.			Black			White			Mex.Am.			Black			White			Mex.Am.					
	M	F	Total	M	F	Total	M	F	Total	M	F	Total	M	F	Total	M	F	Total	M	F	Total	M	F	Total	M	F	Total	M	F	All
1	43	42	85	73	64	137	3	5	8	58	58	116	60	72	132	8	5	13	101	100	201	133	136	269	11	10	21	245	246	491
2	45	41	86	81	86	167	6	4	10	44	67	111	87	61	148	6	8	14	89	108	197	168	147	315	12	12	24	269	267	536
3	55	38	93	97	80	177	6	6	12	48	52	100	87	59	146	10	5	15	103	90	193	184	139	323	16	11	27	303	240	543
4	48	52	100	105	86	191	3	10	13	49	53	102	87	68	155	5	9	14	97	105	202	192	154	346	8	19	27	297	278	575
5	59	59	118	103	89	192	5	6	11	52	47	99	85	79	164	6	9	15	111	106	217	188	168	356	11	15	26	310	289	599
6	35	38	73	98	91	189	7	3	10	46	61	107	77	96	173	5	6	11	81	99	180	175	187	362	12	9	21	268	295	563
7	10	9	19	93	112	205	31	40	71	10	16	26	109	90	199	12	12	24	20	25	45	202	202	404	43	52	95	265	279	544
8	15	7	22	118	115	233	44	40	84	11	6	17	105	90	195	5	8	13	26	13	39	233	205	428	49	48	97	298	266	564
9	10	14	24	121	110	231	32	39	71	11	10	21	95	82	177	13	7	20	21	24	45	261	192	408	45	46	91	282	262	544
10	16	10	26	121	126	247	17	16	33	7	7	14	137	109	246	39	40	79	23	17	40	258	235	493	56	56	112	337	308	645
11	19	29	48	85	79	164	21	14	35	7	7	14	98	107	205	42	33	75	26	36	62	183	186	369	63	47	110	272	269	541
12	12	27	39	69	84	153	21	12	33	9	11	20	84	95	179	22	18	40	21	38	59	153	179	332	43	30	73	217	247	464

GRAND TOTAL: 6,609

Table 4: Distribution of Year 02 Students by Race and Sex and Grade Level Within Treatment Conditions

| | CONTROL SCHOOLS | | | | | | | | | EXPERIMENTAL SCHOOLS | | | | | | | | | ALL SCHOOLS | | | | | | | | | TOTAL | | |
| | Black | | | White | | | Mex.Am. | | | Black | | | White | | | Mex.Am. | | | Black | | | White | | | Mex.Am. | | | | | |
Grade Levels	M	F	Total Black	M	F	Total White	M	F	Total MexAm	M	F	Total Black	M	F	Total White	M	F	Total MexAm	M	F	Total Black	M	F	Total White	M	F	Total MexAm	M	F	ALL
1	31	12	43	62	67	129	9	7	16	38	30	68	25	21	46	0	0	0	69	42	111	87	88	175	9	7	16	165	137	302
2	28	32	60	73	80	153	7	5	12	39	38	77	19	17	36	1	0	1	67	70	137	92	97	189	8	5	13	167	172	339
3	36	32	68	97	90	187	8	6	14	22	33	55	21	18	39	20	26	46	58	65	123	118	108	226	28	32	60	204	205	409
4	24	18	42	90	66	156	6	5	11	41	43	84	21	19	40	2	2	4	65	61	126	111	85	196	8	7	15	184	153	337
5	9	17	26	69	57	126	1	6	7	65	62	127	24	19	43	0	2	2	74	79	153	93	76	169	1	8	9	168	163	331
6	37	37	74	81	82	163	5	6	11	49	46	95	22	14	36	1	2	3	86	83	169	103	96	199	6	8	14	195	187	382
7	—	—	—	—	—	—	—	—	—	10	8	18	41	46	87	3	3	6	10	8	18	41	46	87	3	3	6	54	57	111
8	—	—	—	—	—	—	—	—	—	8	14	22	97	66	163	9	9	18	8	14	22	97	66	163	9	9	18	114	89	203
9	—	—	—	—	—	—	—	—	—	11	5	16	82	70	152	4	5	9	11	5	16	82	70	152	4	5	9	97	80	177
10	0	1	1	48	54	102	4	2	6	12	12	24	102	96	198	21	28	49	12	13	25	150	150	300	25	30	55	187	193	380
11	12	7	19	87	96	183	13	6	19	6	5	11	110	87	197	23	29	52	18	12	30	197	183	380	36	35	71	251	230	481
12	11	24	35	57	62	119	13	9	22	6	7	13	80	75	155	25	24	49	17	31	48	137	137	274	38	33	71	192	201	393

GRAND TOTAL: 3,845

Table 5: Distribution of Year 03 Students by Race, Grade-Level and Sex within Treatment Conditions

Grade Levels	Control Schools						Experimental Schools						All Schools								
	BLACK			WHITE			BLACK			WHITE			BLACK			WHITE			TOTAL		
	M	F	Tot. Bl.	M	F	Tot. Wh.	M	F	Tot. Bl.	M	F	Tot. Wh.	M	F	Tot. Bl.	M	F	Tot. Wh.	M	F	Tot. All
1	34	29	63	35	34	69	31	27	58	32	29	61	65	56	121	67	63	130	132	119	251
2	24	25	49	23	30	53	13	18	31	30	10	40	37	43	80	53	40	93	90	83	173
3	10	8	18	13	15	28	32	24	56	32	26	58	42	32	74	45	41	86	87	73	160
4	17	13	30	23	24	47	37	35	72	32	28	60	54	48	102	55	52	107	109	100	209
5	13	18	31	20	19	39	33	42	75	46	36	82	46	60	106	66	55	121	112	115	227
6	16	11	27	18	20	38	47	49	96	45	38	83	63	60	123	63	58	121	126	118	244
7	19	9	28	29	17	46	22	22	44	43	34	77	41	31	72	72	51	123	113	82	195
8	25	38	63	25	28	53	29	35	64	40	47	87	54	73	127	65	75	140	119	148	267
9	24	17	41	5	27	32	2	10	12	3	7	10	26	27	53	8	34	42	34	61	95
10	18	29	47	15	34	49	5	9	14	5	13	18	23	38	61	20	47	67	43	85	128
11	19	21	40	21	9	30	8	12	20	3	10	13	27	33	60	24	19	43	51	52	103
12	15	23	38	13	15	28	5	14	19	1	10	11	20	37	57	14	25	39	34	62	96

GRAND TOTAL: 2,148

A further edit occurred as each study was conducted. Table 6 displays the gross N and editing criteria for each study and its replications, if any. Sub-group N's for each study will be presented as the studies are described.

Table 6: Individual Study N with Edit Criteria

	Study Number	Year 01	Year 02	Year 03	Edit Criteria
BASIC STUDIES	1	250	--	--	4 tapes submitted; school principal's co-operation
	2	257	--	--	SD and MTAI pre-tests
	3	238	--	--	5 tapes; MTAI pre-test
	4	238	--	--	5 tapes; MTAI pre-test
	5	89	--	--	Secondary teachers; tape for March, 1972
	6	234	--	--	6 tapes including September, 1971 and May, 1972 tapes
	7	121	--	--	Experimental teachers; 4 tapes including May, 1971 and May, 1972
	8	--	--	46	Experimental teachers; September, 1973 tape; Harvard Step-Test
	9	260	192	99	5 tapes submitted during year
APPLIED STUDIES	10	240	155	87	4 tapes each year including pre-post; if experimental, completed training
	11	121	52	41	Experimental teachers; 4 tapes including pre-post; completed training
	12	86	41	--	Experimental teachers grades 1-6; pre-post tapes; completed training
	13	--	--	47	Teachers grades 4-8; pre-post tapes; if experimental, completed training
	14	156*	--	--	Classroom teachers; 4 or more tapes; Secondary teachers restricted to English & Math; their students
		5,003*			
	15	5,796*	2,726*	2,138*	Students of participating teachers; took pre-post tests

-- Study Not Replicated.
* Student N

Study Variables

Data was collected from students, teachers, and principals of the participant schools. The data obtained from the three kinds of participants is discussed separately below.

Student Indices: Table 7 lists the data collected from each student in the study and the schedule of data collection. The achievement tests and self-concept instruments were administered by the classroom teacher utilizing machine-scorable forms which were scored by the publisher. Absentee data was supplied by the school system's central data processing unit and was taken from the official records kept for purposes of determining state aid. Socio-demographic data was also supplied for each student.

Table 7: Schedules of Data Collection

A. Student Outcome Indices

Measures:	Nov. 71	April 72	May 72	Oct. 72	April 73	May 73	Oct. 73	April 74
How I See Myself Tests	X	X		X	X		X	X
Achievement Tests	X	X		X	X		X	X
Attendance Data			X			X		
Socio-Demographic Data		X			X			X

B. Data from Teachers and Principals

Measures:	May 71	Aug. 71	Sept. 71	May 72	Sept. 72	May 73	Sept. 73	April 74
Minnesota Teacher Attitude Inventory		X		X	X	X	X	X
Classroom Climate Semantic Differential		X		X	X	X	X	X
Personal and Professional Information			X		X		X	
Audio Recordings of Classroom Instruction	X		X——*——X		X——*——X		X——*——X	
Audio Recordings of Principal/Teacher Interaction			X——+——X		X——+——X		X——+——X	

*At Monthly Intervals   +Three Times a Year

Teacher Data: Each year, the teacher participants were administered pre and post tests on the Minnesota Teacher Attitude Inventory and the School Climate Semantic Differential. The pre-test was administered by an NCHE trainer during teacher "work days" prior to school opening in the fall and post-test was administered in May. (See Table 7). Each teacher also filled out a Professional Information sheet supplying data on her/his current work assignment, professional preparation, and personal information. The Minnesota Teacher Attitude Inventory (MTAI) and the Semantic Differential (SD) were scored at the NCHE offices.

The study variables of major interest to the NCHE researchers were those derived from the audio tape recordings of classroom interaction supplied by the teachers. Each teacher recorded one continuous hour of instruction during a designated week each month during the school year. The teachers had been directed to teach in their normal manner. These audio recordings were forwarded to the National Consortium for Humanizing Education where they were coded for teacher and student behavorial variables by teams of trained raters who maintained inter-rater reliabilities of above .90.

The raters applied three instruments in their coding of the recordings. The first instrument is a set of 5 Process Scales adapted from Carkhuff (Aspy, 1972; Carkhuff, 1969) which utilize the teacher's vocal tone, choice of emotion words, and selected portions of the communication pattern to measure the level of interpersonal skills exhibited in verbal interaction. (See Appendix for copies of the scales). Each scale defines five levels from 1.0 to 5.0 with intermediate ratings beyond the decimal point; e.g., 1.3 or 4.7. In effect, then, each is applied as a 40 point scale.

The five interpersonal skills measured by the Process scales are:

1. **Meaning** — the teacher's empathy or understanding of the meaning-to-the-student of classroom experiences.
2. **Genuineness** — the teacher's person-to-person basis for interactions with students.
3. **Success Promotion** — the degree to which the teacher promotes the student's attainment of individual goals in moment-to-moment processes.
4. **Respect** — the teacher's regard for the student as an individual with the capacity for achieving.
5. **Student Involvement** — the degree to which the students are involved in and excited about their learning activities.

The raters also applied the Cognitive Functioning Categories adapted from Bloom (Bloom et al, 1956). This is a time-sampling technique for measuring the frequency of occurrence of 8 categories of mental operations as they are indicated by teacher-student verbal products in the classroom. Four of these categories are for teacher products and four are for student products. The instrument further includes two categories for behavior which cannot be codified as to its cognitive level. (For copy of instrument, see Appendix).

The third instrument applied, Flanders' Interaction Analysis (Flanders, 1965), is also a time-sampling technique which supplies the frequency of occurrence in seven categories of teacher behavior, two categories of student behavior, and one category of silence or confusion. (The instrument is displayed in the Appendix). Flanders' Interaction Analysis is the most widely known of the instruments used by the NCHE. Table 8 lists all of the tape data study variables and the symbols for each variable.

Table 8:   Study Variables Assessed
from Audio Tape Recordings

Instru-ment	Variable Name	Abbrev-iation	Regression Equation Symbol
Flanders' Inter-action Analysis Categories	Teacher Accepts Feelings of Student	F-1	F1
	Teacher Praises or Encourages Student	F-2	F2
	Teacher Accepts Ideas of Student	F-3	F3
	Teacher Asks Questions	F-4	F4
	Teacher Lectures	F-5	F5
	Teacher Gives Directions or Commands	F-6	F6
	Teacher Criticizes or Justifies Authority	F-7	F7
	Student Responds	F-8	F8
	Student Initiates	F-9	F9
	Silence or Confusion*	F-10	F0
Cognitive Function-ing Categories	Teacher Recalls Facts	C-1	C1
	Teacher Asks for Facts	C-2	C2
	Teacher Thinks	C-3	C3
	Teacher Asks for Thinking	C-4	C4
	Student Recalls Facts	C-5	C5
	Student Asks for Facts	C-6	C6
	Student Thinks	C-7	C7
	Student Asks for Thinking	C-8	C8
	Non-Cognitive Behavior	C-9	C9
	Silence or Confusion*	C-10	C0
Process Scales	Meaning	M	M
	Genuineness	G	G
	Success Promotion	SP	SP
	Respect	R	R
	Student Involvement	SI	SI

*NOTE: Although these variables have the same name, they are not identical because some behaviors which register in F-10 on the Flanders instrument are redistributed among categories C-5 through C-9 on the Cognitive instrument.

Principal Data: Only tape data was obtained from the principals. Each principal supplied one-hour recordings of faculty meetings and/or other interactions with the teachers in her/his school at the beginning, middle, and end of the school year. These recordings were evaluated using the same instruments as were used on the teacher tapes.

PROCEDURES FOR ASSESSING TAPE DATA

Not every teacher and principal supplied the complete number of tapes requested. Table 9 displays the actual tape data base in terms of the number of teachers and principals participating and the number of hours of instruction coded by the raters.

Table 9:   Tape Data Base

	Year 01	Year 02	Year 03	Total
No. Principals	11	10	6	27
No. Hrs. of Interaction Coded (P - Tapes)	35	31	18	84
No. Teachers	298	211	128	637
No. Hrs. of Interaction Coded (T - Tapes)	2,192	1,632	694	4,518

In assessing the tapes, four 3-minute segments from each of the tapes were selected at random for evaluation. The first segment was taken from the beginning of the hour, the second from about twenty minutes into the hour, the third segment from about forty minutes into the hour, and the fourth segment toward the end of the hour.

Assessment of Interpersonal Processes

The teacher's levels of skills in interpersonal functioning were assessed blind by raters who applied the Process Scales. Each of the raters completed their evaluations separately. The inter-rater reliabilities for the scales ranged from .898 for Respect to .921 for Student Involvement.

Each of the four 3-minute segments selected from each tape was assigned a rating for each scale. The final measurement for each scale was the mean of ratings for the four segments for that scale. This mean for each scale was the score used in the data analysis.

All four 3-minute segments for each tape were coded by trained raters using Flanders' Categories for Interaction Analysis. Coding occurred at 3-second intervals. Inter-rater reliabilities were above .96. The data used in the analysis was the total number of 3-second intervals recorded in each category for the tape.

Assessment of Cognitive Functioning

All four 3-minute segments for each tape were coded by trained raters using the Cognitive Functioning Categories. Coding occurred at 3-second intervals. Inter-rater reliabilities were above .94. The data used in the analysis was the total number of 3-second intervals recorded in each category for the tape.

Independence of Tape Data Instruments

Since both the Process Scales and the Flanders' Interaction Analysis Categories deal with affective aspects of verbal interaction, the question arose as to whether they were independent instruments. Chi-Square analysis was conducted to estimate the independence of the instruments.

The hypothesis for this analysis was that if the instruments were interdependent, then groups which were differentiated by one instrument would also be differentiated by the other instrument at approximately the same level of probability.

Accordingly, the Process Scales were used to identify the twenty highest functioning teachers and the twenty lowest functioning teachers. A middle or "normal" group consisted of those teachers functioning with ± 1 standard deviation of the mean on the Process Scales. T-tests of differences between the group means were significant at $p < .05$ ($\bar{x}_{Hi} \neq \bar{x}_{N} \neq \bar{x}_{Lo}$).

A 10-by-10 Flanders' Interaction Matrix (frequencies of occurrence of Flanders' Categories by sequential pairs) was constructed from the tape data for each teacher. The individual matrixes for the teachers in each of the three groups were then averaged cell-by-cell to obtain a Mean Flanders' Matrix for each group. (See Figures 1, 2, and 3). The Matrix of the "Normal" group was used to provide an estimate of the "expected" frequency for each cell in the Matrix. The Matrix of each of the other two groups was treated as a contingency table and Chi-Square was calculated. (Chi-Square for Low functioners = 7.51; Chi-Square for High functioners = 3.89). Neither Chi-Square was significant at the specified level of probability so the null hypothesis of samples drawn from identically distributed populations was accepted.

The Chi-Square analysis of the Flanders' Interaction Matrixes failed to differentiate groups which **had** been differentiated by the Process Scales. The conclusion of the researchers was that while there may be some interdependence of the two instruments it was not high enough to invalidate the use of either instrument for the purposes of this project.

Fig. 1: Mean Flanders' Matrix for "Normal" Group

2nd Category in Sequence

	F1	F2	F3	F4	F5	F6	F7	F8	F9	F10
F1	0.01	0.00	0.0	0.01	0.02	0.01	0.0	0.01	0.01	0.01
F2	0.0	0.11	0.05	0.32	0.48	0.12	0.01	0.20	0.06	0.12
F3.	0.00*	0.01	0.16	0.34	0.52	0.05	0.00	0.10	0.05	0.06
F4	0.01	0.02	0.03	6.04	1.66	0.23	0.03	10.84	0.27	2.17
F5	0.01	0.15	0.05	6.62	68.05	1.69	0.20	4.46	2.57	4.73
F6	0.0	0.01	0.00	0.40	0.89	2.54	0.05	1.33	0.13	1.01
F7	0.0	0.00	0.00	0.08	0.16	0.05	0.47	0.09	0.04	0.19
F8	0.02	0.98	0.88	4.94	8.64	0.82	0.15	52.26	0.54	2.80
F9	0.01	0.11	0.10	0.47	2.53	0.11	0.04	0.21	5.65	1.02
F10	0.00	0.08	0.03	2.02	5.16	0.75	0.13	2.84	1.08	20.65
Total	0.06	1.47	1.30	21.24	88.11	6.37	1.08	72.34	10.40	32.76

1st Category in Sequence

*0.00 indicates a negligible quantity but one that is not absolute zero as indicated by 0.0

Fig. 2: Mean Flanders' Matrix for Low Functioners

| | | | | 2nd Category in Sequence | | | | | | |
	F1	F2	F3	F4	F5	F6	F7	F8	F9	F10
F1	0.01	0.0	0.0	0.01	0.03	0.0	0.0	0.01	0.0	0.01
F2	0.0	0.04	0.02	0.52	0.52	0.18	0.0	0.34	0.06	0.11
F3	0.0	0.01	0.05	0.19	0.32	0.02	0.01	0.08	0.07	0.05
F4	0.0	0.05	0.01	4.60	1.34	0.19	0.02	11.30	0.45	1.92
F5	0.01	0.15	0.04	5.90	58.05	1.44	0.31	5.20	3.67	5.18
F6	0.0	0.01	0.0	0.38	0.68	1.72	0.05	1.53	0.19	0.98
F7	0.0	0.0	0.0	0.05	0.24	0.03	0.57	0.07	0.07	0.21
F8	0.03	1.37	0.59	5.54	9.04	1.12	0.14	53.43	0.78	3.43
F9	0.01	0.11	0.10	0.63	3.67	0.15	0.05	0.36	8.10	1.53
F10	0.02	0.06	0.01	1.84	5.65	0.64	0.14	3.52	1.47	23.23
Total	0.08	1.80	0.82	19.66	79.54	5.49	1.29	75.84	14.86	36.65

1st Category in Sequence

Fig. 3: Mean Flanders' Matrix for High Functioners

2nd Category in Sequence

	F1	F2	F3	F4	F5	F6	F7	F8	F9	F10
F1	0.0	0.0	0.0	0.01	0.01	0.0	0.0	0.01	0.0	0.01
F2	0.0	0.10	0.04	0.39	0.49	0.19	0.01	0.15	0.11	0.14
F3	0.0	0.01	0.22	0.45	0.49	0.11	0.0	0.10	0.02	0.13
F4	0.0	0.02	0.06	7.37	1.85	0.28	0.03	12.22	0.19	2.22
F5	0.0	0.11	0.08	6.78	61.70	1.82	0.25	4.79	2.71	5.17
F6	0.0	0.03	0.01	0.52	0.92	3.90	0.09	1.56	0.21	1.29
F7	0.0	0.0	0.0	0.10	0.19	0.07	0.49	0.12	0.12	0.20
F8	0.03	1.13	1.01	5.83	8.92	1.04	0.18	49.81	0.74	2.79
F9	0.0	0.10	0.09	0.62	2.87	0.14	0.09	0.37	5.63	0.95
F10	0.0	0.13	0.05	2.20	5.53	0.90	0.17	2.68	1.25	20.06
Total	0.03	1.63	1.56	24.27	82.97	8.45	1.31	71.81	10.98	32.96

1st Category in Sequence

STUDY NUMBER 1

DOES THE PRINCIPAL'S BEHAVIOR
AFFECT TEACHER BEHAVIOR?

PURPOSE OF STUDY

This study asked two questions:

1. *Is there a significant relationship between the principal's functioning and the functioning of the teachers in his/her school?*
2. *What factors of the principal's behavior are the best predictors of his/her teacher's behavior?*

DESIGN

Sample

The study population were the 11 principals and 250 teachers of 11 schools from the Year 01 Sample. The eleven schools included 8 Elementary schools (grades 1-6), 1 Jr. High school (grades 7-9), and 2 Sr. High schools (grades 10-12). The total Year 01 sample included a second Jr. High school but the principal in that school failed to supply his data to be used for this study, although his teachers did participate.

Data Collection

The data was collected from one-hour audio tape recordings supplied by the participants. The principals supplied recordings of their faculty meetings and/or other interaction with their faculty while the teachers recorded instruction in their classrooms. Only teachers who had supplied 4 or more tapes during the year were included in the study. Tapes from both the principals and teachers were coded for the same set of 25 variables: 10 categories of Flanders Interaction Analysis, 10 categories of Cognitive Functioning, and 5 Process Scales.

Assessment of Flanders' Interaction Analysis

The score recorded for each tape was the total number of 3-second periods tallied in each category of Flanders' Interaction Analysis from four 3-minute segments of the tape.

The 10 categories coded were:

F-1	– Teacher (Principal)	Accepts Feelings of Student (Teacher)
F-2	– Teacher (Principal)	Uses Praise or Encouragement
F-3	– Teacher (Principal)	Accepts Ideas of Student (Teacher)
F-4	– Teacher (Principal)	Asks Questions
F-5	– Teacher (Principal)	Lectures
F-6	– Teacher (Principal)	Gives Directions or Commands
F-7	– Teacher (Principal)	Criticizes or Justifies Authority
F-8	– Student (Teacher)	Responds to Teacher (Principal)
F-9	– Student (Teacher)	Initiates Interaction
F-10	– Silence or Confusion	

The same segments of each tape were coded for Cognitive Functioning Categories. The scores recorded for the tape were the total number of 3-second periods tallied for each category. The 10 categories coded were:

C-1	— Teacher (Principal)	Recalls Facts
C-2	— Teacher (Principal)	Asks Someone to Recall Facts
C-3	— Teacher (Principal)	Demonstrates Thinking Above Memory Level
C-4	— Teacher (Principal)	Asks Someone to Demonstrate Thinking
C-5	— Student (Teacher)	Recalls Facts
C-6	— Student (Teacher)	Asks Someone to Recall Facts
C-7	— Student (Teacher)	Demonstrates Thinking Above Memory Level
C-8	— Student (Teacher)	Asks Someone to Demonstrate Thinking
C-9	— Non-Cognitive Behavior	
C-10	— Silence or Confusion	

Assessment of Process Levels

The participant's levels of interpersonal functioning were assessed "blind" by raters who applied 5 Process Scales. Each of the four 3-minute segments selected from each tape was assigned a rating for each scale. The final score recorded for each scale was the mean of ratings on the tape segments for that scale. The five Process Scales used were:

M — Meaning:	The Teacher's (Principal's) empathy or understanding of the meaning-to-the child (teacher) of his/her school-related experiences.
G — Genuineness:	The Teacher's (Principal's) person-to-person basis for interactions.
R — Respect:	The Teacher's (Principal's) respect for the child (teacher) as an individual with the capacity for achieving.
SP — Success Promotion:	The degree to which the Teacher (Principal) promotes the success of the student's (teacher's) goals in moment-to-moment processes.
SI — Student Involvement:	The degree to which the students (teachers) are involved in and excited about their learning (current) activities.

It was necessary to discriminate between variables measuring the teacher-student interaction and those referring to principal-teacher interactions. Therefore, the letter T was prefixed to the variable symbol when it refers to the teacher-student interactions and the letter P was prefixed when reference is to the principal-teacher interaction.

ANALYSIS

The data for the study was the grand mean for the year for each individual participant on each of the variables. With this data, 25 stepwise multilinear regression analyses were carried out, using in turn each of the 25 Teacher Behavior Variables as the dependent variable.

Because the sample included only 11 principals, only 10 of their variables could be used as independent variables in each regression. Therefore 9 variables were selected on theoretical grounds as those more probable to predict the behavior of the teachers. These 9 variables used in **all** the analyses were the principals' scores on:

P-F2 — Use of Praise and Encouragement
P-F3 — Acceptance of Teacher's Ideas
P-F7 — Use of Criticism or Justification of Authority
P-C1 — Recall of Facts (Memory, Lecture)
P-C2 — Asking Fact Questions
P-C4 — Asking Thinking Questions
P-M — Understanding of the Meaning of the Teacher's Experience
P-SP — Promoting the Success of the Teacher's Goals
P-R — Communicating Respect for the Teacher

Additionally, in the 16 analyses in which the dependent variable was **not** the same-named variable **(for teachers)** as one of the 9 independent variables identified above, a tenth independent variable was used. This was, of course, the principal's scores on the variable with the same name as the dependent variable.

RESULTS

Data Parameters

The means and standard deviations for both the principals' and the teachers' scores on the 25 variables are displayed in Table 10. The Flanders' and Cognitive scores are expressed as the number of 3-second intervals tallied for the category during 12 minutes selected at random from an hour of interaction. Thus, a mean of .46 for F-1 indicates that almost ½ of one 3-second interval during the twelve minutes was spent in accepting feelings. (To convert means to Percent of Classtime, divide the mean by 240 — the number of 3-second intervals in twelve minutes).

By examining the data in Table 10, an over-all picture of principal and teacher functioning is revealed. Several items of particular interest are discussed below.

1. In faculty meetings, these principals spent almost 7 times as much time criticizing teachers and justifying authority as they spent in praising them, accepting their ideas, or accepting their feelings. In fact, they spent 3 times as long in Category F-7 as in Categories F-1, F-2, and F-3 combined.
2. On the average, these principals spent 27 times as much meeting time talking as they spent in asking teachers to contribute to the meeting.
3. The ratio of total principal talk (Sum of Categories F1-F7) to total teacher talk (sum of categories F8 and F9) was 3 to 1.
4. Principals ran very businesslike faculty meetings — only 5% of the time was spent in silence or confusion.
5. Principals spent 16,743 times as long in recalling facts as they did in demonstrating thinking, on the average.
6. They asked 24 times as many fact questions as questions eliciting a thinking response.

Comparing Principal versus Teacher Functioning

1. Principals accepted teacher's feelings more than teachers accept students feelings.
2. Principals gave praise and accepted teacher's ideas less than teachers did for their students.
3. Principals asked fewer questions of teachers than teachers ask of their students **but** principals had a higher proportion of time spent asking thinking questions. The ratio of intervals tallied for thinking to fact questions asked by principals was 24-to-1; for teachers, the ratio was 550-to-1.
4. In general, principals functioned at higher levels of inter-personal skills than teachers (scores on Process Scales). The one exception was Student Involvement — Students become more involved in their learning activities than teachers become involved in faculty meetings.
5. In Table 10, asterisks indicate those variables where the standard deviation is larger than the mean. Inspection of the raw data for those variables reveals that there are many cases in which the score for the variable was zero. That is, many individuals had no occurrence of the behavior named by this variable on their tapes; and the mean of the variable was lowered by these incidences of zero. Variables common to both principals and teachers in which **many individuals registered zero** were F-1, F-2, F-7, C-3, C-4, C-7, C-8, and C-9. These categories deal with either affective behaviors or higher levels of thinking behaviors. Principals also scored zero in several cases in F-3 (accepting ideas) and F-6 (giving commands or directions). Teachers registered zero in some cases for C-6 (fact questions asked by their students).

Table 10: Parameters of Data -- Means and Standard
Deviations of Principals' and Teachers'
Scores on Study Variables

	VARIABLES	PRINCIPALS		TEACHERS	
		$\overline{X}$	$\hat{\sigma}$	$\overline{X}$	$\hat{\sigma}$
Flanders' Categories	F-1	0.46	1.26*	0.06	0.15*
	F-2	0.38	0.98*	1.58	1.63*
	F-3	0.29	0.32*	1.38	1.28
	F-4	7.62	5.63	22.56	10.97
	F-5	163.60	25.68	88.00	33.16
	F-6	1.04	1.10*	6.74	4.70
	F-7	3.59	7.52*	.99	1.52*
	F-8	31.91	13.52	74.50	34.15
	F-9	18.84	11.29	10.00	8.73
	F-10	12.22	9.77	34.13	23.68
Cognitive Functioning Categories	C-1	167.43	23.69	97.42	30.76
	C-2	8.45	5.97	22.03	10.43
	C-3	0.01	0.04*	.32	.85*
	C-4	.17	0.24*	.004	.01*
	C-5	38.08	15.85	77.38	31.45
	C-6	3.53	2.88	1.81	2.28*
	C-7	6.71	8.66*	3.12	4.35*
	C-8	1.26	2.29*	0.35	0.73*
	C-9	2.11	2.79*	2.70	3.06*
	C-10	12.19	8.55	33.47	23.09
Process Scales	M	2.8	0.326	2.7	0.219
	G	2.9	0.335	2.7	0.222
	SP	2.8	0.320	2.7	0.232
	R	2.9	0.465	2.8	0.223
	SI	2.7	0.575	2.9	0.202
		N=11		N=250	

*Standard Deviation larger than the mean

The correlations of the principals' and teachers' scores on the same variable are displayed in Table 11. The correlations of each of the dependent variables with the 9 independent variables common to all the regression analyses is displayed in Table 12.

Table 11: Correlation of Principals' and Teachers' Scores on Same Variable

Variable	r
F-1	.20
F-2	.28
F-3	.06
F-4	.07
F-5	.06
F-6	.22
F-7	.11
F-8	-.24
F-9	.12
F-10	-.08
C-1	-.01
C-2	.12
C-3	-.07
C-4	.01
C-5	-.12
C-6	-.11
C-7	.02
C-8	.16
C-9	-.004
C-10	-.09
M	-.12
G	-.11
SP	-.09
R	-.004
SI	-.05

Table 12: Correlation Matrix of Independent Versus
Dependent Variables

| | | Independent Variables — Principals' Scores on Variables | | | | | | | | |
Dependent Variables — Teacher's Scores	P-F2	P-F3	P-F7	P-C1	P-C2	P-C4	P-M	P-SP	P-R
Flanders' Interaction									
Teacher Behaviors									
T-F1	.16	.02	-.12	-.12	-.10	.03	.009	.03	.10
T-F2	.28	-.11	.31	-.03	.23	-.004	-.26	-.31	-.17
T-F3	.28	-.06	.05	-.11	.04	.06	-.05	-.07	.03
T-F4	.16	.07	.23	-.03	.11	.04	.23	-.24	-.25
T-F5	-.16	-.04	-.16	-.01	-.17	-.06	.02	.08	.11
T-F6	.13	.07	.17	-.04	.17	-.04	-.11	-.15	-.12
T-F7	.03	-.14	.11	.17	.06	-.06	-.09	-.004	-.14
Student Behaviors									
T-F8	.08	.25	.11	.11	.03	-.09	-.08	-.09	-.22
T-F9	.07	-.07	-.14	.10	-.08	.07	.11	.11	.20
T-F10	-.06	.02	-.05	-.08	.11	.01	.18	.14	.24
Cognitive Functioning									
Teacher Behaviors									
T-C1	-.13	-.05	.12	-.01	-.15	.05	-.01	.04	.08
T-C2	.21	.09	.25	-.06	.12	.04	.27	.29	-.26
T-C3	-.02	.05	-.10	-.04	-.10	.01	.01	.06	.12
T-C4	-.004	.01	.02	-.01	.004	.01	-.06	-.03	-.03
Student Behaviors									
T-C5	.11	.007	.11	.09	.03	-.08	-.08	-.10	-.21
T-C6	-.11	-.03	-.21	-.10	-.009	.05	.31	.29	.41
T-C7	.01	-.01	.06	-.03	-.02	-.006	-.04	.07	.06
T-C8	-.04	-.03	-.09	-.07	-.08	.03	-.02	.02	.12
T-C9	.05	-.07	-.06	-.03	-.04	.06	-.08	.01	-.01
T-C10	-.06	.02	-.08	-.06	.09	.002	.21	.17	-.24
Inter-personal Processes									
T-M	-.08	-.08	.10	-.01	.06	.01	-.12	-.11	-.05
T-G	-.06	-.08	-.09	-.002	-.04	-.01	-.11	-.10	-.04
T-SP	.07	-.09	-.10	-.02	.07	-.02	-.10	-.09	-.02
T-R	.09	-.09	.11	-.04	.08	.03	-.11	-.11	-.004
T-SI	.12	-.13	-.09	.05	.07	-.07	-.08	-.08	-.06

Table 13 summarizes the results of the 25 multilinear regression analyses. As you can see, it was not possible to build models for 3 of the 25 variables. Of the 22 regressions completed, 16 were significant at the .01 level and three more at the .05 level while the last three were not significant until the .10 level. This means that 19 regressions were at acceptable levels of significance; indicating that there is definitely a non-chance relationship between the principal's functioning and the functioning of the teachers in his/her school. Although the RSQ's achieved are not extremely high (ranging from .01 to .29) this is to be expected since there are many other factors potentially affecting teacher functioning (class size, time of year, subject matter, personal competencies in curriculum and methodology, and even the physical plant of the school). The fact that significant relationships exist at all is important.

To determine which of the principal's behaviors are the most important predictors of teacher behavior, it is necessary to examine the regression analyses more closely. Table 14 shows which independent variable entered into the model for each dependent variable, the amount of increase in RSQ upon entry, and whether entry occurred at the 1st, 2nd, or subsequent steps. It does not report a variable which was entered and later removed **unless** it entered at the 1st or 2nd steps; then the entry is reported with a slash through it to indicate that it was later removed.

Variables F-2 and F-3 were the most active with 11 predictive appearances each. However, all but one of their entries were at the second or later steps. Six of Respect's 8 entries occurred at the 1st step and 2 of C-2's eight entries occurred at the 1st step. M had 10 entries with 4 occurring at the 1st step; however, three of these were in regressions which did not reach a satisfactory level of significance.

In general, then, it would appear that the principal's level of Respect (P-R) for his teachers is the most powerful predictor followed closely by his/her Use of Praise (P-F2) and Acceptance of Ideas (P-F3) in that order. The number of Fact Questions asked by the Principal is also a good predictor of teacher behavior.

From Examination of Regression Equations

A closer examination of selected regression equations supports this general idea. The regressions to be examined more closely were selected on three bases:

1. They reached a meaningful level of RSQ (explaining 20% or more of the variance) in the regression summarized in Table 13.

2. They reached a level of significance of $p < .01$.

3. They were for variables which have been found useful in predicting student gain from teacher behavior. (See Study No.

Table 13: Summary of Full Models for 25 Stepwise Multilinear Regressions of Principal Behavior as Predictor of Teacher Behavior

Dependent Variables	Total RSQ Achieved	F-Ratio For Regression	Sig. Level $p <$	Standard Error of Estimate	# Variables in Final Equation	# Steps Performed
T-F1	.05	7.029	.01	0.1498	2	2
T-F2	.21*	17.849	.01	1.4542	4	4
T-F3	.09	13.483	.01	1.2241	2	2
T-F4	.17	10.592	.01	10.0820	5	5
T-F5	.29*	12.939	.01	28.3502	8	10
T-F6	.18	11.896	.01	4.2795	5	11
T-F7	.10	7.815	.01	1.4482	4	8
T-F8	.13	10.179	.01	31.9599	4	4
T-F9	.11	6.666	.01	8.2931	5	5
T-F10	.10	10.315	.01	22.5061	3	3
T-C1	.22*	10.458	.01	27.4525	7	9
T-C2	.22*	15.071	.01	9.2567	5	7
T-C3	.02	4.300	.05	0.8469	1	1
T-C4			NS			
T-C5	.11	6.341	.01	29.9534	5	5
T-C6	.24*	20.489	.01	2.0033	4	4
T-C7			NS			
T-C8	.03	5.113	.05	0.7260	2	2
T-C9			NS			
T-C10	.10	10.307	.01	21.9385	3	3
T-M	.02	4.121	.05	0.2177	1	1
T-G	.01	3.346	.10+	0.2212	1	1
T-SP	.01	2.880	.10+	0.2317	1	1
T-R	.01	3.609	.10+	0.2200	1	1
T-SI	.02	4.970	.05	0.2005	1	1

NS = $\underline{F}$ - level insufficient for computation of equation
+ Not at acceptable level (p < .05) of significance
* Models accounting for meaningful amounts of variance

93

Table 14: Summary of Increase in RSQ at Entry of Variable into
Model for the 22 Models Constructed

Group	Dependent Variables	Independent Variables										
		P-F2	P-F3	P-F7	P-C1	P-C2	P-C4	P-M	P-SP	P-R	Other	(Var.)(Name)
Flanders	T-F1	.01++									.04+	(P-F1)
	T-F2	.09++	.01	.09+								
	T-F3	.07+					.01					
	T-F4	.03	.02		.01	.03++	.01++			.06+		
	T-F5	.03++	.04	.009	.03	.03+			.05	.008	.04	(P-F5)
	T-F6	.01	.02		.04	.02++					.04+*	(P-F6)
	T-F7	.01			.03+	.02++		.01	.01			
	T-F8	.01	.01		.01++	.03					.05+	(P-F8)
	T-F9		.03			.01++	.01	.01++	.03	.04+		
	T-F10			.01				.01++		.06+		
Cognitive	T-C1	.01++	.04		.02	.02+	.02					
	T-C2	.02	.04		.01	.03		.01	.05	.02++		
	T-C3			.02+								
	T-C5	.01++							.01	.04+		
	T-C6		.01			.01	.02	.02		.17+		
	T-C8		.01++					.03++				
	T-C10							.02++	.02	.06+	.02+	(P-C8)
Process	T-M							.02+				
	T-G							.01+				
	T-SP							.01+				
	T-R							.01+				
	T-SI		.02+									
	# 1st Step Entries	1	1	2	1	2	1	4	1	6		
	# 2nd Step Entries	5	1		1	4	1	3	6	1		
	# Later Steps	5	9	2	5	3	3	3		1		
	Total # Predictive Appearances	11	11	4	7	9	5	10	7	8		

+Entered at 1st Step   ++Entered at 2nd Step   /Subsequent removal of Variable
originally entered at 1st or 2nd step
*Variable (F-6) subsequently re-entered with RSQ increase of .02

14 in which teacher behavior variables F-2, F-3, F-6, F-7, C-3, C-8, M, and SI proved to be predictive of variance in total days absent for the year and of gains on self-concept and achievement indices).

Table 15 displays regression equations for the selected variables. It does not display the full equation summarized in Table 13 and 14, however. Instead, it shows the most **efficient** equation for each variable; that is, the equation which can explain a reasonable amount of the variance with the fewest number of variables.

In the equations shown, the independent variables R, F-2, C-2, C-4, and SP appear frequently. Examination of their functions in the equations yields the following information:

1. As the level of the principal's respect (R) for the teachers in his/her school increases, the teachers . . .
   (a) use slightly more lecture
   (b) give fewer commands and directions to students
   (c) recall more facts
   (d) ask fewer fact questions
   (e) allow children to ask more fact questions

2. As the principal uses more Praise and Encouragement (F-2) with his/her teachers, in their classrooms the teachers . . .
   (a) give more praise and encouragement to students
   (b) accept more student ideas
   (c) use less lecture
   (d) use slightly more criticism and justification of authority
   (e) spend less time recalling facts
   (f) ask more questions of students

3. As the principal asks more fact questions (C-2) of teachers, the teachers when working with their students . . .
   (a) use less lecture
   (b) give more commands and directions
   (c) use less recall of facts
   (d) ask more questions of their students

4. As the principal asks more thinking questions (C-4) of teachers, the teachers when working with their students . . .
   (a) give less praise
   (b) accept more student ideas
   (c) allow more student questions

5. As the principal's level of success promotion (SP) increases, the teachers in his/her school . . .
   (a) use less criticism and justification of authority
   (b) use less lecture
   (c) spend less time recalling facts

Table 15: Selected Regression Equations

RSQ Achieved	F-Ratio For Regression	Sig. Level p <	Standard Error of Estimate	Regression Equation
.21	22.402	.01	1.4614	$T\text{-}F2 = 1.243 + 0.492F2 + 0.085F7 - 0.833C4$
.09*	13.483	.01	1.2241	$T\text{-}F3 = 1.112 + 0.397F2 + 0.682C4$
.16	11.756	.01	30.7152	$T\text{-}F5 = 145.931 - 10.098F2 - 2.791C2 - 3.923SP + 2\ 85R$
.10*	7.399	.05	4.4914	$T\text{-}F6 = 13.082 - .0.709F6 - 0.182F7 + 0.351C2 - 0.323R$
.11*	7.815	.05	1.4482	$T\text{-}F7 = -0.659 + 0.157F2 + 0.009C1 + 0.384M - 0.380SP$
.12	8.946	.02	29.0318	$T\text{-}C1 = 156.120 - 8\ 269F2 - 2.371C2 - 3.68SP + 2.371R$
.17	17.292	.01	9.5741	$T\text{-}C2 = 38.633 + 2.458F2 + 0.435C2 - 0.730R$
.23	25.806	.01	2.0139	$T\text{-}C6 = -8.604 + 1.567C4 + 0.180M + 0.171R$

*Equations reported for these variables because of their utility in predicting student achievement from teacher behavior.

In general, the functions listed above are in a direction consonant with this conclusion: As a principal uses higher levels of interpersonal and interactional skills with his/her teachers, they use higher levels of skills with their students. The exceptions to this are those listed in 1a, 1c, and 2d.

DISCUSSION

Although it seems clear that there is a significant relationship between the principal's behavior and the behavior of the teachers in his/her school, the exact nature of the dynamics of that relationship are not clear. Hypotheses for the possible dynamics for the relationship include the following suggestions.

Selection: The principal generally has some control over the assignment of teachers to the school. He may **select** those teachers who function in ways that he admires and respects . . . probably ways similar to the ways in which he functions. There is no evidence in the data to support this hypothesis; but on the other hand there is no evidence to reject it.

Modeling: The principal may serve as a model of interactive and cognitive behavior for her teachers. In the examination of the functioning of the five independent variables in the regression equations, there is some data to support this conclusion. Particularly the relationships delineated in the "Other" column of Table 14 and in items 2 and 3 above seem to support a modeling association.

Expectation: The principal may express expectancies for his teachers' classroom performance which they, more or less successfully, attempt to meet. There is no evidence in the data to support or to deny this hypothesis.

Facilitation: As the principal uses high levels of interpersonal skills with her teachers, she makes them feel accepted and secure and they then function at higher levels with their students. Some slight evidence for this can be found in items 1 and 5 above although 1a and 1c do not reflect this dynamic.

In all probability, some combination of the hypotheses is the most realistic delineation of the relationship. It may well be, for instance, that as the principal uses high levels of interpersonal skills with teachers he/she comes to be a significant other for them and they therefore try hard to meet his/her expectancies and model their interactive and cognitive behavior after the principal's.

In conclusion, the findings from this study are:

1. *Descriptive data of principal and teacher functioning were presented.*

2. *Significant (p < .05) predictive relationships between the principal's interpersonal behavior and the teacher's classroom behavior were detected for 19 of the 25 dependent variables.*

3. *RSQ's for the 19 significant models ranged from .02 to .29.*

4. *Five of the 19 significant models accounted for meaningful amounts of variance with RSQ > .20.*

5. *The best predictors of the teacher's behavior were identified as the principal's (a) level of Respect for the teacher, (b) Use of Praise, (c) Acceptance of Ideas, and (d) Asking of Fact Questions.*

6. *The functions of the predictive variables in the regression equations support the following statement of the directionality of the relationship: As a principal uses higher levels of interpersonal and interactional skills with his/her teachers, they use higher levels of these skills with their students.*

Implications of these findings for applied research studies are:

1. *Since it seems clear that there is a significant relationship between the principal's behavior and that of the teachers in his/her school, efforts to change teacher behavior should involve the principal as an active participant and supporter and, if possible, as a leader of the innovative efforts.*

2. *Further investigation of this relationship seems indicated in order to determine causative dynamics.*

3. *One hypothesis which should be tested is that **prior** training of the principal and/or other instructional leader (in the specific skills goals for the teacher training program) would enhance the skills acquisition of the teachers. **

*This hypothesis was tested in the Year 03 sample.

DOES THE PRINCIPAL'S BEHAVIOR AFFECT TEACHER PERCEPTIONS OF WORKING ENVIRONMENT AND INSTRUCTIONAL TASKS?

PURPOSE OF STUDY

The purpose of this study was to validate the relationships detected in Study No. 1 by seeing if a similar relationship could be detected in self-report rather than observational data. Therefore, the following question was posed:

When teachers are grouped according to the way in which their school principals are ranked on interpersonal functioning, are there significant differences among the response means of the groups of measures of teacher perception of work environment and instructional tasks?

DESIGN

Sample

The sample for the study consisted of the principals of all 12 Year 01 schools and all Year 01 teachers who (1) had taught the previous full school year in their currently assigned school and (2) had completed both the School Climate Semantic Differential and the Minnesota Teacher Attitude Inventory pretests. Total N for teachers was 257.

Data Collection

The principals were ranked in order of their mean rated levels of interpersonal functioning. Raters were (1) NCHE trainers and (2) local school system Professional Growth and Development Co-ordinators. Ratings were made on the basis of the raters' perceptions of the over-all level of interpersonal functioning of the individual.

Teachers were administered the School Climate Semantic Differential (SD) and the Minnesota Teacher Attitude Inventory (MTAI) by NCHE trainers in August of 1971. The instruments were scored at the NCHE center in Monroe, La.

The MTAI yields one score which can be considered a measure of the "child-centeredness" of the teacher. The SD yields 17 sub-scores on various aspects of school climate and one Total score which is the sum of the 17 sub-scores. Each sub-score is considered to be a measure of "the attractiveness to the teacher" of that particular aspect of the total school operation. Possible range of the sub-scores is from 8 to 54 by intervals of one.

ANALYSIS

The teachers were assigned as intact groups by school to one of three samples on the basis of the rank (see above) of the principal of the school. Faculties of the 4 highest ranked principals were assigned to Sample 1, the middle 4 to Sample 2, and the lowest 4 to Sample 3.

Since the teachers were assigned as intact groups, the data used in the analysis was the school mean (mean of the scores of the individual teachers in the school) on each of the variables. (These means are displayed in Table 16). The means of each variable were converted into ranks and a Kruskal-Wallis One-Way Analysis of Variance by Ranks was conducted separately for each of the 19 variables.

RESULTS

Table 17 displays the results of the analyses. Six of the 19 variables proved to be significant at the $p < .05$ level. So for these six variables, the null hypothesis was rejected and the samples were considered to come from differently distributed populations. Since one of these variables was the Semantic Differential **Total** Score and since 6 out of 19 significant tests is six times the number expected by chance at the .05 level of probability, the following conclusion was drawn: teachers whose principals differ in their levels of interpersonal functioning do, in fact, report different perceptions of their work environment, and instructional tasks.

DISCUSSION

The above conclusion is supported by a closer examination of Table 17. The sum of the ranks for Sample 1 (schools of high functioning principals) is in every case (except the MTAI scores) higher than that of either of the other two groups.

Examination of the nature of the significant variables reveals that three of the five sub-score variables reflect aspects of school organization which are strongly and directly affected by the school principal's functioning. The principal is responsible for requesting and scheduling services from the Central Office (Aspect 3); he/she is the primary Public Relations Officer for the school and hence has a direct effect on school-community relationships (Aspect 16); and he/she is the primary source of teacher evaluation (Aspect 6). Aspect 1 (Present school situation) is certainly affected by the principals' functioning although perhaps not in so **direct** a manner as the other three.

One aspect (Local school leadership) which had been expected to show a significant difference among groups was not significant at the .05 level although it was significant at the .10 level. However, scores on this aspect did provide some degree of anecdotal validation for the rating procedure used to rank the principals. The lowest mean score on this aspect was achieved by the faculty of the school whose principal had received the lowest ratings from both the NCHE trainers and the local school system co-ordinators. He was also the one principal who did not submit tapes for rating during the year.

Table 16: School Means for MTAI and SD Variables by Groups

Variables	Schools of Highest Ranking Principals				Schools of Middle Ranking Principals				Schools of Lowest Ranking Principals			
	B*	E	F	K	A	D	U	I	C	L	G	J
MTAI	25.67	34.61	10.05	19.27	17.65	27.05	31.56	19.02	21.14	29.68	26.92	31.53
#1	48.53	51.72	49.20	53.36	48.20	46.50	43.83	48.77	46.05	45.61	43.24	46.50
#2	42.60	46.11	41.40	44.36	38.10	44.00	44.22	43.32	38.55	41.50	40.48	40.28
#3	41.67	44.78	43.20	45.64	42.05	44.63	40.28	38.77	40.85	38.64	39.60	37.78
#4	47.20	48.33	46.95	53.93	50.45	49.29	42.61	44.84	44.15	46.75	41.60	41.78
#5	44.73	42.00	44.40	49.43	41.40	44.33	44.22	40.77	41.00	43.75	41.64	40.06
#6	44.21	44.35	43.65	47.43	41.10	43.09	43.22	41.23	42.05	41.68	37.63	39.18
#7	41.00	40.28	39.65	38.79	37.05	38.61	42.22	33.27	41.45	31.54	32.38	32.29
#8	44.50	50.28	41.60	48.71	43.42	39.13	41.28	36.79	44.15	38.50	35.83	37.82
#9	47.80	48.61	46.60	53.29	42.85	46.92	49.17	45.52	46.00	46.86	44.76	43.78
#10	37.73	43.47	43.60	49.36	38.60	41.67	42.72	38.28	40.15	39.89	37.32	38.17
#11	41.60	45.28	38.15	40.29	35.75	39.58	37.20	40.82	40.30	37.36	37.64	37.11
#12	47.73	48.00	43.95	50.79	40.21	49.17	48.22	42.66	46.79	42.68	45.63	42.44
#13	52.60	53.67	50.70	52.21	47.58	53.08	52.28	50.00	49.53	50.57	49.00	45.50
#14	51.93	51.89	48.30	51.64	47.32	50.17	45.22	47.20	48.40	47.33	42.64	45.50
#15	43.80	40.50	42.15	42.57	35.30	41.50	39.94	34.88	35.45	33.00	35.48	35.94
#16	49.73	48.56	50.20	47.71	44.65	42.75	43.06	42.36	44.90	43.71	41.28	38.17
#17	45.80	50.72	49.89	50.64	47.50	50.70	47.67	44.71	45.25	49.68	41.84	39.33
Total SD	764.53	793.67	761.10	820.14	712.60	757.96	747.67	706.95	730.20	717.36	681.92	675.56

Aspects (Sub-Scores) of SD

*Code letters for schools are randomly assigned designates to protect anonymity of subjects. Schools are arranged in order from A–L within groups and not by ranks of principals.

Table 17: Summary of Kruskal-Wallis One-Way Analysis of Variance by Ranks for 19 Teacher Perception Variables

Variables	ΣR_1	ΣR_2	ΣR_3	H or H' Statistic[+]
MTAI	23	24	31	0.729
Semantic Differential Total	42	22	14	7.998*
SD Sub-Categories:				
1. Present school situation	41	23.5	13.5	7.495*
2. Teaching educationally disadvantaged students	35	28	15	3.960
3. Leadership and services provided by central office	39	26	13	6.498*
4. Faculty group planning activities	36	29	13	5.344
5. Educational change through innovation	39	23	16	5.344
6. Evaluation of educational practices	42	22	14	7.998*
7. Inservice training activities	34	27	17	2.806
8. Parent interest and cooperation	40	21	17	5.806
9. Individualized instruction	37	24	17	3.960
10. The non-graded organizational structure	35	26	17	3.114
11. The graded organizational structure	37	21	20	3.498
12. Instructional emphasis on pupil self-concept	34	25	19	2.191
13. Your fellow faculty members	37	27	14	5.114
14. Your school philosophy	40	20	18	5.691
15. Action research projects	41	21	16	6.729*
16. School-community relationships	42	19	17	7.421*
17. Local school leadership	36	27	15	4.268

*sig. at p < .05; $\chi^2_{.05, \ 3} = 5.991$ [+]H' is used when there are tied ranks

SUMMARY

The conclusion drawn from this study was that teachers whose principals differ in their levels of interpersonal functioning do, in fact, report different perceptions of their working environment and instructional tasks. Thus, this analysis supports the findings from Study Number 1 and further emphasizes the need to involve the principal as an active supporter of any program designed to change instructional behavior.

ARE THERE EFFECTS OF GRADE LEVEL UPON INTERACTION ANALYSIS?

PURPOSE OF STUDY

This study asked two questions:

1. *Is the grade-level at which the teacher instructs a significant contributor to differences among the means of Flanders' Interaction Analysis Categories?*
2. *When adjusted for appropriate measures of individual teacher characteristics, is there a significant difference among the grade-level means of Flanders' Interaction Analysis Categories?*

DESIGN

Sample

The sample for this study consisted of all Year 01 teachers who (1) had submitted 5 or more tapes during the year and (2) had completed the MTAI pre-test in August, 1971. Total N was 238. The bottom line of Table 18 displays the N by grade-level.

Data Collection

The MTAI (Minnesota Teacher Attitude Inventory) was administered during a pre-school in-service training session and scored at the NCHE offices. Each teacher subsequently submitted to NCHE monthly audio tape recordings of one continuous hour of instruction. These recordings were evaluated by trained NCHE raters for several variables including 10 categories of Flanders' Interaction Analysis and 5 Process Scales. For details of the assessment procedures, see Part I, Procedures for Assessing Tape Data.

For Flanders' Categories, the score recorded for each tape was the total number of 3-second periods tallied in each category during 12 minutes selected at random in four 3-minute segments. For Process Scales, the data recorded for each teacher was the mean of the ratings for the four 3-minute segments. The data used in this analysis was the Teacher's Grand Mean for the year on each category or scale. Table 18 displays the grade-level means of the Flanders' Categories.

ANALYSIS

One series of one-way analysis of variance and two series of one-way analysis of co-variance were planned. Concomitant variables for the two series of analysis of co-variance would include two different kinds of individual teacher characteristics. The measures of individual teacher characteristics selected for the **Series One** analyses were two of the Process Scales (measures of the teacher's interpersonal functioning). The **Series Two** analyses would use the MTAI and a third Process Scale, Success Promotion.

Table 18: Unadjusted Flanders' Means by Grade Level

Flanders' Categories	Grade Levels							
	1	2	3	4	5	6	(7-9)	(10-12)
F-1*	0.0285	0.0427	0.0062	0.0343	0.0583	0.0957	0.0556	0.0920
F-2	2.6410	2.6059	1.8033	1.4373	1.9296	2.0486	0.7982	0.5094
F-3	1.6515	1.8464	1.3371	1.9119	1.7078	1.5081	1.2051	1.0435
F-4	30.8289	27.4167	27.0795	31.6252	27.6743	25.0885	14.2571	16.0882
F-5	77.3794	67.2072	58.5194	83.1528	73.5299	74.7485	86.9145	115.5145
F-6	11.7990	8.7700	8.7500	7.5257	5.9135	7.1024	6.0495	3.7280
F-7	1.7405	1.6391	0.8705	0.9129	1.2748	0.6762	1.1313	0.4365
F-8	75.2039	85.9858	104.4380	73.4237	89.3251	92.2937	66.0386	56.9603
F-9	7.0515	9.0400	6.8838	7.3643	8.8478	6.3471	14.2346	13.5381
F-10	31.6810	35.4549	30.3175	32.6204	29.7482	30.1004	49.3194	32.0937
N	20	22	21	21	23	21	39	71

*See Table 20 for Variable Names

The two process measures selected for use in the **Series One** analyses were Aspy's Genuineness and Respect Scales (1972) which had been derived from Carkhuff's scales for the Measurement of Congruence and Positive Regard (1969). The two scales utilize the teacher's vocal tone, choice of emotion words, and selected portions of the communication pattern to measure the level of interpersonal skills utilized in verbal interaction. Each scale defines five levels from 1.0 to 5.0 with intermediate ratings beyond the decimal point; e.g., 1.3 or 4.7. In effect, then, each is applied as a 40 point scale.

The Genuineness Scale measures the degree to which the teacher operates as an individual involved in person-to-person interactions rather than as a role functionary. It is based on a continuum for ritualistic to spontaneous communication with sub-continua of energy level and use of personal pronouns.

The Respect Scale measures the degree to which the teacher communicates to the students a positive regard for their abilities as individuals. It is based on a continuum from negative to positive regard with sub-continua of energy level and expectation level in terms of cognitive tasks.

These two measures were chosen on theoretical grounds as being two of the variables of interpersonal functioning which would contribute the most to teacher differences in the classes of behavior measured by Flanders' Interaction Analysis. Additionally, prior research with these scales had demonstrated positive relationships with some of the Flanders' Categories but had failed to show a significant relationship with grade level of the teacher.

Because the process measurements would be taken from the same behavior sample which was to be coded for Flanders' Interaction Analysis, an additional analysis which would include a different kind of measure of individual teacher characteristics was undertaken. The MTAI was chosen for the "different" concomitant variable because (1) it is a self-report rather than a process measure and (2) its scores can be considered as a measure of the "child-centeredness" of the teacher – a pattern of behavior which is compatible with that exhibited by teachers utilizing **high** levels of interpersonal skills.

The second concomitant variable for the **Series Two** analyses was a third Process Scale which was expected to be a significant contributor to teacher behavior in the Flanders' Categories. This third Process Scale, Success Promotion, measures the degree to which the teacher promotes the success of the student in attaining his/her individual goals. It is based on a continuum from negative to positive attendance to student goals with sub-continua of directionality of class activities and response to student cues.

To test the co-variance assumption that the concomitant variable(s) is unaffected by the treatments (grade level), one-way analysis of variance was conducted for each of the co-variates. Table 19 displays the results and indicates that the lowest minimum significant probability was .218. Thus, the use of these variables as co-variates is permissible.

Table 19: Tests of Significance for Computed F's of One-Way Analysis of Variance of the Grade Level Means of the Concomitant Variables

| Variables | F-Value* | Prob. | Grade Level Means | | | | | | | |
			1	2	3	4	5	6	(7-9)	(10-12)
Respect	1.3728	0.218	2.93	2.79	2.79	2.77	2.79	2.76	2.75	2.78
Genuineness	1.2978	0.252	2.84	2.76	2.73	2.71	2.72	2.67	2.68	2.72
MTAI	1.1390	0.340	3.60	2.44	0.94	1.46	2.62	1.71	2.43	2.17
Success Promotion	1.3567	0.225	2.86	2.79	2.74	2.73	2.74	2.68	2.72	2.74
N			20	22	21	21	23	21	39	71

*DF = 7,230

From ANOVA

A series of 10 one-way analyses of variance were carried out using, in turn, the incidence of behaviors in each of the 10 Flanders' Interaction Analysis Categories as the dependent variable. Of the ten analyses, all but one reached acceptable levels of significance ($p < .05$) for rejection of the hypothesis that there were no differences among the treatment (grade-level) means. As evident in Table 20, the analysis for Flanders' Category 1 was the only one in which grade-level differences failed to reach significance.

Table 20: Tests of Significance for Computed F's of 10 One-Way
Analyses of Variance for Grade-Level Effects on
Flanders' Categories with Sources of
Significance Indicated

	Dependent Variable	Computed F[+]	Min. Signif. Probability	Summary of Sig. Comparisons Among Grade-Level Means*
F-1:	Accepts Feelings	1.3678	.2199	- - - -
F-2:	Praises	13.5094	.00001	7-12 ≠ 1-6 4 ≠ 1+2
F-3:	Accepts Ideas	2.1169	.0427	10-12 ≠ 2+4
F-4:	Asks Questions	17.6356	.00001	7-12 ≠ 1-6 4 ≠ 6
F-5:	Lectures	17.1357	.00001	10-12 ≠ 1-9 7-9 ≠ 2+3
F-6:	Gives Directions	12.1230	.00001	10-12 ≠ 1-9 1 ≠ 2-12
F-7:	Criticizes	3.0292	.0046	10-12 ≠ 1-6
F-8:	Student Responds	7.8654	.00001	10-12 ≠ 1-6
F-9:	Student Initiates	4.9645	.00001	7-12 ≠ 1-6
F-10:	Silence or Confusion	2.7714	.0088	7-9 ≠ 1-6 7-9 ≠ 10-12

[+]DF - 7,230

*Results of Duncan's New Multiple Range Test

- - - -No differences detected.

In order to determine the source of the grade-level effects demonstrated in the analyses, Duncan's new multiple range test was carried out for each of the dependent variables. The results are summarized in the column on the far left of Table 20, with the significant comparisons being grouped by grade-level.

The major source of difference for each variable was one or more comparisons between secondary and elementary grade levels. For only one dependent variable (F-10) was a comparison **within** the secondary level a major source of variance. Significant comparisons **within** elementary grades were detected only for variables F-2 and F-4.

From Series One Analysis of Co-Variance

A series of 10 analyses of co-variance were carried out using, in turn, each of the Flanders' Interaction Analysis Categories as the dependent variable and a measure of Genuineness as concomitant variable 1 and a measure of Respect as concomitant variable 2. Again, in all but one of the ten analyses, it was possible to reject the hypothesis of no difference among the adjusted treatment means. The dependent variables concerned in the nine significant analyses were the same as in the first series. (See Table 21).

Although Duncan's new multiple range test was carried out for each of the dependent variables associated with the rejection of the null hypothesis, no new information was generated. The pattern of differences among the treatment means detected in the ANOVA series was merely repeated with no significant changes.

The tests of significance for the concomitant variables detected linear relationships at acceptable levels of probability between Respect and four of the dependent variables (F-3, F-4, F-7, and F-10). Genuineness, however, reached acceptable levels of significance for only two variables, F-4 and F-8.

From Series Two Analysis of Co-Variance

A second series of 10 one-way analyses of co-variance were carried out using, in turn, the Flanders' categories as the dependent variables with MTAI and Success Promotion scores as the concomitant variables. Of the ten analyses, seven reached acceptable levels of significance for rejection of the null hypothesis. As evident in Table 22, the analyses for Flanders' Categories 2, 4, 5, 6, 7, 8, and 9 were those in which grade-level effects reached significance.

Results from Duncan's new multiple range test were similar to those from the preceding two series of analyses. The major source of differences between the grade level means remained the comparisons between one or more levels of the secondary schools and one or more grades of the elementary school. The changes in the pattern were that slightly fewer comparisons resulted in the detection of significant differences. For example, the comparison for F-2 that grade 4 ≠ grades 1 and 2 (see Table 20) no longer held for this series of analyses.

In two of the 10 analyses, MTAI showed a linear effect at acceptable levels of probability. These were for dependent variables F-1 and F-3. The other concomitant variable, Success Promotion, evidenced strong linear relationships with 8 of the dependent variables.

From Examination of Regression Coefficients

An examination of the signs of the regression coefficients for the concomitant variables indicated that all but 5 of the 17 significant

Table 21:   Tests of Significance for Computed F's of 10 One-Way
            Analyses of Co-Variance for Grade-Level Effects on
            Flanders' Categories with Genuineness and Respect
            as Concomitant Variables (Series One)

Dependent Variable	Tests for	Computed F	Min. Signif. Probability
Flanders' Category 1	Adj. Treatment Means	1.6168	-- *
	Genuineness Regr. Coeff.	0.3856	--
	Respect Regr. Coeff.	0.5951	--
Flanders' Category 2	Adj. Treatment Means	13.0968	.00001
	Genuineness Regr. Coeff.	0.0859	--
	Respect Regr. Coeff.	3.4130	.0660
Flanders' Category 3	Adj. Treatment Means	2.1082	.0437
	Genuineness Regr. Coeff.	0.0518	--
	Respect Regr. Coeff.	4.1483	.0428
Flanders' Category 4	Adj. Treatment Means	18.1877	.00001
	Genuineness Regr. Coeff.	0.0618	--
	Respect Regr. Coeff.	9.8821	.0019
Flanders' Category 5	Adj. Treatment Means	18.4764	.00001
	Genuineness Regr. Coeff.	4.8905	.0280
	Respect Regr. Coeff.	0.0908	--
Flanders' Category 6	Adj. Treatment Means	11.9713	.00001
	Genuineness Regr. Coeff.	0 8191	--
	Respect Regr. Coeff.	0.8983	--
Flanders' Category 7	Adj. Treatment Means	3.6484	.0009
	Genuineness Regr. Coeff.	0.4026	--
	Respect Regr. Coeff.	5.3719	.0214
Flanders' Category 8	Adj. Treatment Means	8.0629	.00001
	Genuineness Regr. Coeff.	5.3644	.0215
	Respect Regr. Coeff.	1.7148	--
Flanders Category 9	Adj. Treatment Means	5.6245	.00001
	Genuineness Regr. Coeff.	0.8803	--
	Respect Regr. Coeff.	0.6435	--
Flanders' Category 10	Adj. Treatment Means	2.7204	.0100
	Genuineness Regr. Coeff.	0.0311	--
	Respect Regr. Coeff.	8.7330	.0035

*Only probabilities less than .10 are reported; acceptable level
of significance was p <.05.

DF = 7,228 for Adjusted Treatment Means
     1,228 for Concomitant Variable 1
     1,228 for Concomitant Variable 2

Table 22: Tests of Significance for Computed F's of 10 One-Way
Analyses of Co-Variance for Grade-Level Effects on
Flanders' Categories with Success Promotion and MTAi
as Concomitant Variables (Series Two)

Dependent Variable	Tests for	Computed F	Min. Signif. Probability*
Flanders' Category 1	Adj. Treatment Means MTAI Regr. Coeff. Success Promotion Regr. Coeff.	1.4888 5.0916 9.7473	-- * .0251 .0020
Flanders' Category 2	Adj. Treatment Means MTAI Regr. Coeff. Success Promotion Regr. Coeff.	12.7563 0.3866 16.7151	.00001 -- .0001
Flanders' Category 3	Adj. Treatment Means MTAI Regr. Coeff. Success Promotion Regr. Coeff.	1.8962 9.1079 20.2039	.0714 .0029 .00001
Flanders' Category 4	Adj. Treatment Means MTAI Regr. Coeff. Success Promotion Regr. Coeff.	16.1766 2.4991 27.1642	.00001 -- .00001
Flanders' Category 5	Adj. Treatment Means MTAI Regr. Coeff. Success Promotion Regr. Coeff.	17.3360 0.6995 8.7112	.00001 -- .0035
Flanders' Category 6	Adj. Treatment Means MTAI Regr. Coeff. Success Promotion Regr. Coeff.	12.5912 0.3966 0.0273	.00001 -- --
Flanders' Category 7	Adj. Treatment Means MTAI Regr. Coeff. Success Promotion Regr. Coeff.	3.3924 0.3012 6.9623	.0021 -- .0089
Flanders' Category 8	Adj. Treatment Means MTAI Regr. Coeff. Success Promotion Regr. Coeff.	7.2036 0.1663 0.4475	.00001 --
Flanders' Category 9	Adj. Treatment Means MTAI Regr. Coeff. Success Promotion Regr. Coeff.	5.1340 1.8916 8.0949	.00001 -- .0049
Flanders' Category 10	Adj. Treatment Means MTAI Regr. Coeff. Success Promotion Regr. Coeff.	2.1205 3.5383 38.4725	.0427 .0613 .00001

*Only probabilities less than .10 are reported; acceptable level
of significance was $p < .05$.

DF = 7,228 for Adjusted Treatment Means
     1,228 for Concomitant Variable 1
     1,228 for Concomitant Variable 2

relationships with dependent variables were in theoretically expected directions. The twelve valid relationships were:

1. Respect was related positively with F-2 (Praise), F-3 (Acceptance of Ideas), F-4 (Asking of Questions) and negatively with F-7 (Criticism or Justification of Authority), and F-10 (Silence or Chaos).
2. MTAI was related positively with F-3.
3. Success Promotion was related positively with F-1 (Acceptance of Feelings), F-2, F-4, and F-9 (Student Initiates) and negatively with F-7 and F-10.

The five relationships in directions not expected were:

1. Genuineness was related positively to F-5 (Lecture) and negatively to F-8 (Student Responds).
2. MTAI was related negatively to F-1.
3. Success Promotion was related negatively to F-3 and positively to F-5.

DISCUSSION

In general, significant differences among the grade level means of Flanders' Categories were detected. Only one Flanders' Category (F-1) failed to register grade-level effects. This failure to register grade-level effects may be an artifact of the extremely small size of the response means due to the fact that many individuals had **no** occurrence of F-1 in their data. If F-1 had been treated as a dichotomous variable (present or not-present), perhaps a relationship might have been detected.

The detected grade-level effects seem to be much stronger and more stable in some categories than in others. The minimum significant probability for Categories 2, 4, 5, 6, 8, and 9 remained at approximately the same level in all three series while that of the other variables more readily reflected the effects of the concomitant variables. In Category 7, however, the fluctuation was minor.

SUMMARY

In conclusion, the findings from this study are:

1. *Significant differences among the grade level means of Flanders' Categories were detected for all categories except F-1.*
2. *The sources of these grade-level differences were primarily a result of differences among the means of one or more of the levels of the secondary schools and one or more of the elementary grades.*
3. *Significant relationships were also detected between the concomitant and dependent variables.*
4. *The relationships with the co-variates were generally (but not always) in theoretically expected directions.*

The implication of this study for applied research studies is that when Flanders' Categories are to be study variables and the research involves teachers from several grade-levels, provision must be made for the effects of grade-level as a confounding variable. At a minimum, correction must be made for the effect of secondary versus elementary level membership.

ARE THERE EFFECTS OF GRADE LEVEL UPON COGNITIVE FUNCTIONING CATEGORIES?

PURPOSE OF STUDY

This study asked two questions:

1. *Is the grade-level at which the teacher instructs a significant contributor to differences among the means of Cognitive Functioning Categories?*
2. *When adjusted for appropriate measures of individual teacher characteristics, is there a significant difference among the grade-level means of Cognitive Functioning Categories?*

DESIGN

Sample

The sample for this study was the same as for Study No. 3. The bottom line of Table 23 displays the N by grade-level.

Data Collection

Data collection procedures were the same as for Study No. 3. The Cognitive Functioning Categories were coded from the same tape segments as the Flanders' Interaction Analysis Categories and the Process Scales.

For Cognitive Categories, the score recorded for each tape was the total number of 3-second periods tallied in each category during 12 minutes selected at random in four 3-minute segments. For the Respect scale, the data recorded for each teacher was the mean of the ratings for the four 3-minute segments. The data used in this analysis was the Teacher's Grand Mean for the year on each category or scale. Table 23 displays the grade-level means of the Cognitive Categories while Table 19 (cf. ante) lists the grade-level means for Respect and MTAI.

ANALYSIS

One series of one-way analysis of variance and one series of one-way analysis of co-variance were planned. The analysis of co-variance would use two different kinds of individual teacher characteristics as concomitant variables. The measures of individual teacher characteristics selected were the MTAI and the Respect scale (a measure of the teacher's interpersonal functioning).

Respect is one of a set of 5 Process Scales developed by Aspy (1972) which utilize the teacher's vocal tone, choice of emotion words, and selected portions of the communication pattern to measure the level of interpersonal skills utilized in verbal interaction. Each scale defines five levels from 1.0 to 5.0 with intermediate ratings beyond the decimal point; e.g., 1.3 or 4.7. In effect, then, each is applied as a 40 point scale.

Table 23: Unadjusted Cognitive Means by Grade Level

Cognitive Categories	Grade Levels							
	1	2	3	4	5	6	Jr. Hi. (7-9)	Sr. Hi. (10-12)
C-1*	92.208	80.149	71.120	92.708	83.614	84.900	93.195	119.971
C-2	32.390	25.389	25.927	30.882	26.519	25.144	14.008	15.547
C-3	0.032	0.113	0.250	0.070	0.279	0.702	0.391	0.565
C-4	1.337	1.645	1.741	1.872	1.892	1.217	0.935	0.238
C-5	77.888	89.205	104.828	74.889	88.883	91.796	71.012	62.608
C-6	0.433	0.675	0.531	1.132	1.260	1.594	4.103	2.762
C-7	1.538	2.788	3.526	3.441	5.115	3.604	3.883	3.123
C-8	0.095	0.096	0.263	0.055	0.722	0.332	0.356	0.569
C-9	3.248	3.301	1.909	3.438	2.187	1.853	3.301	2.301
C-10	30.840	36.650	29.911	31.520	29.536	28.865	48.821	31.321
N	20	22	21	21	23	21	39	71

*See Table 24 for variable names

The Respect Scale measures the degree to which the teacher communicates to the students a positive regard for their abilities as individuals. It is based on a continuum from negative to positive regard with sub-continua of expectation level in terms of cognitive tasks and energy level.

Respect was chosen on theoretical grounds as being the one variable of interpersonal functioning which would contribute the most to teacher differences in the classes of behavior measured by the Cognitive Categories. Additionally, prior research with this scale had demonstrated positive relationships with some of the Cognitive Categories but had failed to show a significant relationship with grade level of the teacher.

Because the process measurement would be taken from the same behavior sample which was to be coded for Cognitive Categories, a different kind of measure of individual teacher characteristics was selected for the second concomitant variable. The MTAI was chosen as the "different" co-variate because (1) it is a self-report rather than a process measure and (2) its scores can be considered as a measure of the "child-centeredness" of the teacher — a pattern of behavior which is compatible with that exhibited by teachers utilizing high levels of interpersonal skills.

Analysis of variance for the effect of treatments (grade-level) on the concomitant variables was performed in Study No. 3. Both MTAI and Respect were tested at that time. Table 19 (cf. ante) displays the results.

RESULTS

From ANOVA

A series of 10 one-way analyses of variance were carried out using, in turn, the incidence of behaviors in each of the 10 Cognitive Categories as the dependent variable. Of the ten analyses, six reached acceptable levels of significance ($p < .05$) for rejection of the hypothesis that there were no differences among the adjusted treatment (grade-level) means. As evident in Table 24, the analyses for Categories C-3, C-4, C-7, and C-9 were those in which grade-level differences failed to reach significance.

In order to determine the source of the grade-level effects demonstrated in the analyses, Duncan's new multiple range test was carried out for each of the dependent variables. The results are summarized in the column on the far left of Table 24, with the significant comparisions being grouped by grade-level.

Although the major source of differences between the grade-level means were the comparisons between one or more levels of the secondary schools and one or more grades of the elementary school, there were significant differences for four variables (C-1, C-2, C-5, and

Table 24: Tests of Significance for Computed F's of 10 One-Way
Analyses of Variance for Grade-Level Effects on
Cognitive Functioning Categories with Sources
of Significance Indicated

	Dependent Variable	Computed F^+	Min. Signif. Probability	Summary of Sig. Comparisons Among Grade Level Means*
C-1:	Teacher Recalls Facts	12.6903	.00001	10-12 ≠ 1-6, 7-9 3 ≠ 1,4, 7-9
C-2:	Teacher Asks for Facts	21.1849	.00001	7-12 ≠ 1-6 1 ≠ 2,3,5,6 4 ≠ 6
C-3:	Teacher Thinks	1.9266	.0663	- - - -
C-4:	Teacher Asks for Thinking	1.0583	.3914	- - - -
C-5:	Student Recalls Facts	6.6554	.00001	10-12 ≠ 2,3,5,6, 5 ≠ 1,4, 7-9
C-6:	Student Asks for Fact	12.9114	.00001	7-12 ≠ 1-6
C-7:	Student Thinks	1.0935	.3681	- - - -
C-8:	Student Asks for Thinking	3.0181	.0047	5 ≠ 1,2,4 4 ≠ 10-12
C-9:	Non-Cognitive Behavior	1.3044	.2490	- - - -
C-10:	Silence or Confusion	3.0519	.0043	7-9 ≠ 1-6, 10-12

+DF = 7, 230

*Results of Duncan's New Multiple Range Test

- - - - No difference detected

C-8) **within** the elementary grades. Significant comparisons between secondary levels were detected only for variables C-1 and C-10.

From Analysis of Co-Variance

A series of 10 analyses of co-variance were carried out using, in turn, each of the Cognitive Categories as the dependent variable and a measure of Respect as concomitant variable 1 and MTAI scores as concomitant variable 2. (See Table 25). In seven of the ten analyses, it was possible to reject the hypothesis of no difference among the adjusted treatment means. The ANOVA series had detected significant differences for only 6 variables. The new variable in which grade-level differences were detected was C-3. The significant comparisons among the treatment means for C-3 were: 1 ≠ 6 or 10-12; 6 ≠ 4.

Changes from unadjusted to adjusted grade-level means resulted in some slight changes in the significant comparisons among the means for some variables. These changes were:

For C-1, the adjusted mean of secondary level 10-12 was no longer different from 7-9.

For C-2, adjusted mean of 4 was not different from 3 but was different from 6.

For C-6, adjusted means 10-12 ≠ 7-9.

For C-8, adjusted mean of 4 was not different from 5.

The tests of significance for the concomitant variables detected linear relationships at acceptable levels of probability between Respect and five of the dependent variables (C-1, C-2, C-4, C-7, and C-10). All five relationships were in theoretically expected directions. Two of these relationships were for variables in which grade-level differences at acceptable levels were not detected. That is, only the teacher's Respect for students was significantly related to C-4 (Teacher Calls for Thinking) and C-7 (Student Thinks).

Table 25: Tests of Significance for Computed F's of 10 One-Way Analyses of Co-Variance for Grade Level Effects on Cognitive Categories with Respect and MTAI as Concomitant Variables

Dependent Variable	Tests for	Computed F	Min. Signif. Probability
Cognitive Category 1	Adj. Treatment Means	12.9608	.00001
	Respect Regr. Coeff.	12.3681	.0005
	MTAI Regr. Coeff.	.0.9545	-- *
Cognitive Category 2	Adj. Treatment Means	20.3062	.00001
	Respect Regr. Coeff.	34.8379	.00001
	MTAI Regr. Coeff.	3.9059	.0494
Cognitive Category 3	Adj. Treatment Means	2.3632	.0240
	Respect Regr. Coeff.	0.8428	--
	MTAI Regr. Coeff.	0.3498	--
Cognitive Category 4	Adj. Treatment Means	1.0571	--
	Respect Regr. Coeff.	14.3780	.0002
	MTAI Regr. Coeff.	0.0613	--
Cognitive Category 5	Adj. Treatment Means	5.3519	.00001
	Respect Regr. Coeff.	0.5900	--
	MTAI Regr. Coeff.	0.0769	--
Cognitive Category 6	Adj. Treatment Means	11.8814	.00001
	·Respect Regr. Coeff.	0.1502	--
	MTAI Regr. Coeff.	0.7597	--
Cognitive Category 7	Adj. Treatment Means	1.7519	.0985
	Respect Regr. Coeff.	14.0689	.0002
	MTAI Regr. Coeff.	0.0208	--
Cognitive Category 8	Adj. Treatment Means	2.9709	.0054
	Respect Regr. Coeff.	0.0692	--
	MTAI Regr. Coeff.	0.1185	--
Cognitive Category 9	Adj. Treatment Means	1.1029	--
	Respect Regr. Coeff.	0.3553	--
	MTAI Regr. Coeff.	0.0370	--
Cognitive Category 10	Adj. Treatment Means	2.3599	.0242
	Respect Regr. Coeff.	45.3410	.00001
	MTAI Regr. Coeff.	2.1674	--

*Only probabilities less than .10 are reported; acceptable level of significance was p < .05.

DF = 7,228 for Adjusted Treatment Means
     1,228 for Concomitant Variable 1
     1,228 for Concomitant Variable 2

DISCUSSION

In general, significant grade-level effects on the variance of Cognitive Functioning Categories were detected. Three Categories (C-4, C-7, C-9) failed to register grade-level effects. For categories C-4 and C-7, this may be related to the strong relationships with Respect. The failure of C-9 to show grade-level differences may be an effect of the nature of the variable in that it has no **distinctive** characteristic. That is, it serves as an escape or catch-all category for behaviors not classifiable as to level of cognitive functioning. For example, many behaviors which register in Flanders' Categories 1, 3, 6, 7, and 9 may be classified as C-9 on the Cognitive Functioning instrument.

Contrary to expectations, the largest means for student and teacher "thinking" behavior were not at the secondary levels. For unadjusted C-3 (Teacher Thinks), the largest means were registered by grade 6, Senior High (10-12), and Junior High (7-9), in that order. When the means were adjusted for Individual Teacher Characteristics, the mean for the Jr. Hi. moved to fourth place while 5th grade took third position. In C-7 (Student Thinks), the three highest unadjusted means were achieved by grade 5, Jr. Hi., and grade 6, in that order, while the Sr. Hi. (10-12) was the **third lowest** mean. (It was higher than grades 1 and 2). In the adjusted means, grade 6 is replaced in third position by grade 3.

SUMMARY

In conclusion, the findings from this study are:

1. *Significant differences among the grade-level means of Cognitive Functioning Categories were detected for all categories except C-4, C-7, and C-9.*

2. *The sources of these grade-level differences were primarily a result of differences among the means of one or more of the levels of the secondary school and one or more of the elementary grades.*

3. *There were significant differences among the means of the elementary grades for variables C-1, C-2, C-5, and C-8.*

4. *There were significant differences between the two levels of secondary schools for variables C-1 and C-10.*

5. *Significant relationships were also detected between concomitant and dependent variables.*

6. *The relationships of the dependent variables with Respect were in theoretically expected directions, but that between MTAI and C-2 was not.*

The implication of this study for applied research studies is that when Cognitive Functioning Categories are to be study variables and the research involves teachers from several grade-levels, provision must be made for the effects of grade-level as a confounding variable. At a minimum, some consideration must be made of the effect of secondary versus elementary school membership. The effect of grade-level differences among the elementary grades is more critical for the Cognitive Functioning Categories than for Flanders' Interaction Analysis.

ARE THERE EFFECTS OF SUBJECT MATTER UPON TEACHER BEHAVIOR STUDY VARIABLES?

PURPOSE OF STUDY

This study posed the question:

Is the subject matter which the Junior or Senior High School teacher presents a significant contributor to differences among the means of Classroom Functioning as measured by Flanders' Interaction Analysis Categories, Cognitive Functioning Categories, and Process Scales?

DESIGN

Sample

The sample for this study consisted of Year 01 Junior or Senior High School teachers who submitted a tape for the month of March, 1972. Total N was 89. The bottom line of Table 27 displays the N by Subject Matter and Grade-level groups.

Data Collection

Data for the study consisted of the individual's scores on 10 Flanders' Interaction Analysis Categories, 10 Cognitive Functioning Categories, and 5 Process Scales. The data was collected through the normal procedures for assessment of tape data described in Part I.

The month from which data was to be taken for this analysis was chosen through random number procedures from all months available for Year 01, exclusive of May, 1971 and May, 1972 which were reserved for analyses using pre and post test data. The study was restricted to data from one month to avoid contamination from time-of-year. (See Study No. 6).

ANALYSIS

Twenty-five two-way analyses of variance were conducted, using in turn each of the Flanders', Cognitive, and Process scores as the dependent variable. Factors were grade-level on which the teacher instructed and subject matter presented. Grade-level was included as a factor on the basis of results from Studies 3 and 4.

There were two grade-level groups: (1) Junior High, grades 7-9 and (2) Senior High, grades 10-12. Subject matter groups were: (1) Math, (2) English, (3) Social Sciences, (4) Science and (5) Applied Subjects. "Applied Subjects" included such courses as Home Economics, Vocational Education, Business Education, Shop, etc.

RESULTS

Table 26 presents the results of the 25 analyses. It lists by source of variation all significance levels less than .10 which were detected.

Table 26: Significance Levels Less Than .10 by Sources of
Variation for 25 Two-Way Analysis of Variance
by Grade and Subject Matter for
Classroom Functioning Variables

	Grade	Subject Matter	G X S	Significant Grade Comparisons	Sources of Significance for Subject Matter*
F-1					
F-2	--	--			
F-3	--	.0731			Applied Subjects <Math and Social Studies
F-4	--	--			
F-5	.0381	--		7-9 <10-12	
F-6	--	--			
F-7		--			
F-8		--			
F-9		--	.0316		
F-10		--			
C-1					
C-2	.0489	.0006	.0022	7-9 <10-12	Math> all others
C-3					
C-4	.0543			10-12 <7-9	
C-5					
C-6	.0128	.0030		10-12 <7-9	Math and Science> others
C-7					
C-8					
C-9					
C-10	.0453			10-12 <7-9	
M					
G					
SP					
R					
SI					

*Results of Duncan's New Multiple Range Test.

Table 27: Means for Variables in which Significant Differences by Grade, Subject Matter or GXS Interactions were Detected

Variables	Means[++] by Grade		Means[++] by Subject Matter Taught				
	7-9	10-12	Math	English	Social Sciences	Science	Applied Subjects*
F-5: Teacher Lectures	93.55	119.07	121.25	115.56	93.86	83.83	118.45
F-9: Student Initiates	14.52	10.54	14.38	10.88	12.14	11.42	11.83
C-3: Teacher Thinks	0.0[+]	0.96	2.94	0.12	0.0[+]	0.0[+]	0.18
C-4: Teacher Calls For Thinking	1.97	0.48	2.56	1.32	1.14	0.0[+]	0.09
C-6: Student Asks For Facts	4.00	1.82	5.18	1.60	1.93	5.08	1.05
C-10: Silence or Confusion	56.18	36.48	47.06	32.76	55.21	46.00	45.13
N	33	56	16	25	14	12	22

*Home Economics, Vocational Education, Business Education, Shop, etc.

[++]Data is reported as total number of 3-second intervals coded in category during 12 minutes selected at random in four 3-minute segments from a one-hour tape.

[+]Absolute zero. No occurrence of variable for any member of this group in segments coded.

Only 7 variables reached this level of significance for any source of variation. Table 27 presents the means by Grade and Subject Matter groups for these 7 variables.

Subject matter had a significant main effect for only three variables, F-3, C-3, and C-6. Of these, F-3 was not at the acceptable ($p < .05$) level.

Two variables (F-9 and C-3) achieved significant grade-by-subject matter interactions. The cell means for these variables are presented in Table 28.

DISCUSSION

With only two out of 25 analyses yielding subject matter as a significant source of variation at the .05 level, the conclusion drawn by the researchers was that subject matter was not an important enough confounding variable to cause problems within the scope of the present study. Grade-level was again found to have an important effect on the study variables.

The occurrences of cell means of absolute zero for C-3 in Table 28 proved of much interest to the researchers. Examination of the raw data for this variable showed that the means for the non-zero cells were accounted for by 6 of the 9 Sr. High Math teachers, 4 of the 18 Sr. Hi. Applied Subjects teachers, and 3 of the 16 Sr. Hi. English teachers. Altogether, these 11 teachers achieved a total of 54 3-second intervals of Thinking behavior during the 132 minutes coded at random from their tapes (12 minutes from each tape). Since the instructional hour for these teachers was 50 minutes long, multiplying by 4.16 (the number of 12 minute periods in 50 minutes) provides an estimate of the total amount of C-3 occurring in the tapes of these 11 teachers.

This estimate indicates that out of the 89 class hours of instruction represented by the tapes submitted by secondary teachers during the second week of March, 1972, students were exposed to models of thinking behavior for slightly less than 12 minutes. And, then, only if they attended the class of one of 11 particular teachers was thinking behavior exhibited to them.

That this is not an unusually or exceptionally low incidence of C-3 is borne out by data from another study in which 607 hours of instruction supplied by 98 secondary teachers yielded a mean for C-3 of 0.52. This is approximately 1½ seconds of C-3 for every tape coded or a total of a little less than 16 minutes for all 607 tapes. Using the estimation procedure (multiplying coded quantity by 4.16), the estimate of total C-3 in 607 hours of secondary instruction is 1 hour and 6 minutes.

The rest of the study variables were examined for frequently occurring cell means of zero. Variables F-1 and F-2 were found to have zero means for all cells except that of Senior High English. Examination of the raw data indicated that the non-zero mean for both these

Table 28: Rank Order of Means for Significant Grade
by Subject Matter Interactions

F-9: Student Initiates			C-3: Teacher Thinks		
Mean	Group	N	Mean	Group	N
30.75	Jr. Hi. Applied Subjects	4	5.22	Sr. Hi. Math	9
22.83	Sr. Hi. Social Studies	6	0.22	Sr. Hi. Applied Subjects	18
17.14	Jr. Hi. Math	7	0.18	Sr. Hi. English	16
16.78	Jr. Hi. English	9	0.0	Jr. Hi. Math	7
12.22	Sr. Hi. Math	9	0.0	Jr. Hi. English	9
12.14	Sr. Hi. Science	7	0.0	Jr. Hi. Social Sciences	8
10.40	Jr. Hi. Science	5	0.0	Sr. Hi. Social Sciences	6
7.61	Sr. Hi. Applied Subjects	18	0.0	Jr. Hi. Science	5
7.56	Sr. Hi. English	16	0.0	Sr. Hi. Science	7
4.12	Jr. Hi. Social Science	8	0.0	Jr. Hi. Applied Subjects	4

variables was accounted for by the behavior of one teacher who had scored one 3-second interval each of F-1 (Accepting Student Feelings) and F-2 (Giving Praise).

SUMMARY

In conclusion, the findings of this study include:

1. *The subject matter represented by the teacher was a significant ($p < .05$) source of variation only for variables C-3 (Teacher Thinks) and C-6 (Student Asks for Facts).*

2. *For both variables, Math teachers attained the highest mean. For C-6, Science teachers scored a mean slightly lower than, but not different from, that of the Math teachers.*

3. *Significant grade-by-subject matter interactions were detected for F-9 (Student Initiates) and C-3.*

4. *Largest means for F-9 were attained by teachers of Jr. Hi. Applied Subjects and Sr. Hi. Social Sciences; for C-3 the highest mean was that of the Sr. Hi. Math teachers.*

5. *Of the 89 class hours of instruction represented by the tapes submitted during the second week of March, 1972, students were exposed to models of thinking behavior for slightly less than 12 minutes. This is a total,* **not** *a mean, and is the sum of behaviors by 11 of the 89 teachers; the other 78 teachers registered no occurrences of C-3 (Teacher Thinks).*

Since only two out of 25 analyses yielded significant differences among the subject matter means at the .05 level, the implication for the applied research studies was that subject matter was not an important enough confounding variable to cause problems within the scope of the present study.

IS TEACHER BEHAVIOR AFFECTED BY
THE TIME OF YEAR?

PURPOSE OF STUDY

This study posed two questions:

1. *Will sixth degree orthogonal polynomial multilinear regression analysis yield significant non-linear trends across time among Classroom Functioning Variables (as measured by Flanders' Interaction Analysis Categories, Cognitive Functioning Categories, and Process Scales) for Control (No-Training Condition) groups and/or for Experimental (Training Condition) groups?*
2. *Are the trends for the Experimental groups different from those of the Control groups?*

DESIGN

Sample

The sample for this study consisted of all Year 01 teachers who submitted 6 or more tapes, two of which were the September, 1971 and May, 1972 tapes. Total N for the study was 234. Table 29 displays the N by grade-level groups within treatment conditions.

Table 29:   Teacher Sample for Trend Analysis by Grade Level Groups Within Treatment Conditions

Grade Level Groups	Number of Teachers	
	Control	Experimental
1	9	11
2	12	10
3	11	10
4	11	10
5	11	12
6	10	11
7-9	11	26
10-12	29	40
Totals 1-6	64	64
Totals 7-12	40	66
Totals 1-12	104	130

Data Collection

Data for the study was the individual's score for each tape (month) on each of 10 Flanders' Interaction Analysis Categories, 10 Cognitive Functioning Categories, and 5 Process Scales. The data was collected by the regular procedures for assessment of tape data described in Part I.

ANALYSIS

The levels of the independent variable for this analysis were the nine months of the school year from September, 1971 to May, 1972 during which tapes were obtained from teachers at monthly intervals. The procedure used was a sixth-degree orthogonal polynomial multilinear regression analysis across time (months). Each regression coefficient was computed* independently of the others and each was tested for significance at the $p < .05$ level. If more than three coefficients were significant, they were eliminated on the basis of R^2 until only the three components achieving the highest R^2 remained. The resulting regression equation was used to generate the curve representing the trend of the behavior across time.

This procedure was repeated for each of the 25 study variables for each of the groups within each of the conditions. Since there were 10 groups (Grades 1, 2, 3, 4, 5, 6, all Elementary, grades 7-9, grades 10-12, All Secondary) for each of two conditions (Control and Experimental) for each of 25 variables, a total of 500 regressions were completed.

RESULTS

From Control Group Data

A question of some concern to the researchers was whether time of year might be a confounding factor for the study variables. Thus, the analyses of most interest in this study were those utilizing the data from the control groups. Table 30 displays the significant components of the polynomial expressions of the fitted curves for each analysis in which a significant trend was detected in the control data. Of the 250 analyses conducted with this data, 79 significant trends were detected. Twenty-four of these were in the 50 analyses with the data from School Level groups (All Elementary and All Secondary). When the teachers in the School Level groups were treated separately in grade level groups, the resulting 200 analyses yielded 55 significant trends with 41 occurring among the elementary grades and 14 occurring among the secondary groups.

Of the 79 significant trends, 70 were fitted with polynomial expressions which contained a linear term; 57 had a cubic component, and 32 had a quartic component. The majority of the curves had a decreasing function. (See further discussion below).

*Using procedures to compensate for unequal N of observations at time points.

Table 30: Significant Components of the Polynomial Expressions for Significant Trends Detected in Control Group Data

	By School Level		By Grade Level Groups							
	All Elem.	All Sec.	1	2	3	4	5	6	7-9	10-12
F-1	2,3,5	--	--	--	--	--	1,2,3	--	--	--
F-2	1,3,5	--	--	1,3,5	--	1,3	1,3,5	--	--	--
F-3	1,4,5	1,3	--	--	--	1,2,4	1,3,5	--	--	1,3
F-4	1,2,3	--	--	--	1,2	--	--	1,4	--	--
F-5	--	--	--	--	--	--	--	--	--	--
F-6	1,3,5	1,3,5	--	--	--	--	--	--	2,3,5*	--
F-7	--	--	--	--	--	--	--	--	--	--
F-8	1,3	--	1,3	--	--	--	--	--	--	--
F-9	--	--	1 *	--	--	--	--	--	--	--
F-10	1,3,5	--	--	--	--	--	--	--	--	1,3,5*
C-1	2,3,6	--	--	--	--	--	--	--	--	--
C-2	1,2,3	1,3	--	1,2,3	1,2	--	1,3	1,2,6	--	1,2,3
C-3	--	--	--	--	--	--	--	--	--	--
C-4	--	--	--	--	--	--	--	--	--	--
C-5	1,3	--	1,3	--	1,3,5	--	--	--	--	--
C-6	--	2,4,6*	1,2	3	--	1,3 *	--	--	--	2,3,5*
C-7	--	--	--	--	1,3	--	--	--	--	--
C-8	--	--	--	--	--	--	--	--	--	--
C-9	--	--	1,3,5*	--	--	--	--	--	--	--
C-10	--	--	--	--	--	--	--	--	--	--
M	1,3	2,3	--	1,2	--	1,2	1,3,5	--	2,3,5	1,2
G	1,3	1,2,3	1,3	1,3	1,3,4	1,3	1,3,5	--	2,3,5	1,2
SP	1,3	1,2	--	--	1,2,3	1,2	1,3,4	--	1,2	1,2
R	1,3	1,3	1,2	--	1,3,5	1,2	1,3,4	1,2	1,2	1,3
SI	1,3	1,3	1,2	--	1,3,5	1,3	1,3	--	--	1,3

* = in same direction as the expected direction of treatment benefits for Experimental Groups

Three major forms of fitted curves occurred in this data. They are represented in Figure 4. The most commonly fitted curve was one with both linear and cubic terms. Thirty-nine curves were of this form but 14 of those had an added 5th degree component. (When compared with observed data, this quintic component usually occurred when there had been an April or May "recovery" from a decreasing function). Twenty-two trends were expressed with linear and quadratic components and 8 of these included a cubic term. (Again, this cubic term was associated with "recovery" from decreasing function in the observed data). The third repeated form was that of a fifth degree polynomial expression with the linear and quartic terms eliminated as insignificant. This form occurred five times and four of these were in the secondary grade-level groups (7-9 and 10-12).

Figure 4: General Forms of Commonly Occurring Significant
Negative Trends in Control Group Data

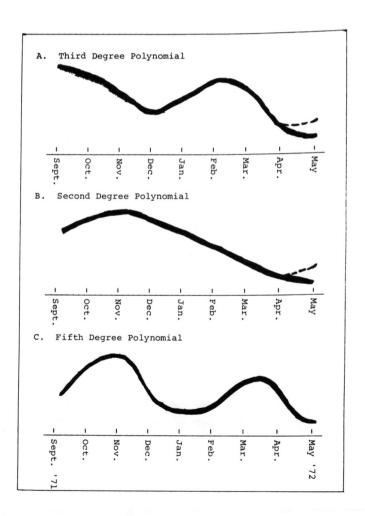

Table 31: Significant Components of the Polynomial Expression for Significant Trends Detected in Experimental Group Data

	By School Level		By Grade Level Groups							
	All Elem.	All Sec.	1	2	3	4	5	6	7-9	10-12
F-1	--	--	--	--	--	--	--	--	1,2,3+	1,2,3
F-2	1,3,5+	1,2,3+	--	3,5,6+	2,3,5+	--	1,3,5+	2,3,6+	--	2,3,6+
F-3	--	1,2,3	--	--	2,5,6+	--	--	--	--	--
F-4	1,2,6	1,3,4	--	--	--	--	--	--	--	2,5
F-5	1,2,6	--	--	2,3,5+	--	--	--	--	2,3,4+	--
F-6	--	3,4 +	3,4	1,2,3	1,3 +	1,2,3+	2,3,6	2,3,5	1,2,3+	1,2,3
F-7	--	--	--	--	--	--	1,2,6	1,2,3	3,4,5	--
F-8	2,3,5	--	1,3	3,5,6	--	--	--	--	2,3,4	--
F-9	--	--	--	--	--	--	--	--	--	3,5,6+
F-10	2,3,5	1,6	--	2,3,6+	--	--	--	1,2,3+	1,2,3	2,5,6+
C-1	1,2,6	--	1,3,5	2,3,5	1,2,3	--	--	--	2,3,4	--
C-2	1,3,6+	1,6	--	2,3,5	--	--	2,3,5+	--	--	2,3
C-3	--	--	--	--	--	--	--	--	--	--
C-4	--	1,5,6	--	--	--	--	--	--	1,2,3	--
C-5	2,3,6	--	1,2,3	3,5,6	--	--	--	--	2,3,4	2,3,5
C-6	--	--	--	--	--	--	--	--	--	--
C-7	--	1,2,3	--	--	1,2,3	2,3,4	--	--	--	1,2,4
C-8	--	--	--	--	--	--	--	--	--	2,3,5
C-9	--	--	--	--	--	--	--	--	1,2,3+	--
C-10	2,4,6	3,5,6	--	--	--	--	--	1,5,6+	1,2,3	2,5,6
M	1,2,3+	3,4	--	--	--	2,3,5+	--	1,2,4+	2,3,4	1,2,3
G	1,2,6+	3,4	--	--	2,3,5+	2,3,5+	--	1,4 +	2,3,4	2,4,5
SP	1,2,5+	4	2,3,5+	--	2,3,5+	--	--	1,4 +	2,3,4	1,2,4
R	1,2,5+	4	--	--	--	2,4,6+	--	--	2,3,4	3,5,6
SI	1,2,5+	4	--	1,2,5+	1,2,3+	--	--	--	3,4,5	--

+ = in expected direction of treatment benefit

Table 31 displays the significant polynomials of the fitted curves for each analysis in which a significant trend was detected in the data from Experimental groups. Of the 250 analyses conducted with this data, 97 significant trends were detected. Twenty-eight of these were in the 50 analyses with the data from School Level groups (All Elementary and All Secondary). When the teachers in the School Level groups were treated separately in grade level groups, the resulting 200 analyses yielded 69 significant trends with 38 occurring among the elementary grades and 31 occurring among the secondary groups.

Of the 97 significant trends, 46 were fitted with polynomial expressions which contained a linear term; 70 had a quadratic component, and 68 had a cubic component. About half of the curves had a decreasing function. (See further discussion below).

The forms of the fitted curves were not as consistent in the Experimental Data as in the Control Data. However, of the 38 significant **positive** trends (in the direction* of anticipated treatment benefits) two general forms of fitted curves occurred commonly. They are represented in Figure 5. The arrows in the figure represent those points in time at which treatment (training of teachers) was applied. The most commonly fitted curve was one with **both** quadratic and cubic terms. Nineteen curves had this form, but 12 of those were cases in which the quadratic and cubic terms were components of a 5th or 6th degree expression. The second generally occurring form in this data was that of a 5th or 6th degree polynomial expression which included a significant quadratic component as one of three terms. This form occurred 8 times.

From Comparison of Control versus Experimental Trends

The trends for each dependent variable were compared for each of the grade-level groups. Of the 400 trend analyses carried out with data from **grade-level** groups, the regression was significant in 124 cases. These cases were so distributed that at least one regression of the pair was significant in 102 of a possible 200 **paired** comparisons (the comparison of the trend of a behavior variable in grade-level matched experimental vs. control groups).

Table 32 displays the results of the comparison. The symbols used are defined in the table; but, to summarize, the "+" and "−" symbols denote the direction of the behavior trends while the letters and numbers indicate significance. Specifically, a "+" denotes a favorable comparison; i.e., one in which it can be considered that the Experimental group has moved in the expected direction of treatment benefit as indicated by (1) **a significant positive trend of the experimental**

---

*Either an increasing or a decreasing function, depending upon whether high or low levels of the specific behavior were desired treatment benefits. Positive directions are indicated in Table 31 by a +.

132

Figure 5: Two General Forms of Commonly Occurring Significant
Positive Trends in Experimental Group Data With
Applications of Treatment Indicated

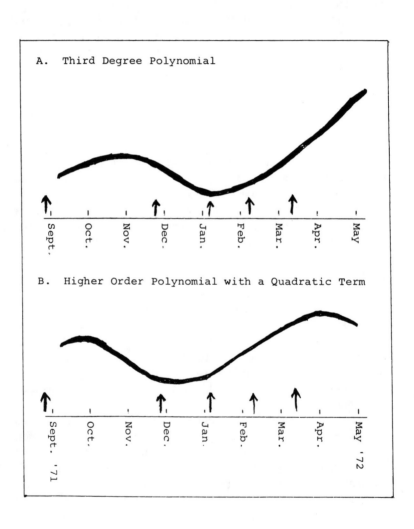

Table 32: Summary of 6-Degree Polynomial Multilinear Regression Analysis Across Time -- Direction & Treatment Assignment of Significant Behavior Trends for 200 Paired Analyses of Experimental & Control Grade-Level Groups

Variables	Elementary Schools by Grade						Secondary by Grade	
	1	2	3	4	5	6	7-2	10-12
F-1	--	--	--	--	+C	--	+X	-XND
F-2	--	+2	+X	+C	+2	+X	--	+X
F-3	--	--	+X	+C	+C	--	--	+C
F-4	--	--	+C	--	--	-2ND	--	-XND
F-5	--	+X	--	--	--	--	-XND	--
F-6	-XND	-XND	+XND	+XND	-XND	-XND	+2ND	-XND
F-7	--	--	--	--	--	-XND	-XND	--
F-8	-2ND	-XND	--	--	-XND	--	-XND	--
F-9	-C	--	--	--	--	--	-XND	+X
F-10	--	+X	--	--	--	+XND	-XND	+2ND
C-1	-XND	-XND	-XND	--	--	--	-XND	--
C-2	--	-2ND	+C	--	+2	-CND	--	-2ND
C-3	--	--	--	--	--	--	--	--
C-4	--	--	--	--	--	--	-XND	-XND
C-5	-2ND	-XND	-CND	--	--	--	-XND	--
C-6	+CND	+C	--	+CND	--	--	--	-C
C-7	--	--	-XND	-XND	--	--	--	-XND
C-8	--	--	--	--	--	--	--	-XND
C-9	+CND	--	--	+X	--	--	+X	--
C-10	--	--	--	--	--	+XND	+XND	+XND
M	--	+C	--	+2	+C	+X	-2ND	-2ND
G	+C	+C	+2	+2	+C	+X	-2ND	-2ND
SP	+XND	--	+2	+C	--	+X	-2ND	-2ND
R	+C	--	+C	+2	+C	+C	-2ND	-2ND
SI	+C	+X	+2	+C	+C	--	-XND	+C

Symbols Used

When only Experimental Trend is Significant:

+X Experimental trend toward, and control away from, expected direction.
-X Experimental trend away from, and control toward, expected direction.
+XND No Difference -- both trends away from desired direction: control non-sig.
-XND No Difference -- both trends away from desired direction: control non-sig.

When both Experimental and Control Trends are Significant:

+ 2 Experimental trend toward and control away from expected direction.
- 2 Experimental trend away from and control toward expected direction.
+ 2ND No Difference -- both trends significant in expected direction.
- 2ND No Difference -- both trends significant away from expected direction.

When only Control Trend is Significant:

+ C Experimental non-sig. trend is desired direction with control away from it.
- C Experimental non-sig. trend away from desired direction with control toward expected direction.
+ CND No Difference -- both trends in expected direction; experimental non-sig.
- CND No Difference -- both trends away from expected direction; experimental non-sig.

-- Neither group significant

group paired with either a **significant** control group trend in the opposite direction or with a **non-significant** control group in the same or opposite direction or (2) a **non-significant positive trend** of the experimental group paired with a **significant** control group trend in the opposite direction.

Similarly, a "−" denotes an unfavorable movement of the Experimental group away from the expected direction of treatment benefit as indicated by (1) a **significant negative trend of the experimental group** paired with either a **significant** control group trend in the positive direction or with a **non-significant** control group trend in the same or opposite directions or (2) a **non-significant negative trend** of the experimental group paired with a **significant** control group trend in a positive direction.

The letters "ND" indicate that both trends were in the same direction. A "+X" or "−X" standing alone or with the letters "ND" indicates that only the experimental trend was significant. The letter "C" immediately following the directional symbol ("+" or "−") indicates that only the control trend was significant while the number "2" following the directional symbol indicates that both the control and the experimental trends were significant.

The incidence of favorable and unfavorable comparisons are summed by grade-level groups in Table 33. Elementary Teachers have more favorable than unfavorable comparisons (44 to 23) while the Secondary teachers have more unfavorable ones.

Table 33: Summary of Favorable Versus Unfavorable
Comparisons of Experimental Group
Trends with Control Group Trends

	Grade-Level Groups	No. Favorable* Comparisons	No. Unfavorable Comparisons
Elementary	1	6	5
	2	7	5
	3	8	5
	4	10	2
	5	8	2
	6	7	4
Secondary	7-9	4	13
	10-12	6	11
Totals	Elementary	46	23
	Secondary	10	24
	All	56	47

*Favorable comparison: one in which it can be considered that the Experimental group has moved in the expected direction of treatment benefit.

Closer examination of Table 32 indicates that the Elementary school teachers generally have favorable comparisons on the Interpersonal Process (M, G, SP, R, SI) and Indirect Behavior (F-1, F-2, F-3, F-4) variables. The picture for the Secondary Schools is not as favorable as that of the Elementary Schools but the Senior High School (grades 10-12) does better than the Junior High (grades 7-9).

Although the data exhibits negative movement for the experimental groups, these are usually accompanied by negative movement of the matching control group as well. There is no case in which the experimental group had a **significant negative direction** accompanied by a significant **positive** direction for the control group. There are two cases (indicated by "−C" in Table 32) in which the experimental group had a non-significant negative movement paired with a significant positive movement of the control group.

DISCUSSION

The "−XND", "−2ND", "+C", and "−CND" symbols registered in Table 32 are reflective of a general tendency which was found in the data. This tendency was most marked in the significant trends for the control group data. (See Table 30).

That is, in general* the behavior trend for the control group was a movement across the year from September to May towards increased amounts of direct teacher behavior (F-5, F-6, F-7, C-1), increased amounts of Silence and Chaos (F-10, C-10) lower levels of student participation (F-8, F-9, C-5, C-6, C-7, and C-8), and less facilitative levels of interpersonal processes. This was not strictly a linear trend and, of course, it varied considerably among grade-levels and variables but, in general, it showed a decreasing function from September through December or January, a partial recovery in January or February, and a second downward trend through May. For some variables there was a second slight recovery in May, ending the downward trend with April. (See A and B of Figure 4).

Thus, for the experimental group to show positive movement, they had to over-come this general downward trend before positive movement could be evidenced. The symbol "+C" in Table 32 indicates cases in which a significant negative trend in the control group is paired with a non-significant positive trend of the experimental group. These cases are interpreted as being instances in which the experimental group succeeded in breaking up the negative trend but not in making significant positive movement. The symbols "−ND", "−2", "−2ND" in Table 32 indicate those cases in which the experimental group reflected the general negative tendency of the data.

The general trend across time for the experimental groups was not

---

* Exceptions are indicated by * in Table 30.

136   as consistent as for the control groups, which also substantiates the concept of the experimental treatment benefits being in a direction opposed to the direction of the normal processes evidenced across the school year. Of the 97 significant trends detected in the experimental data, 38 were in the direction of expected treatment benefits. For the control groups, only 7 of the 79 significant trends were in this direction.

While examining the behavior trends across time, anecdotal evidence was discovered indicating that the measures selected for the study do reflect classroom processes accurately. This was found in the data taken in the week immediately following two racial incidents (a rape and a stabbing) in one of the secondary schools. The data for that time period (Feb., 1972) supplied by the faculty of the school which was involved in the racial incidents exhibited a severe depression in the variables most directly related to facilitative interpersonal processes. Thus, the data for that month **for that school** showed (1) marked decreases (from the levels attained in both the month preceding and the month following) in amount of praise given, questions asked by pupils, and student ideas accepted, and (2) a sharp increase in criticism and justification of authority and the amount of silence or confusion in the classroom. Decreases were also registered in the levels of the teacher's Meaning, Genuineness, Respect for Students, Success Promotion, and in the degree of Student Involvement in classroom processes.

SUMMARY

In conclusion, the findings from this study were:

1. *The data supplied anecdotal validation that the measures selected for the project do reflect classroom process accurately.*
2. *Significant trends across time were found in the Control group data.*
3. *These trends were consistent with the interpretation that there is a deterioration across the year from September till May in the levels of facilitative conditions offered students.*
4. *Significant trends across time were detected in the Experimental Group data.*
5. *These trends were not as consistent as the trends from the Control data but were compatible with the interpretation that the benefits of the treatment applied (training of teachers) were in directions opposed to the direction of the normal processes evidenced across the school year.*
6. *Of the 97 significant trends in the Experimental data, 38 were in the direction of expected treatment benefits.*

The first implication of this study for the applied research studies was that time of year was a confounding factor for the study variables and must be taken into consideration in the interpretation of research results. Secondly, a comparison of (1) the variables in which positive movement was evidenced and (2) the content of the training sessions for the year indicates a correspondence between the skills in which instruction was explicit and the variables in which movement was exhibited. This comparison led to the hypothesis that for the attainment of desired treatment benefits in additional variables, specific skills development training programs for those behaviors should be applied. To test this hypothesis, the training modules for the second year would have to undergo revision.

STUDY NUMBER 7
ARE INITIAL LEVELS OF THE TEACHER BEHAVIOR RELATED TO RACE, SEX AND EXPERIENCE?
PURPOSE OF STUDY

The study posed the question:

> *Are teacher characteristics of sex, race, and years of teaching experience significant contributors to differences among the means of Classroom Functioning variables as measured by Flanders' Interaction Analysis Categories, Cognitive Functioning Categories, and Process Scales?*

DESIGN

Sample

The sample for this study consisted of all Year 01 experimental (Training Condition) teachers who submitted at least 4 tapes during the year, two of which were the May, 1971* and May, 1972 tapes. Total N was 121. The bottom lines of Table 34 and 35 display the N by Sex, Race, and Teaching Experience groups.

Table 34: Significance Levels Less Than .05 by Sources of Variation for 25 Analyses of Variance by Sex, Race, and Years of Teaching Experience for Classroom Functioning Variables

Variables*	Main Effects			Interaction Effects		
	SEX	RACE	YTEA	SxR	SxY	RxY
F-1	--	--	--	--	--	--
F-2	--	--	--	--	--	--
F-3	--	--	.0276	--	--	--
F-4	--	--	--	--	--	--
F-5	.0024	--	--	--	--	--
F-6	--	--	.0015	--	--	--
F-7	--	--	--	--	--	--
F-8	.0046	--	--	--	--	--
F-9	.0142	--	--	--	--	--
F-10	--	--	--	--	--	--
C-1	.0014	--	--	--	--	--
C-2	--	--	--	--	--	--
C-3	--	--	--	--	--	--
C-4	--	--	--	--	--	--
C-5	.0214	--	--	--	--	--
C-6	.0211	--	--	--	--	--
C-7	--	--	--	--	--	--
C-8	.0129	--	--	.0079	.0155	--
C-9	--	--	--	--	--	--
C-10	--	--	--	--	--	--
M	--	--	--	--	--	--
G	.0459	.037	--	--	--	.0477
SP	.0480	--	--	--	--	--
R	--	--	--	--	--	--
SI	--	--	--	--	--	--
DF	1, 106	1, 106	5, 106	1, 106	3, 106	3, 106

*See Table 8, Part I, for names of Variables.
+Results of Duncan's New Multiple Range Test.

*For the thirteen teachers who had not been employed by the school system in May, 1971, the September, 1971 tape was used as the pre-test tape.

Table 35:   Means for Sex and Race Groups for   139
Variables in which Significant
Differences by Sex or Race were Detected

Dep. Var.	Means by Sex		Means by Race	
	Male	Female	Black American	White American
F-5	113.87	69.12	--	--
F-8	47.25	84.32	--	--
F-9	22.75	9.72	--	--
C-1	123.75	79.03	--	--
C-5	55.12	89.72	--	--
C-6	4.81	1.67	--	--
C-8	3.25	0.23	1.42	0.32
G	2.65	2.39	2.30	2.47
SP	2.73	2.45	--	--
N	16	105	33	88

Data Collection

Data for the study consisted of the individual's pretest (May, 1971) scores on 10 Flanders' Interaction Analysis Categories, 10 Cognitive Functioning Categories, and 5 Process Scales. The data was collected through the normal procedures for assessment of tape data described in Part I.

ANALYSIS

Twenty-five analyses of variance were conducted, using in turn each of the Flanders', Cognitive, and Process scores as the dependent variable. Factors were teacher characteristics of sex, race, and years of teaching experience. The groups by characteristic and code number were as follows:

Sex
1 — Male
2 — Female

Race
1 — Black American
2 — White American

Years of Teaching Experience
1 — 1 Year
2 — 2 Years
3 — 3 to 7 Years
4 — 8 to 15 Years
5 — 16 to 24 Years
6 — Over 25 Years

The current school year was counted as 1 year since it would be completed by the time of the post-test. Thus, for number of years experience **prior** to the current year, subtract 1 from each of the figures above. That is, a "1 year" teacher is in his 1st year of teaching and has had 0 years of prior experience. A "2 years" teacher is in her second year of teaching and has had 1 year of prior experience, etc.

RESULTS

Table 34 presents the results of the 25 analyses. It lists by source of variance all significance levels less than .05 which were detected.

This level of significance was reached by one or more factors for 11 of the 25 variables. Interaction effects were significant for two variables. Tables 35 and 36 present the means of the significant factors for the variables affected.

Sex was the greatest contributor to variation, affecting 9 of the twenty-five variables. Of these 9 variables, 4 were teacher behavior variables (F-5, C-1, G, SP) and 5 were student behavior variables (F-8, F-9, C-5, C-6, C-8).

Race did not appear to have an important effect on the study variables. It showed up only once in main effects (G) and twice in interactions (C-8, G).

Years of teaching experience was slightly more important than race. It showed up twice in main effects (F-3, F-6) and twice in interactions (C-8, G).

DISCUSSION

Sex contributed the most systematic information from the analyses. Male teachers in general lectured more than female teachers (F-5) but they also allowed or elicited more student initiated responses (F-9). These student initiated responses included students asking more fact and more thinking questions (C-6, C-8) of male teachers than of female teachers. Female teachers elicited more directed student

Table 36: Means for Teaching Experience Groups for Variables in which
Significant Differences by Years of Teaching
Experience were Detected

Dep. Var.	Means of Teaching Experience Groups						Significant Comparisons*
	1 Yr.	2 Yrs.	3-7 Yrs.	8-15 Yrs.	16-24 Yrs.	Over 25 Yrs.	
F-3	5.50	2.81	0.69	1.74	3.56	1.55	3 < 1, 5 6 < 1
F-6	25.5	11.00	5.80	5.93	7.56	6.61	2-6 < 1
G	2.37	2.43	2.41	2.56	2.40	2.24	6 < 4
N	10	11	26	31	25	18	

*Results of Duncan's New Multiple Range Test.

response (F-8) and more student recall of facts (C-5) than did male teachers, and spent less time presenting facts (C-1) and slightly more time modeling thinking for students. However, there was no **significant** difference in the amounts of time male and female teachers spent in the C-3 (Teacher Thinks) category. (Mean for males was 0. 15; for females, 0.17). Males were higher than females in both of the Process Scales in which sex reached .05 significance.

The above results must be considered in view of the fact that the sample included only 16 male teachers and 13 of these were secondary school teachers, whereas a majority of the female teachers were elementary teachers. Reference to Studies No. 3 and 4 (cf. ante.) indicates that the pattern of differences due to grade-level (secondary vs. elementary) is the same for variables F-5, F-8, F-9, C-1, C-5, and C-6 as the pattern for male/female differences on those variables. That is, both males and secondary teachers are higher on variables F-5, F-9, C-1, C-6 and both males and secondary teachers are lower on variables F-8 and C-5. So it is not possible to make a clear-cut determination as to whether sex or grade-level or an interaction of these two factors is the primary source of differences on these variables. Since the sex/grade-level distributions for the sample in Studies 3 and 4 were 5 males to 123 females at the elementary level and 29 males to 81 females at the secondary level, it appears more probable that at least on the factors F-5, F-9, C-1, C-6, F-8, and C-5 grade level contributed to apparent sex differences and not the reverse.

However, for variables G and SP, grade level was not a significant factor in prior studies (See Table 19, Study No. 3) and for variable C-8 the elementary vs. secondary pattern did not hold; so for these three variables, sex can be clearly considered a significant contributor to the variance. That is, male teachers functioned at higher levels of the two Process Scales (G, SP) and were asked significantly more thinking questions by their students (C-8).

The information from race was not systematic. White Americans had higher means in the variable (G) in which race was a significant main effect but had lower means in the variable (C-8) in which race showed as one of two significant interactions with sex.

Teaching experience also offered little systematic information but what there was seemed to indicate that teachers who were starting their first year were different from other teachers, at least on variables F-3 and F-6. They gave more directions to students and accepted more student ideas than did other teachers.

SUMMARY

In conclusion, findings from this study were:

1. *Of the three factors, (sex, race, and years of teaching experience), sex contributed more to the variation of the*

classroom functioning variables than did either of the other two factors.

2. *Sex contributions to the variation of G (Genuineness of the teacher), SP (Success Promotion), and C-8 (Student asks for Thinking) seemed to be clear-cut, with male teachers functioning at higher levels than female teachers.*

3. *Sex contributions to the variation of F-5, F-8, F-9, C-1, C-5, and C-6 may have been contaminated by grade-level differences detected for these variables in the present study indicated that male teachers lectured more (F-5), allowed or elicited more student initiated responses (F-9), were asked more fact questions (C-6) by their students while female teachers elicited more directed student response (F-8) and more recall of facts (C-8) by their students and spent less time presenting facts (C-1) to their students.*

4. *Race did not seem to have important effects on the study variables and the information provided by its one significant main effect and two significant interactions (with sex) were in opposite directions.*

5. *Teaching experience showed as a significant factor in four variables; as a main effect for variables F-3 and F-6 and in interactions for variables C-8 and G. The information provided by these analyses seemed to be that teachers beginning their first year of teaching were different from other teachers in that they gave more directions (F-6) and accepted more student ideas (F-3).*

The implications of these findings for applied research were that studies of differential response to training should include correction of post-test scores for pre-test standing on at least sex and teaching experience characteristics.

IS THERE A RELATIONSHIP BETWEEN THE LEVEL
OF PHYSICAL FUNCTIONING OF THE TEACHER
AND TEACHER BEHAVIOR?

PURPOSE OF STUDY

Because the results of Study No. 11 for years 01 and 02 indicated that there were unsystematic effects of sex and years of teaching experience on response to training, the researchers wondered if the teacher's level of physical functioning might be an underlying factor which was related to these results. Therefore, the following question was posed:

> *Are there significant correlations between the teacher's level of physical functioning (as measured by the Harvard Step Test) and Classroom Functioning Variables as measured by Flanders' Interaction Analysis, Cognitive Functioning Categories, and Process Scales?*

DESIGN

Sample

The sample for this study was the 46 Year 03 experimental teachers who (1) submitted a tape in September, 1973 and (2) completed the Harvard Step Test.

Data Collection

The Harvard Step-Test was administered by an NCHE trainer who visited the experimental schools for this purpose. The individual's scores on 10 Flanders' Interaction Analysis Categories, 10 Cognitive Functioning Categories, and 5 Process Scales was collected through the normal procedures for assessment of tape data described in Part I.

The Harvard Step-Test is reported as the total number of pulse beats in two minutes immediately subsequent to cessation of controlled exercise. (The higher the number, the poorer the physical condition). The mean for elementary teachers was 170.2; for secondary teachers, 177.3.

ANALYSIS

Pearson's Correlation Coefficients were calculated for each classroom functioning variable. The calculations were carried out separately for elementary and secondary school teachers.

RESULTS

Table 37 presents the correlation coefficients for both elementary and secondary teachers. Seven coefficients were high enough to be significant at $p < .05$. This is approximately three times as many significant correlations as would be expected by chance at the .05 level.

DISCUSSION

Since seven of the 50 coefficients reached acceptable levels of significance, the conclusion was that there is a non-chance relationship between the level of physical functioning and the Classroom Functioning of the teacher. This relationship seemed to be stronger for secondary than for elementary teachers.

The relationship also seemed to occur in different directions for the two sets of teachers. Comparing the signs of the correlation coefficients in Table 37 reveals that for 13 of the twenty-five variables, elementary and secondary teachers have signs in opposite directions. Four of these 13 variables were ones in which at least one of the coefficients was significant.

SUMMARY

This study indicated that there was a non-chance relationship between the teacher's level of physical functioning and Classroom Functioning variables. On this basis, the researchers decided to use the Harvard Step-Test Score as a second concomitant variable for the replication of Study No. 11 to be carried out in Year 03.

Table 37: Correlation Coefficient for Harvard Step-Test
Score with Pre-Test Scores of 25 Classroom
Functioning Variables for Elementary and
Secondary Teachers

	Elementary		Secondary	
	r	p <	r	p <
F-1	0.0	--	0.0	--
F-2	-.04	--	.03	--
F-3	-.34	.05	.36	--
F-4	.06	--	.46	--
F-5	-.21	--	.69	.02
F-6	.18	--	-.29	--
F-7	.05	--	-.48	--
F-8	.12	--	.78	.01
F-9	.23	--	-.74	.01
F-10	-.09	--	-.57	--
C-1	-.03	--	.48	--
C-2	-.06	--	.44	--
C-3	0.0	--	0.0	--
C-4	.07	--	.05	--
C-5	.08	--	-.13	--
C-6	.35	.05	-.80	.01
C-7	.13	--	-.01	--
C-8	.08	--	0.0	--
C-9	.09	--	.80	.01
C-10	-.10	--	-.46	--
M	.003	--	.10	--
G	.02	--	.34	--
SP	.05	--	.05	--
R	.02	--	.36	--
SI	.11	--	.26	--
	N=34		N=12	

RESPONSE SURFACE ANALYSIS
PURPOSE OF STUDY

This study posed four questions:

1. *Can replicable, predictable, and significant relationships be detected among Classroom Functioning Variables as measured by Flanders' Interaction Analysis Categories, Cognitive Functioning Categories, and Process Scales?*
2. *Will these relationships be different at the elementary and secondary levels?*
3. *Can specific recurring predictors be identified for each of the Classroom Functioning Variables?*
4. *Can response surfaces generated from the regression equations resulting from backward elimination multilinear regression analysis provide information that will be useful in guiding the design of training programs?*

DESIGN

Sample

The sample for this study was all Year 01, Year 02, and Year 03 teachers who submitted 5 or more tapes during the year. Table 38 presents the data base for the study.

Table 38: Data Base for Response Surface Analysis

	Elementary			Secondary		
	Yr. 01	Yr. 02	Yr. 03	Yr. 01	Yr. 02	Yr. 03
No. of Teachers	162	132	55	98	60	44
No. of Hours of Instruction Coded	1,194	974	322	607	376	225

Data Collection

Study variables were the individual's scores on 10 Flanders' Interaction Analysis Categories, 10 Cognitive Functioning Categories, and 5 Process Scales. The data was collected through the normal procedures for assessment of tape data described in Part I.

ANALYSIS

Response Surface Analysis was carried out for each of the 25 study variables. The procedure used was to designate each of the study variables in turn as the dependent variable with the remaining 24 variables being considered as independent. The computer was then loaded with the linear, quadratic, and cross-product values of the independent variables and backward elimination multilinear regression analysis was carried out. The procedure was continued until only two variables were left in the model. The resulting regression equation was used to generate points with which to plot the response surface. The regression equation with 3 variables was also identified and a 3-variable response surface was generated for each study variable.

The analysis for each study variable was carried out separately for elementary (grade 1-6) and secondary (grade 7-12) teachers as it was anticipated that the relationships would be different at the two levels. Since there were three samples (Year 01, Year 02, and Year 03) at each level which were analyzed separately, a total of 150 analyses were conducted. Each analysis yielded two response surfaces — a 2-variable surface and a 3-variable surface — for a total of 300 surfaces which were constructed.

RESULTS

From Regression Analysis

A majority of the regressions were significant at $p < .001$; however, they ranged as high as $p < .75$. Acceptable levels of significance were $p < .05$. Only 19 of the 150 regressions failed to achieve this level of significance. Variable F-7 at the Secondary Level was the only variable which was consistently insignificant; it failed to reach the .05 level in all three samples.

Achieved R^2 for the three-variable equations ranged from .01 to .99. Some variables were predictable at approximately the same levels of R^2 from sample to sample (within a school level) while other variables showed wide differences in achieved R^2 among samples. A methodical comparison of the R^2's provided an estimate of the **stability** of predictability of the study variables from sample to sample. Table 39 summarizes the results of this comparison.

Some study variables consistently predicted the same dependent variables from sample to sample within a school level. These predictors were designated "Recurring Variables." Table 40 presents the Recurring Variables for each dependent variable at each school level.

It is obvious from scanning Table 40 that some variables featured more frequently as predictors of the other study variables. The relative frequency of each of the study variables **as a predictor** is summarized in Table 41.

From Construction of Response Surfaces

The 300 response surfaces generated from the 150 2-variable and the 150 3-variable regression equations derived from the three samples at each of two school levels were examined for information as to the dynamic relationships among the variables. Each surface presented its own exhibit of the dynamics of the inter-relationships of the study

Table 39: Stability of Predictability of Study Variables from Sample to Sample within School Levels

		Elementary Level	Secondary Level
Stable	With Consistently Ample R²	F-5 C-2 C-4 C-7 C-10 M G SP R SI	F-5 F-10 C-2 C-10 M R SI
	With Consistently Low R²	F-2	F-7* F-8*
Not Characterized as to Stability	Ample R²	F-4 F-10	F-3 C-4 C-5* C-9* SP
	Low R²	F-6 F-8* F-9 C-1*	F-6* F-9 C-8*
Unstable	With Inconsistently Ample R²	C-9	F-4 C-7 G
	With Inconsistently Low R²	F-1* F-3* F-7 C-3* C-5* C-6 C-8*	F-1* F-2* C-1* C-3* C-6

*Indicates that at least one of the 3 regressions within the school level for the variable did not reach $p < .05$.

+Ample R^2 was defined as $R^2 > .35$ in at least two of the three samples.

Table 40: Recurring* Predictive Variables

Dependent Variable	Elementary Teachers — Variables Recurring as Predictive of Dependent Variable in Equations for		Secondary Teachers — Variables Recurring as Predictive of Dependent Variable in Equations for	
	2 Samples	3 Samples	2 Samples	3 Samples
F-1	M, C-7	F-9	M, SI	C-7
F-2	SI	C-2, M	C-7, C-5	SI
F-3		C-7, SI	C-4, SI	C-2
F-4	R, C-5, C-7	C-6	SP, R, C-7	C-5
F-5	R, C-3	C-5	C-5, R	M
F-6	M, C-1, C-2, SI		SI	F-10, C-1
F-7		C-1, M, C-2		C-1, M
F-8	C-2	F-7, R	R, C-2	F-2
F-9	C-2	M	C-2, SP, F-2, F-1	
F-10	SI, C-2	C-1	C-2, SI	C-1
C-1	M, R, C-6	C-8	C-6	R, M
C-2	M	F-4, C-7		F-4, R, C-7
C-3	F-2	F-5, C-8	F-5, C-8	G
C-4		C-7, F-4, M	F-3, F-4, M	C-7
C-5	F-4, F-7	R	R, F-4	F-7
C-6	F-4, F-8, SI		F-3, SI, F-8	
C-7	F-8, SP	C-4		C-4. F-1
C-8	M, SI, C-3, C-4		C-3, M, F-1, SI	
C-9	F-1	F-7, M	F-3, F-7, C-7	M
C-10	C-4, F-5	SI	F-6	F-5, SI
M	F-7, M	R, F-2	C-1, C-7	R
G	F-2, C-4, M, C-1	F-2	F-7, F-2, M	C-1
SP	C-7, F-3		M, C-1, F-2	
R	F-1, C-7	G	F-1, C-7	G
SI		G		G, C-7

*Recurring - from sample to sample as predictor for same dependent variable.

Table 41: Summary of Predictive Appearances
of Recurring Variables

	Predictive Variables	No. of Appearances		
		Total	Elementary Data	Secondary Data
M:	Meaning	53	29	24
C-7:	Student Thinks	39	17	22
SI:	Student Involvement	34	16	18
R:	Respect	32	15	17
C-1:	Teacher Recalls Facts	25	10	15
C-2:	Teacher Asks for Facts	23	14	9
F-2:	Teacher Praises	19	10	9
F-4:	Teacher Asks Questions	17	10	7
F-7:	Teacher Criticizes	17	10	7
G:	Genuineness	15	6	9
C-4:	Teacher Asks for Thinking	14	9	5
F-1:	Teacher Accepts Feelings	13	4	9
C-5:	Student Recalls Facts	12	5	7
F-5:	Teacher Lectures	10	5	5
F-3:	Teacher Accepts Ideas	8	2	6
C-8:	Student Asks for Thinking	8	6	2
C-3:	Teacher Thinks	7	5	2
C-6:	Student Asks for Facts	7	5	2
F-8:	Student Responds	6	4	2
SP:	Success Promotion	6	2	4
F-9:	Student Initiates	3	3	*
F-10:	Silence or Confusion	3	*	3
F-6:	Teacher Gives Directions	2	*	2
C-9:	Non-Cognitive Behavior	*	*	*
C-10:	Silence and Confusion	*	*	*

*Variable occurred only at random in this data; i.e., it did
not recur from sample to sample within a level as predictor
for the same dependent variable.

variables; however, two general observations could be made of the surfaces as a set.

First, many of the variables were related to the dependent variable in a curvilinear rather than a linear fashion. All but 11 of the 150 2-variable regression equations contained at least one quadratic or cross-product term, while 146 of the 3-variable equations contained such a term.

Second, the surfaces emphasized the dynamic quality of the inter-relationships of the predictor variables. In several cases, the directionality of the relation between the dependent variable and a predictor variable was **completely** reversed as the value of a second predictor variable changed.

DISCUSSION

One of the major reasons for conducting this extensive examination of the relationships between Classroom Functioning variables was the need of the researchers to be able to specify the expected direction of treatment benefit for **each** of the 25 study variables. The National Consortium for Humanizing Education had hypothesized that a humane classroom was characterized by four types of behavior:

1. Frequent acceptance of student feelings.
2. High amounts of student participation.
3. High levels of student thinking beyond the use of facts, and
4. High degree of student involvement.

From this hypothesis, the expected direction of treatment benefits was self-evident for variables F-1, F-8, F-9, C-7, and the Process Scales. And from the implications of directionality of these variables, expected direction could be derived for variables F-2, F-3, F-4, C-2, and C-4. However, the implications for F-5, F-6, F-10, C-1, C-3, C-5, C-6, C-9 and C-10 were not so clear. By examining the response surfaces generated in this study, it was possible to specify the expected direction of treatment benefit for all variables.

Examination of the individual response surfaces also provided guidance for focusing training to change specific aspects of teacher or student behavior. For example, examination of the response surfaces for F-9 (Figure 6 & 7) suggested that in order to increase the amount of Student Initiation at the elementary school level, training should focus on helping the teacher to understand the meaning-to-the-student of his classroom experiences and to communicate acceptance of the student's feelings. At the high school level, training to increase Student Initiation should focus on helping the teacher (1) to raise her levels of skills in promoting the student's achievement of individual goals and (2) reduce the amount of time she spends asking students to recall facts. (See Figures 6 and 7).

Figure 6: Response Surface for
F-9: STUDENT INITIATES at the Elementary School Level

$$F\text{-}9 = 6.59066 - 47.9076\text{F1F1} + 15.013\text{F1M}$$

$R^2 = 0.172$ $\qquad$ $s_E = 5.945$ $\qquad$ $\underline{F} = 16.559$

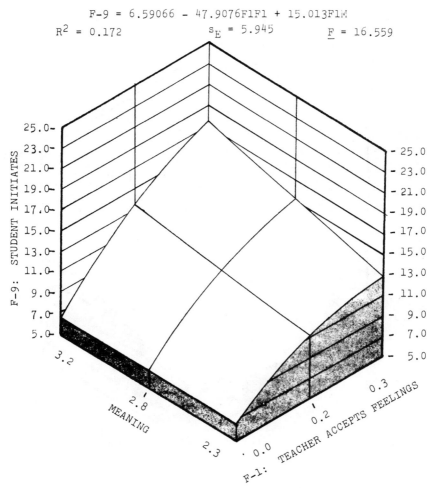

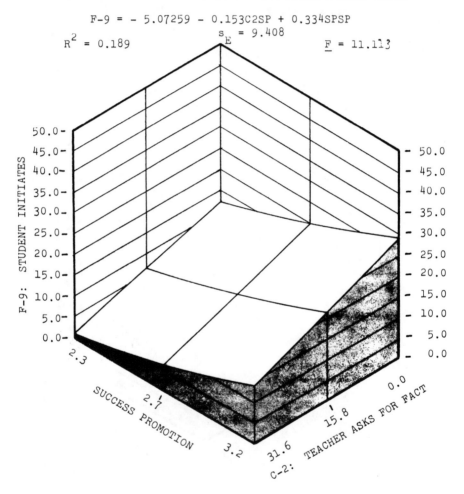

Figure 7:   Response Surface for
F-9:   STUDENT INITIATES at the Secondary School Level

$$F-9 = - 5.07259 - 0.153C2SP + 0.334SPSP$$

$$s_E = 9.408$$

$$R^2 = 0.189 \qquad\qquad \underline{F} = 11.113$$

In conclusion, the findings from this study are:

1. **Replicable, predictable,** *and* **significant** *relationships were detected among variables of teacher and student classroom functioning.*

2. *These* **relationships were different** *at the secondary and elementary school levels.*

3. **Specific recurring predictors** *for each of the study variables were identified.*

4. *Some of the classroom functioning variables* **co-varied significantly** *and* **frequently** *with a large number of the other study variables, and these predictors were few enough in number to suggest that efficient programs for changing overall classroom functioning could be developed by focusing training efforts on these few highly predictive variables.*

5. *The* **individual response surfaces** *generated for each study variable* **provide specific suggestions** *for focusing training efforts aimed at changing selected aspects of teacher or student behavior.*

6. *Two of the 4 most* **frequently recurring predictors** *(and 3 of the top 10) were variables which had been postulated by Rogers as being positively related to effective learning environments.*

7. *Most of the* **frequently recurring predictors** *were related to the kinds of behavior classified by Flanders' as "Indirect."*

8. *The kinds of behavior hypothesized by the National Consortium for Humanizing Education as characterizing a humane classroom were also the kinds of behavior which were* **frequently recurring predictors** *of the other study variables.*

9. *The* **curvilinear relationships** *detected were strong enough and constant enough to suggest that educational researchers need to emphasize the building and testing of* **at least** *quadratic models.*

The most important implication of this study for the NCHE applied studies was the specification of the expected direction of treatment benefits for each of the 25 classroom functioning variables. However, the other findings from this study have important implications for applied reasearch in education in general. Also, the methodology (Response Surface Analysis) seems a promising one for researchers in education and other social sciences.

STUDY NUMBER 10

DOES INTERPERSONAL SKILLS TRAINING FOR TEACHER MAKE A DIFFERENCE IN TEACHER BEHAVIOR?

PURPOSE OF STUDY

This study posed two questions:

1. *When adjusted for pre-test standing, is there a significant difference between the treatment (Training vs. No Training Condition) post-test means on the Classroom Functioning variables as measured by Flanders' Interaction Analysis Categories, Cognitive Functioning Categories, and Process Scales?*
2. *Are the differences cumulative across two years' treatment?*

DESIGN

Sample

This study utilized three samples consisting respectively of all Year 01, 02, and 03 teachers who met the inclusion criteria for their samples. Criteria for each sample were:

1. Year 01 sample included all teachers who (a) had submitted four or more tapes, two of which were the May, 1971 and May, 1972 tapes and (b) if in experimental group, had completed the training program.
2. Year 02 sample included all teachers who (a) had submitted four or more tapes during the second year, one of which was the May, 1973 tape, (b) had previously submitted the May, 1971 and May, 1972 tapes, and (c) if in experimental group, had completed the training program.
3. Year 03 sample included all teachers who (a) had submitted four or more tapes, two of which were the September, 1973 and the April, 1974 tapes and (b) if in experimental group, had completed the training program.

Table 42 displays the N by grade-level and treatment groups for each sample. Total N for three years was 482; however, the Year 02 N (155) was contained within the Year 01 N. (See above).

Data Collection

Data for this study was the individual's scores on each of the pre and post-test (as specified above for each sample) audio tape recordings of classroom instruction on each of the 10 Flanders' Interaction Analysis Categories, 10 Cognitive Functioning Categories, and 5 Process Scales. The data was collected by the regular procedures for assessment of tape data described in Part I. For names of variables, see Table 8 in Part I.

| Samples | Grade Levels | Treatment Conditions | | | | Total Sample |
| | | Training | | No Training | | |
		Experi.	1C2X	1X2C	Control	
Year 01	Elementary (1-6)	55	--	--	66	121
	Special Teachers*	14	--	--	13	27
	Secondary (7-12)	52	--	--	40	92
	Total	121	--	--	119	240
Year 02	Elementary (1-6)	25	8	20	39	92
	Special Teachers*	7	0	2	5	14
	Secondary (7-12)	20	0	3	26	49
	Total	52	8	25	70	155
Year 03	Elementary (1-8)+	46	--	--	23	79
	Secondary (9-12)+	10	--	--	8	18
	Total	56	--	--	31	87

+ This change in the grade levels included in Secondary Schools was occasioned by organizational pattern of schools in the replication site.

*These are non-classroom teachers in grades 1-6 who provide special services (such as speech therapy) or special subject matter (such as art) for students from more than one grade level.

ANALYSIS

The procedure used in the analysis was a two-way analysis of co-variance with pre-test score as the concomitant variable. Factors were grade-level at which the teacher instructs and treatment condition. Grade-level was included as a factor on the basis of Studies No. 3 and 4. (cf. ante).

There were two treatment conditions: Training and No-Training. These are referred to respectively as Experimental and Control groups. In Year 02 only, both groups were subdivided by rotating one control school into the experimental (Training) condition and by rotating one experimental school into the No-Training (Control) condition. These groups are referred to respectively as 1C2X and 1X2C while the groups which remained in the same condition for a second year are referred to as 2YrX (Training) and 2YrC (No-Training).

Grade-level groups for the three samples are as follows:

Years 01 and 02	**Year 03**
Grade 1	Grades 1-3
Grade 2	Grades 4-6
Grade 3	Grades 7-8
Grade 4	Grades 9-12

Grade 5
Grade 6
Special Teachers-Service (1-6)*
Special Teachers-Subject (1-6)*
Junior High (7-9)
Senior High (10-12)

*These two groups were collapsed into one group for Year 02.

"Special Teachers" included those non-classroom teachers in grades 1-6 who provide special services (e.g., speech therapy) or special subject matter (e.g., art) for students from more than one grade level. The grade level groups were collapsed for Year 03 because of small N and because no grade-by-treatment interaction effects **within** the limits of the collapsed groups had been detected in Years 01 and 02.

The data for each year was analyzed separately to determine the treatment effects for that year. In order to test for cumulative differences across two years, the Year 02 post-test (May, 1973) data for groups 2YrC and 2YrX was re-run, using the pre-test data from Year 01 (May, 1971) as the concomitant variable.

Prior to conducting the analyses, the results of Study 9 (cf. ante.) were used to specify the expected direction of treatment (training) benefit for each of the 25 classroom functioning variables. It was determined that **treatment benefits** should result in **increases** in F-1, F-2, F-3, F-4, F-8, F-9, C-2, C-3, C-4, C-5, C-6, C-7, C-8, C-9, M, G, SP, R, and SI while **decreases** should be registered in F-5, F-6, F-7, F-10, C-1, and C-10. The asterisks in Tables 43 - 49 indicate the direction of treatment benefit for each variable.

RESULTS

From Year 01 Data

Twenty-five analyses of co-variance were conducted using in turn each of the Flanders', Cognitive, and Process scores as the dependent variable. Table 43 displays the results of the analyses. It lists by sources of variation all significance levels less than .10 which were detected.

As indicated by the asterisks in Table 43, the experimental group mean was closest to the anticipated direction of treatment benefit for 14 out of the twenty-five variables; and this was a significant difference (at the .05 level) for eight variables (F-2, F-3, C-2, M, G, SP, R, SI). Five other variables (F-4, F-10, C-4, C-7, and C-10) reached the level of significance specified, but in these variables, the control group mean was the farthest in the direction of treatment benefit.

From Year 02 Data

Two series of Analysis of Co-variance were planned using the Year 02 post-test (May, 1973) data. One series (referred to as Year 02 series) would use the data from all four treatment groups with the May, 1972

Table 43: Significance Levels Less Than .10 by Source of Variation for 25 Analyses of Co-Variance of Grade-Level and Treatment Means of Classroom Functioning Variables for Year 01 Teachers in Grades 1-12

Dep. Var.	Min. Sig. Prob. by Source of Variation			Adj. Post-Test X̄		Sig. Grade Comparisons+
	Grade	Treatment	G x T	Experi.	Control	
F-1	--	--	--	0.01	0.08*	--
F-2	.0007	.0001	.0072	4.59*	1.33	1-6, 10-12<7-9
F-3	.0749	.0001	.0433	1.63*	0.29	10-12<1-9
F-4	.0001	.0014	--	17.69	23.00*	7-12<2&6
F-5	--	--	--	85.57*	93.00	--
F-6	.0005	--	--	10.00	9.02*	2-12<1
F-7	.0097	--	.0613	1.44*	1.64	2-12<1
F-8	--	--	--	58.10	66.24*	--
F-9	--	--	--	10.23	10.58*	--
F-10	--	.0010	--	50.00	34.48*	--
C-1	--	--	--	104.61*	104.97	--
C-2	.0001	.0078	--	20.09*	15.92	7-12<1,4, & 6
C-3	--	--	--	0.23*	0.13	--
C-4	--	.0116	--	0.67	2.22*	--
C-5	--	--	--	65.86*	64.57	--
C-6	--	--	--	1.75	2.34*	--
C-7	--	.0085	--	1.43	5.56*	--
C-8	--	--	--	0.03	0.06*	--
C-9	--	--	--	3.52*	3.22	--
C-10	--	.0159	--	47.09	35.71*	--
M	--	.0001	.0589	2.63*	2.46	--
G	--	.0008	.0142	2.60*	2.45	--
SP	--	.0144	.0519	2.57*	2.46	--
R	--	.0001	.0135	2.63*	2.48	--
SI	--	.0036	--	2.73*	2.61	--
	DF = 9, 219	DF = 1, 219	DF = 9, 219	N = 121	N = 119	

+Results of Duncan's New Multiple Range Test.
*Mean Associated with direction of expected treatment benefits

pre-test as co-variate. To test for cumulative differences **across both years,** the second series (called, obviously, Cumulative Differences series) would use only the data for the teachers in groups 2YrC and 2YrX with the May, 1971 pre-test as co-variate.

Because the five significant main effects of grade-level and the seven significant grade-by-treatment interactions in the Year 01 data seemed to suggest that differences between secondary and elementary schools might be masking treatment differences* and because there were no Secondary teachers in the 1C2X group and only 3 in the 1X2C group, it was decided that the analysis for both the **Year 02 series** and the **Cumulative Differences series** should be run a second time using only data from grades 1-6.

This meant a total of 100 analyses of co-variance in 4 runs of 25 analyses each. The series are presented separately below.

Year 02 Series: Tables 44 and 45 present the results of the two runs of the Year 02 series. Summarizing data for grades 1-12, Table 44 reveals significant differences among the treatment means for only two variables (C-9 and SI). However, for **every variable,** the asterisk indicating the mean which is farthest in direction of treatment benefit is on an experimental mean — 13 on the means of the 2YrX groups and 12 on the means of the 1C2X group.

Removal of the effect of the Secondary School data changes the picture. Table 45 displays the results of the analysis of Year 02 data, using only grade levels 1-6.

The first thing of interest in Table 45 is the inflation (in positive directions) of the means of the 2YrX group with the removal of the influence of the Secondary School Data. Thus, the 2YrX group means now register 18 of the "benefit" asterisks with the 1C2X group accounting for the remaining seven variables.

Significant ($p < .05$) differences were detected among the treatment means for three variables (F-10, C-7, C-9) and two other variables (F-2, F-9) approach this level. All five variables are ones in which the two year continuous experimental group (2YrX) achieved the mean associated with treatment benefits.

Cumulative Differences Series: Tables 46 and 47 display the results of the analyses of co-variance of the Year 02 Post-Test means for groups 2YrX and 2YrC using the May, 1971 pre-test as co-variate. The analyses using the data from all grade levels is in Table 46 while Table 47 displays the results from grades 1-6.

As indicated in Table 46, significant differences among the treatment means were detected on variables F-2, F-10, and C-9. In each case, the mean associated with treatment benefits is that of the experimental group.

---

*This hypothesis had been tested with **a posteriori** analysis in the Year 01 data and had been supported.

Table 44: Significance Levels Less Than .10 by Source of Variation for 25 Analyses of Co-Variance of Grade-Level and Treatment Means on Classroom Functioning Variables for Year 02 Teachers in Grades 1-12

Dep. Var.	Min. Sig. Prob. by Source of Variation			Adjusted Treatment Means				Sig. Grade Comparisons[+]
	Grade	Treatment	G x T	2YrX	1C2X	1X2C	2YrC	
F-1	--	--	.0004	0.77*	0.25	0.03	0.04	--
F-2	.0010	.0982	--	2.44*	1.82	1.47	0.91	10-12< 1
F-3	--	--	--	1.33*	0.09	0.09	0.01	--
F-4	.0763	--	--	18.01	19.02*	14.31	16.63	--
F-5	.0742	--	--	70.36*	79.01	78.10	84.63	--
F-6	--	--	.0803	4.72*	7.75	7.51	6.08	--
F-7	--	--	--	1.51	0.40*	1.36	0.77	--
F-8	.0154	--	--	65.28	103.77*	54.27	72.21	7-9< 2
F-9	--	--	--	15.25*	12.92	13.93	13.63	--
F-10	--	.0516	--	24.30	18.22*	21.73	36.68	--
C-1	.0155	--	--	77.86*	78.36	80.37	93.76	--
C-2	--	--	.0557	15.48	21.93*	15.67	15.59	7-9< 1,2,&4
C-3	--	--	--	0.27*	0.00	0.00	0.04	--
C-4	.0272	--	--	1.64*	0.18	0.22	0.93	3< 5
C-5	.0051	--	--	71.35	117.64*	67.62	84.18	7-12< 1-3
C-6	.0289	--	--	1.62*	0.51	0.68	1.46	1< 6
C-7	--	--	--	3.04*	0.13	0.17	1.74	--
C-8	--	--	--	0.06*	0.00	0.00	0.04	--
C-9	.0429	.0490	--	3.84*	2.79	3.50	1.69	10-12< 1,1,&5
C-10	--	--	--	28.16	20.59*	24.66	33.91	--
M	.0289	--	--	2.34	2.63*	2.14	2.52	7-9< 1-6,10-12
G	.0389	--	--	2.32	2.58*	2.15	2.51	7-9< 1-6
SP	.0448	--	--	2.35	2.58*	2.18	2.52	7-9< 1-6
R	.0278	--	--	2.41	2.66*	2.16	2.51	7-9< 1-6
SI	.0026	.0481	--	2.52	2.90*	2.33	2.75	7-9< 1-6,10-12
	DF = 8, 122	DF = 3, 122	DF = 20, 122	N = 52	N = 8	N = 25	N = 70	

[+]Results of Duncan's New Multiple Range Test.

*Mean associated with direction of expected treatment benefits.

Table 45: Significance Levels Less Than .10 by Source of Variation for 25 Analyses of Co-Variance of Grade-Level and Treatment Means on Classroom Functioning Variables for Year 02 Teachers in Grades 1-6

Dep. Var.	Min. Sig. Prob. By Source of Variation			Adjusted Treatment Means				Sig. Grade Comparisons[+]
	Grade	Treatment	G x T	2YrX	1C2X	1X2C	2YrC	
F-1	--	--	.0006	.13*	.25	0.05	0.02	--
F-2	.0630	.0562	--	3.53*	1.87	1.40	1.33	--
F-3	--	--	--	2.16*	0.06	0.09	.01	--
F-4	.0414	--	--	23.93*	19.22	16.07	17.68	--
F-5	--	--	--	65.59*	79.01	82.40	70.70	3 < 4
F-6	--	--	--	6.07*	6.21	7.92	10.68	--
F-7	--	--	--	2.25	0.47*	1.57	0.99	--
F-8	--	--	--	86.24	104.19*	60.10	85.77	--
F-9	--	.0790	--	18.18*	12.99	15.39	9.70	--
F-10	--	.0423	--	17.59*	18.38	23.85	32.69	--
C-1	.0707	--	--	75.88*	78.75	83.70	83.37	--
C-2	.0703	--	.0625	20.66	22.02*	17.65	15.99	--
C-3	--	--	--	0.44*	0.0	0.0	0.0	--
C-4	.0663	--	--	2.13*	0.20	0.17	1.13	--
C-5	--	--	--	92.94	117.99*	75.07	95.08	--
C-6	.0092	--	--	1.31*	0.50	0.68	0.84	--
C-7	--	.0450	--	3.38*	0.14	0.20	0.88	--
C-8	--	--	--	0.09*	0.0	0.0	0.02	--
C-9	--	.0358	--	5.59*	2.87	3.82	2.08	--
C-10	--	--	--	23.23	20.77*	27.56	30.26	--
M	--	--	--	2.64*	2.63	2.31	2.45	--
G	--	--	--	2.62*	2.58	2.52	2.44	--
SP	--	--	--	2.64*	2.59	2.36	2.47	--
R	--	--	--	2.60	2.66*	2.33	2.44	--
SI	--	--	--	2.75	2.90*	2.55	2.71	--
	DF = 6, 77	DF = 3, 77	DF = 18, 77	N = 32	N = 8	N = 22	N = 44	

[+]Results of Duncan's New Multiple Range Test.

*Mean associated with direction of expected treatment benefits.

Table 46: Significance Levels Less Than .10 by Source of Variation for 25 Analyses of Co-Variance of Grade-Level and Treatment Means of Classroom Functioning Variables for Two-Year Teachers (Cumulative Differences) in Grades 1-12

Dep. Var.	Min. Sig. Prob. by Source of Variation			Adj. Treatment $\overline{X}$		Sig. Grade Comparisons[+]
	Grade	Treatment	G x T	2YrX	2YrC	
F-1	--	--	--	.09*	.04	--
F-2	.0001	.0019	--	2.51*	.90	10-12< 1-9
F-3	--	--	.0138	1.47*	.01	--
F-4	.0477	--	--	19.38*	16.63	10-12< 1-9
F-5	--	--	--	71.54*	84.59	--
F-6	.0565	--	.0941	4.97*	7.74	--
F-7	--	--	--	1.59	.77*	--
F-8	.0084	--	--	67.76	72.16*	10-12<1,2,3,6
F-9	--	--	--	16.36*	13.62	--
F-10	--	.0412	--	23.72*	36.66	--
C-1	--	--	--	79.11*	93.67	--
C-2	.0076	--	.0498	16.68*	15.58	10-12< 4
C-3	--	--	.0221	.30*	.04	--
C-4	.0363	--	--	1.57*	.93	--
C-5	.0228	--	--	75.40	84.12*	10-12< 2,3
C-6	--	--	--	1.74*	1.45	1-5, 7-9 <6,10-12
C-7	--	--	--	2.38*	1.74	--
C-8	--	--	--	0.06*	0.04	--
C-9	.0236	.0118	--	3.97*	1.68	6, 10-12 <1-5
C-10	--	--	--	28.17*	33.87	--
M	--	--	.0283	2.42	2.52*	--
G	--	--	.0339	2.40	2.51*	--
SP	--	--	.0661	2.42	2.52*	--
R	--	--	.0597	2.39	2.50*	--
SI	--	.0881	.0788	2.50	2.74*	--
	DF = 7,100	DF = 1, 100	DF = 7, 100	N = 47	N = 70	

[+] Results of Duncan's New Multiple Range Test.

* Mean associated with direction of expected treatment benefits.

Table 47: Significance Levels Less Than .10 by Source of Variation for 25
Analysis of Co-Variance of Grade-Level and Treatment Means on Classroom
Functioning Variables for Two-Year Teachers (Cumulative Differences)
in Grades 1-6

	Min. Sig. Prob. by Source of Variation			Adj. Post Test X̄		Sig. Grade Comparisons
	Grade	Treatment	G x T	2YrX	2YrC	
F-1	--	--	--	.13*	.03	--
F-2	.0101	.0042	--	3.53*	1.32	4 < 1
F-3	--	--	.0956	2.16*	0.01	--
F-4	--	.0451	--	23.88*	17.67	--
F-5	--	--	--	65.35*	70.56	--
F-6	--	--	--	6.03*	10.66	--
F-7	--	--	--	2.25	0.98*	--
F-8	--	--	--	86.04*	85.56	--
F-9	--	.0302	--	18.13*	9.68	--
F-10	--	.0126	--	17.54*	32.64	--
C-1	--	--	--	75.57*	83.13	--
C-2	.0088	--	.0779	20.63*	15.98	4 <1-3, 5-6
C-3	--	--	--	.01	0.43*	--
C-4	--	--	--	2.13*	1.14	--
C-5	--	--	--	92.78	94.87*	--
C-6	.0021	--	--	1.31*	0.84	6 <1-5
C-7	--	.0483	--	3.38*	0.88	--
C-8	--	.0819	--	.09*	0.03	--
C-9	--	.0102	--	5.59*	2.07	--
C-10	--	--	--	23.14*	30.19	--
M	--	.0498	--	2.64*	2.43	--
G	--	--	--	2.62*	2.43	--
SP	--	--	--	2.64*	2.46	--
R	--	--	--	2.60*	2.43	--
SI	--	--	--	2.75*	2.70	--
	DF = 6, 61	DF = 1, 61	DF - 6, 61	N = 32	N = 44	

+Results of Duncan's New Multiple Range Test.
*Mean associated with expected direction of treatment benefits.

Table 47 indicates that (for grades 1-6) seven variables registered significant differences between the treatment means. In addition to F-2, F-10, and C-9, there are significant differences on F-4, F-9, C-7, and M. An eighth variable (C-8) approaches significance. In all 8 variables, the mean associated with treatment benefits is the experimental group mean.

From Year 03 Data

For the Year 03 study, the project was replicated in a different site, moving from an urban north central Texas school system to a rural northeast Louisiana system. Two series of Analysis of Co-variance were conducted using the September, 1973 and May, 1974 data for grades 1-12 and 1-8, respectively. Grades 7-8 were included in the elementary school data because of the way in which the schools were organized — the seventh and eighth grades were included in either elementary schools or in middle schools (grades 4-8). The results of the analyses are displayed in Table 48 (for grades 1-12) and in Table 49 (for grades 1-6).

In Table 48, significant differences between the group means were detected for two variables (F-2 and F-7) and differences approaching significance were registered for four other variables (F-4, C-3, M, and G). Of these six variables, the mean associated with treatment benefits was the experimental mean in 4 cases (F-2, F-4, M, and G).

In the analysis for only grades 1-8 (Table 49), significant differences between the treatment means were detected for five variables (F-2, F-7, F-9, M, G) and five others (F-4, C-3, C-4, C-9, SP) approached significance. Of these ten variables, the mean associated with treatment benefits was the experimental mean for eight variables (F-2, F-4, F-9, C-4, C-9, M, G, SP).

DISCUSSION

Direction of Differences

Because multi-variate analysis was beyond the capability of the computer facility available to the researchers, the data was handled in the manner presented above. In an effort to retrieve at least an estimate of the information that would have been available through multi-variate analysis, a supplementary analysis was conducted. In this procedure, the incidence of adjusted post-test means associated with the expected direction of treatment benefits was submitted to Chi-Square analysis.

Very simply, the incidence of means associated with treatment benefits was counted for Training and No-Training conditions in Tables 43, 44, and 48. Chi-Square was calculated separately for each table and for all tables together. Expected incidence for each condition for a table was 12.5 and expected incidence for all tables together was 37.50. Table 50 displays the results.

By this analysis using the data for all grades 1-12, for two out of three years, and for all three years together, when only the **direction** of

Table 48: Significance Levels Less Than .10 by Source of Variation for 25 Analyses of Co-Variance of Grade-Level and Treatment Means on Classroom Functioning Variables for Year 03 Teachers in Grades 1-12

	Min. Sig. Prob. By Source of Variation			Adj. Post-Test $\bar{X}$		Sig. Grade Comparisons+
	Grade	Treatment	G x T	Experi.	Control	
F-1	--	--	--	0.04*	0.00	--
F-2	--	.0129	--	2.02*	0.30	--
F-3	--	--	--	0.09*	0.03	--
F-4	--	.0950	--	13.20*	9.27	--
F-5	--	--	--	93.87*	98.91	--
F-6	--	--	--	4.00	3.42*	--
F-7	--	.0236	--	1.15	0.22*	--
F-8	--	--	.0308	54.53	57.20*	--
F-9	--	--	--	12.48*	10.07	--
F-10	.0881	--	--	58.77*	60.92	--
C-1	--	--	--	92.76*	87.97	--
C-2	--	--	--	13.25*	11.41	--
C-3	--	.0684	--	0.02	0.32*	--
C-4	--	--	.0215	1.07*	0.71	--
C-5	--	--	--	67.34*	62.83	--
C-6	--	--	--	1.98*	1.83	--
C-7	--	--	--	1.41*	1.03	--
C-8	--	--	--	0.00	0.00	--
C-9	--	--	--	4.04	5.16*	--
C-10	.0325	--	--	58.25*	68.99	4-8 < 1-3, 10-12
M	--	.0905	.0796	2.74*	2.60	--
G	--	.0608	.0157	2.77*	2.61	--
SP	--	--	.0981	2.78*	2.69	--
R	--	--	.0869	2.82*	2.72	--
SI	.0049	--	.0615	2.95*	2.86	10-12 < 4-8; 1-3 < 4-6
	DF = 3, 78	DF = 1, 78	DF = 3, 78	DF = 3, 78 N = 56	N = 31	

+Results of Duncan's New Multiple Range Test.

*Mean associated with expected direction of treatment benefits.

Table 49: Significance Levels Less Than .10 by Source of Variation for
25 Analyses of Co-Variance of Grade-Level and Treatment
Means on Classroom Functioning Variables for
Year 03 Teachers in Grades 1-6

	Min. Sig. Prob. by Source of Variation			Adj. Post-Test X̄		Sig. Grade Comparisons+
	Grade	Treatment	G x T	Experi.	Control	
F-1	--	--	--	0.04*	0.00	--
F-2	--	.0325	--	2.30*	0.40	--
F-3	--	--	--	0.10*	0.04	--
F-4	--	.0947	--	14.07*	9.41	--
F-5	--	--	--	93.39*	99.38	--
F-6	--	--	--	4.59	4.05*	--
F-7	--	.0248	--	1.33	0.25*	--
F-8	--	--	.0239	60.93	63.80*	--
F-9	--	.0463	--	11.79*	5.89	--
F-10	--	--	--	51.63*	57.30	--
C-1	.0725	--	--	94.22	86.86*	--
C-2	--	--	--	14.31*	12.72	--
C-3	--	.0830	--	0.02	0.39*	--
C-4	--	.0993	--	0.96*	0.77	--
C-5	--	--	.0146	72.11*	63.19	--
C-6	--	--	--	2.17*	1.91	--
C-7	--	--	--	1.37*	1.26	--
C-8	--	--	--	0.00	0.00	--
C-9	--	.0809	--	6.61*	3.93	--
C-10	--	--	--	51.38*	66.67	--
M	--	.0206	--	2.76*	2.55	--
G	--	.0057	--	2.81*	2.50	--
SP	--	.0539	--	2.80*	2.65	--
R	--	--	--	2.84*	2.65	--
SI	.0856	--	--	2.97*	2.84	--
	DF = 2, 62	DF = 1, 62	DF = 2, 62	N = 46	N = 23	

+Results of Duncan's New Multiple Range Test.
*Mean associated with expected direction of treatment benefits.

Table 50:   Chi-Square Statistics for Number of Means
Associated with Expected Direction of
Treatment Benefit for Teachers at All
Grade Levels (1-12)

Table Displaying Means	N of Means		Calculated x^2
	Training	No Training	
Table 43: Year 01 (1-12)	14	11	0.36
Table 44: Year 02 (1-12)	25	0	25.00*
Table 48: Year 03 (1-12)	19	5	7.88*
Total Tables 43, 44, 48	58	32	12.00*

*Significant at $x^2_{.05, 1}$ = 3.84

differences between the means (but not the **magnitude** of differences) is considered for all variables together, training did make a difference in the expected directions. The results of the Analyses of Co-Variance presented above demonstrated that when the **magnitude** of differences between the adjusted means is considered, training also made a difference in anticipated directions. This difference was greater for elementary teachers than for secondary teachers.

Magnitude of Change

The next question then becomes, "Is the difference **meaningful** (not trivial) as well as statistically significant?" To answer this question, it was necessary to look at raw means. Accordingly, the unadjusted means for the group which received two years of training were examined. The **unadjusted** pre-test mean was subtracted from the **unadjusted** post-test mean to derive mean change. This mean change was then divided by the unadjusted pre-test mean to yield an index of the magnitude of change in terms of entering levels. The results are displayed in Table 51.

The data displayed in Table 51 supports the following conclusions:
1. The magnitude of the change occurring was large enough to be meaningful.
2. Elementary teachers (grades 1-6) responded better to the training than Secondary teachers (grades 7-12).
3. The major effect of the training was a change in the quality of the interactions between student and teacher with a smaller but supporting change in the proportions of teacher/student participation in classroom verbal interchanges.

Table 51: Magnitude of Change in Experimental Teacher Behavior with 27 Hours of Training in Interpersonal Skills over a 2 Year Period

		2YrX Teachers of Grades 1-6			2YrX Teachers of Grades 7-12		
		Pre-Test X	Change X	Index	Pre-Test X	Change X	Index
Teacher Talk	F-1	0.00	0.15	15.00	0.00	0.003	--
	F-2	1.09	2.45	2.25	0.82	0.45	0.52
	F-3	0.97	1.21	1.25	2.50	-0.68*	0.27*
	F-4	21.90	1.97	0.09	20.38	-0.55*	0.02*
	F-5	79.28	-5.97	0.08	113.24	-5.30	0.04
	F-6	11.72	-3.28	0.28	3.92	0.65*	0.16*
	F-7	1.87	1.06*	0.57*	0.45	0.25	0.55*
Student Talk	F-8	78.25	8.81	0.11	60.33	14.67	0.24
	F-9	7.25	11.88	1.64	13.01	2.72	0.20
	F-10	37.84	-18.75	0.49	25.26	-11.39	0.45
Teacher Cognition	C-1	92.41	-5.42	0.05	116.92	-5.15	0.04
	C-2	20.84	-1.57*	0.08*	19.53	-1.55*	0.07*
	C-3	0.22	0.09	0.41	0.07	0.15	2.14
	C-4	0.19	2.94	15.47	0.75	0.98	1.30
Student Cognition	C-5	80.41	16.37	0.20	67.75	14.06	0.20
	C-6	0.81	0.50	0.61	3.60	-1.63*	0.45*
	C-7	1.44	1.93	1.34	7.57	1.83	0.24
	C-8	0.50	-0.40*	0.80*	0.21	0.35	1.66
Inter-personal Processes	C-9	3.45	5.46	1.58	1.45	1.65	1.13
	C-10	40.16	-19.75	0.49	23.52	-11.66	0.49
	M	2.47	0.68	0.26	2.71	0.32	0.11
	G	2.47	0.65	0.25	2.70	0.28	0.10
	SP	2.41	0.69	0.27	2.74	0.27	0.09
	R	2.66	0.63	0.22	2.75	0.28	0.09
	SI	2.59	0.81	0.30	2.77	0.35	0.12

+ Index = Mean Change + Pre-Test Mean

* Not in expected direction of treatment benefit

Specifically, the larger indexes in Table 51 call attention to those variables in which the largest **proportionate** mean change occurred. A change of 2.45 for Praise (F-2) is not a large amount but it represents more than twice the amount of Praise exhibited on the pre-test tapes. Similarly an increase in the amount of student thinking (C-7) of 1.93 is not large, but it is a third again as much as on the pre-test. In contrast, a change of 8.81 in student response (F-8) seems large but represents an increase of only 10% over the pre-test tape.

In terms of the Process scales, the five levels on the scale are described by the general effect on students of teachers operating at each level as:

1.0 Crippling
2.0 Hurting
3.0 Minimally Effective
4.0 Adding Significantly
5.0 Adding, Encouraging, Exploring

Both elementary and the secondary teachers started in the middle of Level Two, with the secondary teachers higher than elementary teachers. Both groups of teachers moved in desired directions but the change for secondary teachers was not as great as for the elementary group. However, the amount of change for both groups was enough to put them over the 3.0 threshold.

The changes displayed in Table 51 represent the largest changes achieved during the three project years. Both Year 01 and Year 02 changes (taken separately) were still large enough to be meaningful on variables specific to the training carried out each year. (See discussion below). The Year 03 changes were larger than the changes for either Year 01 or Year 02, taken separately, but not for both together as in the data displayed in Table 51.

Change Related to Training Content

Training for Year 01 concentrated solely on facilitative interpersonal skills. In order to reach the expected treatment benefits, it had been anticipated that there would be a **transfer** of increased levels of the Process Skills to classroom "learning" interactions dealing with subject matter and content as well as to those more strictly interpersonal interactions occurring. Comparison of training content with the variables in which positive differences occurred for the training groups made it evident that this hypothesis of transfer of skills must be rejected. (See Table 43). Of the eight variables in which significant positive experimental group differences occurred, only one of them (C-2) was in a content-concerned category. Five of the significant differences occurred in the variables (M, G, SP, R, SI) which directly measure the levels of facilitative interpersonal conditions offered in the classroom and two were in the indirect behavior categories of Flanders which are highly reflective of the affective tone of the classroom. This conclusion was supported by the information generated from trend analysis. (See Study 6).

Accordingly, plans for the second year's training were revised. Modules were developed which concentrated on **applying** interpersonal skills in the "learning" context as well as the "personal" one. These modules were utilized in the training with the 2YrX group. The training modules from the first year were also revised and used with the school which had been rotated into the training condition for the second year of the study.

During the second year, movement for the 2YrX group occurred in content oriented measures (specifically: F-3, F-5, F-6, F-9, C-1, C-3, C-4, C-5, C-6, C-7, and C-8) in anticipated directions. Movement on C-2 and C-5 was not in the desired direction. For the 1C2X group (receiving revised modules from first year), movement occurred in F-2, F-3, F-7, F-8, C-5 and the Process Scales towards the desired direction. Comparisons of the means associated with treatment benefit from Table 43 for the experimental group and Table 44 for the 1C2X group indicate that the two groups moved in similar manner in the two years in which they, respectively, received the **same** content. Similarly, comparisons between the 2YrX and 1C2X groups **within** Table 44 reflect the different pattern of movement for the two groups during the year in which they received different content.

For the Year 03, the training modules from both Years were combined and revised again.* The goal was to produce a program which would obtain movement on both interpersonal processes and processes applied to "learning" interactions within one year's training. Although the small N of the Year 03 study resulted in fewer significant differences between the control and experimental groups, comparison of (1) the magnitude of the differences between the means of control and experimental groups in Tables 43 and 48 and (2) comparisons of the patterns of the means associated with treatment benefits in the same two Tables indicate that the Year 03 training did result in movement on both cognitive and affective oriented behaviors. Again, the elementary teachers responded better to the training than did the secondary teachers.

The number of actual **contact** hours between NCHE trainer and teacher trainees was 20 hours in Year 01, 18 hours in Year 02, and 21 hours in Year 03. Of this, actual **skills training time**** was 15 hours in Year 01, 12 hours in Year 02, and 16 hours in Year 03. The remainder of the contact time was utilized in test administration and other procedural matters.

*For further description of revised program and results of evaluation of Pilot for Year 03 training program, see Study No. 12.
**Presentation of modules.

SUMMARY

In conclusion, the findings from this study were:

1. *Significant differences were detected between control and experimental groups for all three years of the study.*

2. *Elementary teachers responded better to the training than secondary teachers.*

3. *The changes of experimental groups (teachers receiving Interpersonal Skills Training) were of magnitudes large enough to be both statistically significant and not trivial; i.e., they were meaningful in the real-world.*

4. *The variables on which movement occurred were directly and positively related to the specific content of the training program and varied when the content varied.*

5. *The major effect of the training was a change in the quality of the interactions between student and teacher with a smaller but supporting change in the proportions of teacher/student participation in classroom verbal exchanges.*

The Interpersonal Skills Training program was demonstrated to produce changes in the Classroom Functioning variables (teacher and student behaviors in classroom/learning interactions). In effect, then, intervention to change the teacher's input to learning interactions resulted in changes in student behaviors in those interactions.

IS TEACHER RESPONSE TO INTERPERSONAL SKILLS TRAINING AFFECTED BY RACE, SEX OR EXPERIENCE?

PURPOSE OF STUDY

One of the concerns of the researchers was whether the training was responded to similarly by sub-groups of teachers. Therefore this study posed the question:

Are teacher characteristics of sex, race, and years of teaching experience significant contributors to differences among the means of Classroom Functioning variables as measured by Flanders' Interaction Analysis Categories, Cognitive Functioning Categories, and Process Scales when those means are adjusted for pre-test scores?

DESIGN

Sample

The sample for this study consisted of all Year 01, Year 02, and Year 03 experimental (Training Condition) teachers who met the inclusion criteria for Study Number 10. Table 52 displays the N by Sex, Race, and Teaching Experience groups.

Data Collection

Data for the study consisted of the individual's scores on the 10 Flanders' Interaction Analysis Categories, 10 Cognitive Categories, and 5 Process Scales coded from the respective pre and post-test audio recordings of classroom functioning. For Year 01, the pre and post-test tapes were May, 1971 and May, 1972. For Year 02, they were May, 1972 and May, 1973. For Year 03, they were September, 1973 and April, 1974. The data was collected through the normal procedures for assessment of tape data described in Part I. See Table 8, Part I, for names of variables.

ANALYSIS

For each year, twenty-five analyses of co-variance were conducted, using in turn each of the Flanders', Cognitive, and Process post-test scores as the dependent variable with pre-test scores as the concomitant variable. Factors were teacher characteristics of sex, race, and years of teaching experience. The groups by characteristic and code number were as follows:

Sex	Years of Teaching Experience
1 – Male	1 – 1 Year
2 – Female	2 – 2 Years
	3 – 3 to 7 Years

Race   4 — 8 to 15 Years
           1 — Black American   5 — 16 to 24 Years
           2 — White American   6 — Over 25 Years

The current school year was counted as 1 year since it would be completed by the time of the post-test. Thus, for number of years experience **prior** to the current year, subtract 1 from each of the figures above. That is, a "1 year" teacher is in his 1st year of teaching and has had 0 years of prior experience. A "2 years" teacher is in her second year of teaching and has had 1 year of prior experience, etc.

Because Study Number 8 (cf. ante) indicated that there might be some relationship between the teacher's level of physical functioning and the Classroom Functioning variables, the study for Year 03 included the Harvard Step-Test* Scores as a second concomitant variable. Also, the Year 03 analysis did not include tests for interaction effects because of the small N.

Table 52:   Distribution of Experimental Teachers by Sex, Race and Years of Teaching Experience within Three Samples

	Group	Yr. 01	Yr. 02	Yr. 03
Sex	Males	16	5	5
	Females	105	47	36
Race	Black American	34	12	26
	White American	87	40	15
Years Teaching Experience	1 Year	10	--	10
	2 Years	11	9	5
	3-7 Years	26	10	10
	8-15 Years	31	12	16
	16-25 Years	25	11	--
	Over 25 Years	18	10	--
	Total N	121	52	41

*For description of variable and manner of collection, see Study No. 8.

Table 53: Significance Levels Less Than .05 by Source of Variation for 75 Analyses of Co-Variance for Sex, Race, and Teaching Experience Effects on the Classroom Functioning Variables with Pre-Test as Covariate

| | Min. Sig. Prob. by Source of Variation | | | | | | Most Responsive Group(s)* | N of MR Group(s) |
| Dep. Var. | Main Effects | | | Interactions | | | | |
	Sex	Race	YTEA	SxR	SxYT	RxYT		
Year 01								
F-1	.022	--	--	.004	.002	--	Males/Black/3-7 Yrs.	16/1/4
F-4	.013	--	--	--	--	--	Females	105
F-6	.027	--	--	--	--	--	Females	105
F-9	--	--	.009	--	--	.032	1 Yr./Black 1 Yr.	10/2
C-2	.02	--	--	--	--	--	Females	105
C-6	--	--	--	--	--	.030	Black 1 Yr.	2
DF	1,104	3,104	5,104	1,104	3,104	3,104		
Year 02								
F-5	.018	--	--	--	--	--	Females	47
C-1	.034	--	--	--	--	--	Females	47
C-3	--	--	--	--	.039	--	Females, 15-24 Yrs.	9
C-4	.054	--	--	--	.001	--	Males/Male 2 Yrs.	5/1
C-7	--	--	--	--	.016	--	Male 2 Yrs.	1
DF	1, 37	1, 37	5, 37	1, 37	2, 37	3, 37		
Year 03								
F-9	.016	--	--				Males	5
C-6	.007	--	--				Males	5
DF	1, 33	1, 33	3, 33					

*Results of Duncan's New Multiple Range Test.

RESULTS

Table 53 displays the results of the analyses for all three years. It lists all minimum significant probabilities less than .05 which were detected in the analyses for all 25 variables for each of the three years.

Out of the 25 analyses conducted in Year 01, significant differences at the .05 level were detected in only six variables. Of these, sex showed up as a main effect for four variables. Years of teaching experience was a significant contributor to differences between the means for only three variables — once in main effects and three times in interactions. Race showed up only twice, both times in interactions.

For Year 02, race did not appear at all. Sex showed up in main effects three times and three times in interactions with years of teaching experience.

Sex was the only significant source of variation for Year 03. It showed up twice. The regression coefficient for the Harvard Step-Test was not significant ($p < .05$) for any variable.

DISCUSSION

In general, it appeared that most sub-groups were equally responsive to the training. Out of the 75 analyses conducted with the data from training groups over a three year period and two states, significant differences between the means of sub-groups were detected 13 times. Two of these thirteen analyses (and three interaction effects in other analyses) have to be discounted because of the small size of the sub-groups.* The remaining eleven analyses are a few more than could have been expected by chance, but the information generated in these analyses was not systematic.

According to the main effects detected in the remaining eleven analyses, the most responsive group was females in five analyses, males in four analyses, and first year teachers in one analysis. Interaction effects indicated male teachers with 3-7 years experience in one analysis and female teachers with 15-24 years experience in another analysis as the groups most responsive to training. Of these eleven analyses, the only variable that appears in more than one year is F-9.

SUMMARY

In conclusion, the finding from this study is that there is no systematic differential response to Interpersonal Skills training by sub-groups of teachers differentiated according to teacher characteristics of race, sex, or years of teaching experience.

*The results of the analyses for C-6 (Year 01) and C-7 (Year 02) were discounted because of group N's of 1 and 2 respectively. Interaction effects for black males in F-1 (Year 01), Black teachers with 1 year experience in F-9 (Year 01), and Males with 2 years experience in C-4 (Year 02) were also discounted because of small N's.

WHAT IS THE RELATIVE EFFECTIVENESS OF DIFFERENT TYPES OF INTERPERSONAL SKILLS TRAINING?

PURPOSE OF STUDY

The researchers had developed two sets of training modules by Year 02. Set one focused on the interpersonal process skills **per se.** They had been administered to the Year 01 experimental (Training Condition) teachers and a revision of this set would be administered to a new group of experimental trainees during Year 02. A second set of modules focused on training teachers to **apply** increased levels of interpersonal process skills in classroom "learning" interaction (rather than just "personal" ones) and would be applied as a second year of training for the experimental teachers from Year 01. In preparation for the third year of the study, the researchers developed and piloted a program that combined Sets One and Two into a **one-year** program rather than a two-year program. Since the researchers were concerned with the relative effectiveness of this pilot (Program Two) in achieving increased levels of interpersonal skills, it was evaluated against the gains made by the teachers receiving Program One (Set One) training in Year 01 and in Year 02 (revised Set One). The question proposed for this study was:

Can significant differences be detected between the post-test response means of treatment groups receiving different versions of Interpersonal Skills Training when Analysis of Co-Variance is conducted on the Classroom Functioning Variables with pre-test standing as the concomitant variable?

DESIGN

Sample

There were three groups in this study. Group P1Y1 consisted of all the experimental teachers in grades 1-6 who received Program One in Year 01. Group P1Y2 consisted of all the teachers who received Program One (revised) in Year 02. This included all the 1C2X teachers (See Study No. 10) and all other **new** teachers in the experimental elementary schools for the basic project; i.e. all teachers who were receiving their first year of Interpersonal Skills Training in Year 02. The third group (P2Y2) consisted of the faculty of a school not in the basic research projects which had consented* to receive pilot Program Two during Year 02. The bottom line of Table 54 displays the N by group.

*Through "informed consent" procedures.

Data for the study consisted of the individual's scores on the 10 Flanders' Interaction Analysis Categories, 10 Cognitive Categories, and 5 Process Scales coded from the respective pre- and post-test audio recordings of classroom functioning. For group P1Y1, the pre- and post-test tapes were May, 1971 and May, 1972. For group P1Y2, they were May, 1972 and May, 1973. For group P2Y2, they were September, 1973 and May, 1973. The data was collected through the normal procedures for assessment of tape data described in Part I. See Table 8 for names of variables.

ANALYSIS

Since there were two programs and two years, a two-way analysis of co-variance was conducted. The dependent variables were the individual's post-test scores on the Flanders, Cognitive, and Process variables with pre-test scores as co-variate. Factors were Year (01 and 02) and Program (One and Two) with the cell for Program One Year 01 being an empty cell.

Table 54: Significance Levels Less Than .05 by Source of Variation for 25 Analyses of Co-Variance for Program and Year Effects on the Classroom Functioning Variables with Pre-Test as Covariate

	Min. Sig. Prob. by Source of Variation		Adj. Post-Test Means		
	Program	Year	P1Y1	P1Y2	P2Y2
F-1	--	--	.00	.05*	.00
F-2	--	.002	6.52*	1.52	2.99
F-3	.0077	.0001	1.99*	1.58	.14
F-4	--	--	21.00*	17.52	20.35
F-5	--	--	65.45*	68.23	79.46
F-6	--	.0048	12.05	4.65*	6.50
F-7	--	.0410	2.48	.84	.05*
F-8	--	.0210	50.99	86.76*	56.31
F-9	.0001	.0001	7.00	12.54	19.80*
F-10	.0025	.0001	41.00	22.09	14.31*
C-1	--	--	90.12	71.79*	87.38
C-2	--	--	18.67	18.72	20.09*
C-3	--	--	0.02*	0.00	0.00
C-4	--	--	1.36	0.19	2.04*
C-5	--	.0001	53.37	99.75	110.47*
C-6	.0002	--	.85	1.15	1.27*
C-7	--	--	1.39	.23	3.00*
C-8	--	--	.02	.0	0.00
C-9	--	--	3.55*	2.21	2.13
C-10	.0058	.0002	39.94	20.43	13.61*
M	--	--	2.36	2.38	2.63*
G	--	.0453	2.32	2.37	2.58*
SP	.0166	--	2.28	2.35	2.72*
R	.0474	--	2.36	2.43	2.72*
SI	.0194	.0147	2.40	2.63	2.88*
	DF = 1, 123	DF = 1, 123	N = 86	N = 19	N = 22

* = Mean associated with expected direction of treatment benefit.

Table 54 displays the results of the twenty-five analyses of co-variance which were conducted. It presents all sources of significance less than .05 which were detected in the 25 analyses. The mean associated with the expected direction of treatment benefit is indicated with an asterisk. (These expected directions were specified on the basis of Response Surface Analysis carried out in Study No. 9 and were discussed in Study No. 10).

Significant differences between Program means were detected for eight variables (F-3, F-9, F-10, C-6, C-10, SP, R, SI). The mean associated with the treatment benefit in seven of the eight variables was for Program Two.

Significant differences between Year means were detected for eleven variables. In nine variables, the mean associated with the treatment benefit was a Year 02 mean. **Within** Year 02, the "best" mean was achieved by the P1Y2 group for variables F-6 and F-8. In the other seven variables, the "best" group mean **within** Year 02 was achieved by the P2Y2 group.

In all, there were fourteen variables for which the analysis detected significant differences between either Program means or Year means. In these fourteen variables, the group mean associated with the expected direction of treatment benefits was achieved by the P1Y2 group two times, by the P1Y2 group two times, and by the P2Y2 group nine times.

DISCUSSION

No conclusion was drawn as to the relative effectiveness of the original and the revised versions of Program One from this analysis, although the revised versions seemed to be slightly more effective. In nine of the 11 analyses in which significant differences were detected between Year means, the direction of treatment benefits were associated with Year 02 means. When just the means for the two groups (P1Y1 and P1Y2) are compared for direction of treatment benefit, sixteen of the P1Y2 means are in the desired direction. However, when the means for all three groups are compared in this manner, the P1Y1 group did achieve two more means associated with the direction of treatment benefit than did the P1Y2 group, but they were not significant for either Program or Year factors.

Program Two in Year 02 had fourteen means associated with the direction of treatment benefit and ten of these were for variables in which Analysis of Co-Variance detected significant differences between either Program means or Year means. For 7 of eight variables in which significant differences between Program means were detected, the group receiving Program Two in Year 02 achieved the mean associated with treatment benefit. It was concluded that Program Two (combining modules which focused on interpersonal skills with modules focusing on applying the skills within a one-year program) was more effective than either version of Program One.

SUMMARY

No conclusion was drawn as to the relative effectiveness of the original and the revised versions of Program One. However, it was concluded that Program Two was more effective than either version of Program One. Accordingly, it was determined that the Training Program for Year 03 should combine (in a **one**-year program) modules which focused on increasing levels of interpersonal skills with modules focusing on applying the skills in "learning" interactions.

ARE INTERPERSONAL SKILLS TRAINING
EFFECTS ENHANCED WHEN THE PRINCIPAL
OF THE SCHOOL IS TRAINED?

PURPOSE OF STUDY

As a result of Studies Number 1 and 2, the researchers had hypothesized that teacher response to interpersonal skills training would be enhanced by prior training of the school principal (or other local instructional leader) in the same skills. Since one of the experimental school principals in Year 03 had previously taken a graduate course ("Effective Teaching" taught by one of the researchers) in which most of the content of the training modules had been covered, the data from his teachers offered the possibility of a small N testing of the above hypothesis. Accordingly, the following question was posed:

Can significant differences be detected between grade-level or treatment post-test means for the Classroom Functioning Variables as measured by Flanders' Interaction Analysis Categories, Cognitive Functioning Categories, and the Process Scales when post-testing means are adjusted for pre-test standing?

DESIGN

Sample

The sample consisted of three groups of Year 03 teachers who met the inclusion criteria for Study No. 10. Group XwTP were Year 03 experimental (Training Condition) teachers whose principal had received prior training in Interpersonal Skills. The second group (Xw/oP) were Year 03 experimental (Training Condition) teachers whose principals had **not** received prior training in Interpersonal Skills. The third group were Year 03 control (No-Training) teachers.

Since the school whose principal had received prior training was a Middle School (grades 4-8), the study was restricted to teachers teaching on those grade levels. Total N was 47. The N by treatment groups is displayed on the bottom line of Table 55.

Data Collection

Data for the study consisted of the individual's scores on 10 Flanders' Categories, 10 Cognitive Categories and 5 Process Scales from pre- and post-test audio recordings of Classroom instruction. For all groups, the pre-test was the September, 1973 tape and the post-test was the April, 1974 tape. Data was collected in the regular manner for assessment of tape data described in Part I. For names of the variables, see Table 8 in Part I.

Table 55: Significance Levels Less Than .05 by Source of Variation for 25 Analyses of Co-Variance for Grade Level and Treatment Effects on Classroom Functioning Variables with Pre-Test as Covariate

	Min. Sig. Prob. by Source of Variation			Adj. Post-Test Means		
	Grade	Treatment	G x T	XwTP	X w/o P	Control
F-1	--	--	--	.04*	0.00	0.0
F-2	--	--	--	2.32*	1.58	0.15
F-3	--	--	--	0.19*	0.01	0.00
F-4	--	.0479	--	14.41	17.19*	9.65
F-5	--	.0171	--	97.94*	104.27	110.44
F-6	--	--	--	4.78*	4.86	5.33
F-7	--	--	--	1.06	0.40*	3.47
F-8	--	--	.0110	59.79	69.83*	59.14
F-9	--	.0474	--	13.33*	9.33	5.56
F-10	--	--	.0209	46.81	31.13*	50.60
C-1	--	--	--	99.09*	109.23	100.02
C-2	--	--	--	15.34	17.42*	12.12
C-3	--	--	--	0.00	0.00	0.43*
C-4	--	--	--	1.14*	0.02	0.74
C-5	--	--	.0089	73.06	75.63*	64.35
C-6	--	--	--	2.92*	1.33	1.86
C-7	--	--	--	1.79*	1.33	0.99
C-8	--	--	--	0.00	0.00	0.00
C-9	--	--	--	3.81*	5.64	5.64
C-10	--	--	--	44.73	31.02*	53.45
M	--	--	--	2.98*	2.78	2.62
G	--	.0103	--	3.05*	2.79	2.61
SP	--	--	--	3.02*	2.86	2.69
R	--	.0459	.1014	3.07*	2.92	2.72
SI	--	--	--	3.21*	3.06	2.85
	DF = 1, 40	DF = 2, 40	DF = 2, 40	N = 20	N = 13	N = 14

* = Mean associated with expected direction of treatment benefit.

Twenty-five Analyses of Co-variance were conducted using, in turn, each of the Flanders', Cognitive and Process post-test scores as dependent variables with pre-test scores as the concomitant variable. Factors were Treatment and Grade-level. There were three treatment groups: XwTP (training condition teachers **with** prior trained principal), Xw/oP (training condition teachers **without** trained principal), and Control (No-Training condition) teachers. Grade-level groups were (1) teachers in grades 4-6 and (2) teachers in grades 7-8.

RESULTS

Table 54 displays the results of the analyses. It presents all sources of significance less than .05 which were detected in the 25 analyses. The mean associated with the expected direction of treatment benefit is indicated with an asterisk. (These expected directions were specified on the basis of Response Surface Analysis carried out in Study No. 9 and were discussed in Study No. 10).

For 16 out of the 25 variables, the adjusted treatment mean associated with expected directions of treatment benefit was that of the XwTP group. Six of the remaining variables were accounted for by the other experimental group. In only one variable (C-3) was the control mean associated with the expected direction of treatment benefit.

Significant differences between treatment means were detected for five variables: F-4, F-5, F-9, G, R. For all five of these variables, the adjusted post-test mean associated with the expected direction of treatment benefit was the XwTP mean.

There were no significant grade-level main effects. Grade by treatment interaction effects were detected for only four variables.

DISCUSSION AND SUMMARY

In spite of the small N for the study, the null hypothesis of no difference among the treatment means was rejected in five instances and in each case the group with the mean associated with treatment benefits was that of the experimental teachers whose principal had received prior training in the Interpersonal Skills in which the teachers were subsequently trained. Furthermore, this group of teachers had the mean associated with the expected direction of treatment benefit for sixteen out of 25 variables. The researchers concluded that the alternative hypothesis was sufficiently supported and that, in fact, prior training of the principal enhances teacher response to interpersonal skills training.

STUDY NUMBER 14

IS TEACHER BEHAVIOR RELATED TO STUDENT OUTCOMES ON INDICES OF MENTAL HEALTH AND COGNITION?

PURPOSE OF STUDY

This study posed two questions:

1. *When Student Outcome Measures of change have been adjusted for pre-test standing, will multi-linear regression analysis detect significant relationships between the adjusted change measures and the Classroom Functioning variables?*
2. *Which Classroom Functioning variables are the better predictors of the adjusted change measures?*

DESIGN

Sample

The Teacher sample for this study included all Year 01 experimental and control classroom teachers who submitted four or more tapes during the year. "Special teachers" (art, music, speech therapy, etc.) were not included and the study was restricted to Math and English Teachers at the secondary level. The student sample was formed of all students who (1) had been taught by "included" teachers and (2) had taken pre- and post-test of student outcome measures. Table 56 displays student and teacher N by grade level.

Table 56: Distribution of Sample for Study 14 by Grade Level

Grade Levels		Teacher N	Student N
1		20	442
2		22	488
3		21	451
4		21	492
5		23	532
6		15	485
7-12	Math	16	1,365*
	Engligh	18	2,113
Total		156	5,003

*These students contained within English N.

Data for the independent variables in the study were the individual's scores on all submitted audio tape recordings of classroom instruction on each of the 10 Flanders' Interaction Analysis Categories, 10 Cognitive Functioning Categories, and 5 Process Scales. The data was collected by the regular procedures for assessment of tape data described in Part I.

The dependent variables were pre- and post-test measures on Metropolitan Achievement Tests (for students in grades 1-6), California Achievement Tests (for students in grades 7-12), How I See Myself Tests (students in grades 3-12), and total days absent for the year (for all students). The pre-tests were administered in November, 1971 and the post-tests in April, 1972 by the students' regular classroom teachers and scored by the test publishers.

ANALYSIS

Sixty-four multi-linear regression analyses were carried out. The dependent variables were adjusted change* scores on student tests. Table 59 lists the dependent variables. Separate analyses were carried out for grade levels 1, 2, 3, 4, 5, 6, and 7-12. Grades 7-12 were run as one level because of organizational factors of the schools; i.e., all students changed classes thus limiting the number of teachers in a particular subject matter to two or three per grade.

Independent variables were means and standard deviations of measures of selected Classroom Functioning variables. The teacher's Grand Mean** for the year was used as a measure of **average level of functioning**. The standard deviation of the teacher's scores around **his own mean** was used as an estimate of **stability** of functioning. In all there were 28 Independent Variables, as follows:

$\bar{X}$ and $\hat{0}^-$ of F-1:   Accepts Student Feelings

$\bar{X}$ and $\hat{0}^-$ of F-2:   Use of Praise and Encouragement

$\bar{X}$ and $\hat{0}^-$ of F-3:   Accepts Student Ideas

$\bar{X}$ and F-6:   Give Directions or Commands

$\bar{X}$ and $\hat{0}^-$ of F-7:   Use of Criticism and Justification of Authority

$\bar{X}$ of F-9:   Student Initiated Response

---

*Adjusted change was post-test minus pre-test to yield raw change which was then adjusted for pre-test standing. This was done for all variables except (1) first grade tests where absolute post-test scores were used as no pre-test data was available and (2) absence where total days absent was the dependent variable.

**Grand Mean = average over all tapes submitted.

$\bar{X}$ of C-1:   Teacher Recalls Facts

$\bar{X}$ of C-2:   Teacher Asks for Facts

$\bar{X}$ and $\hat{\bar{0}}$ of C-3:   Teacher Thinks

$\bar{X}$ and $\hat{\bar{0}}$ of C-4:   Teacher Asks for Thinking

$\bar{X}$ of C-5:   Student Recalls Facts

$\bar{X}$ of C-6:   Student Asks for Facts

$\bar{X}$ of C-7:   Student Thinks

$\bar{X}$ of C-8:   Student Asks for Thinking

$\bar{X}$ and $\hat{\bar{0}}$ of M: Teacher's Understanding of Meaning to Student of Classroom Experiences

$\bar{X}$ and $\hat{\bar{0}}$ of G: Teacher's Genuineness in Person-to-Person Interactions

$\bar{X}$ of SP: Teacher's Promotion of Success of Student's Goals

$\bar{X}$ of R: Teacher's Respect for Students

$\bar{X}$ and $\hat{\bar{0}}$ of SI: Student's Involvement in **Learning** Activities

In carrying out the regressions, the measures of each teacher's functioning were regressed against the **Mean Change** on the dependent variable for the students taught by that teacher. Therefore, degrees of freedom for each analysis were based on N of classrooms (teachers) rather than N of students. Since the N of classrooms was in all cases smaller than the number of independent variables to be considered, the computer was programmed to halt computation when the degrees of freedom for regression were equal to residual degrees of freedom minus one.

RESULTS

Prediction of Change

The R-squares displayed in Table 57 represent the amount of remaining variance predicted by Classroom Functioning variables **after** the variance due to Pre-test Standing had been removed. In other words, once you have accounted for change related to where the student was on entering, then these R-squares tell you how good teacher behavior was as a predictor of change. All regressions for which R-square is reported were significant at $p < .05$.

Classroom Functioning as a predictor of change varied with the

Table 57: Results of Multilinear Regression Analysis: Variation (R^2) in Adjusted* Mean Gain Predicted by Teacher Behavior Factors

	Dependent Variables	Grade Levels						
		1	2	3	4	5	6	7-12
Self-Concept Factors	Teacher School Acceptance	X	X	.41**	.23	.53	.61	.73
	Physical Appearance	X	X	.78	NS	.64	.45	.82
	Interpersonal Adequacy	X	X	.81	NS	.85	.48	.86
	Autonomy	X	X	.63	.19	.75	.45	.88
	Academic Adequacy	X	X	.29	.14	.73	.69	.84
	Total Days Absence	.71	.84	NS	.14	.42	.38	.54
Achievement	Reading Vocabulary	.68	.35	.83	.50	.75	X	.39
	Reading Comprehension	.43	.80	.89	.88	.42	X	X
	Word Analysis	NS	.37	.90	.85	X	X	X
	Language Usage	X	X	X	.85	.88	X	.39
	Language Mechanics	X	X	X	X	X	X	.59
	Spelling	X	X	.84	.53	.70	X	X
	Math Computation	X	X	.73	.56	.64	X	.86
	Math Concepts	X	X	.86	.35	.15	X	.78
	Math Problem-Solving	X	X	.83	.42	.72	X	X

X = No data at this level on this variable   NS = Regression not Significant at acceptable level ($p < .05$)

*Adjusted for Pre-test standing except 1st grade data uses absolute post-test standing (no pre-test available) and Total Days Absence uses raw totals.

**Numbers Represent R^2

dependent variable and with the grade level. However, there were several patterns in the data presented in Table 57.

First, teacher functioning was a good predictor of absolute standing at the end of the year for first grade students, in all areas except word analysis skills.

Second, except for the third and fourth grades, teacher functioning was a good predictor of the total days absent for her students. The relationship was an inverse one for all predictors except F-6 and F-7. The same trend was observed in third and fourth grades but it did not reach significance in the third grade regression and was not a high predictor at the fourth grade level.

Third, in general, teacher functioning was not as good a predictor of student gain in the fourth grade as it was for the other levels of students.

Fourth, above the fourth grade, teacher functioning was a better predictor of gain in skills than of gain in concepts. For example, in grades 7-12, the R-square for Language Mechanics was .59 but was only .39 for Language Usage. For Math Computation, the MCR square was .86 but, for Math Concepts, it was .78. The same situation was observed at grade 5. Reading Vocabulary was .75 and Comprehension was .42; Math Computation was .64, Math Problem-Solving was .72, and Math Concepts was .15. At the fourth grade level, prediction of change in Math followed the same pattern but not in reading. Below the fourth grade level, only the prediction of post-test standing for first grade follows the pattern, with Reading Vocabulary registering an R-square of .68 and first grade Reading Comprehension registering .43.

Identification of Predictors

The regression equations were examined to determine the relative predictive power of the independent variables. The dependent variables were grouped in three categories: (1) Absence, (2) Self-Concept Measures, and (3) Achievement Measures. Then the regression equations for each category were examined and the number of times a variable appeared as a predictor of change in regression equations at each level for each category was counted. This was divided by the number of equations for the category to get the percent of equations for the category in which the variable appeared as a predictor of gain. This operation was repeated for each category and for the total of all categories. The results are displayed in Table 58.

Single Predictors

The most highly predictive single variables were F-1, F-2, F-3, F-7, F-9, C-3, C-8, M and SI. Cognitive 1 (Teacher Recalls Facts) was a predictor only for elementary Achievement and was negatively correlated with achievement. Cognitive 2 (Teacher Asks for Facts) was predictive for elementary students but not for secondary students. Of the Student Behavior variables, the most highly predictive were F-9 (Student Initiates) and Cognitive 8.

Table 58: Percent of Equations for Category in which Variable Appears* as a Significant Predictor of Gain

	Independent Variables	CATEGORY & LEVEL PREDICTED								
		ABSENCE		SELF-CONCEPT		ACHIEVEMENT		ALL CATEGORIES		
		EL.	SEC.	EL.	SEC.	EL.	SEC.	EL.	SEC.	1-12
Teacher Behaviors	F-1	20%	--	16%	20%	42%	--	30%	9%	26%
	F-2	20	200%+	50	20	30	40%	36	45	38
	F-3	20	--	22	--	30	40	26	18	25
	F-6	--	100	33	20	23	--	24	18	23
	F-7	40	--	33	20	46	80	40	45	41
Interpersonal Processes	C-1	--	--	--	--	3	--	--	--	--
	C-2	20	--	11	--	23	--	18	--	15
	C-3	20	--	44	40	15	20	26	27	26
	C-4	40	--	--	40	19	20	14	27	16
	Meaning	20	100	11	40	34	20	24	36	26
	Genuineness	40	100	11	--	34	--	26	9	23
	Success	20	--	5	--	3	--	6	--	5
	Promotion	20	--	--	--	7	--	6	--	5
	Respect	--	--	--	--	--	--	--	--	--
Student Behaviors	Student Involvement	20	--	38	40	15	20	24	27	25
	F-9	20	100	22	--	30	60	22	36	25
	C-5	--	--	11	--	15	20	12	9	11
	C-6	--	100	16	20	34	--	24	9	21
	C-7	--	--	11	--	34	40	22	18	21
	C-8	--	--	22	20	38	--	28	9	25
	N of Equations	5	1	18	5	26	5	49	11	60

EL: Elementary (1-6)
SEC: Secondary (7-12)

*Variable is counted as appearing if either $\bar{X}$ or σ appeared as predictor in regression.

+Variable appeared as both $\bar{X}$ and σ in the regression.

To simplify this rather complex picture of the relative predictive power of the variables, the **independent** variables were grouped into four clusters according to the kind of behavior being measured. Then for each category of dependent variables, the predictive appearances of the independent variables were summed over each cluster and divided by the total number of predictive appearances of all variables for the category. This provided a picture of the relative power of the different clusters of Classroom Functioning Variables in predicting change. The results are displayed in Table 59.

The teacher's Cognitive Behaviors had relatively little predictive power except for Self-Concept at the secondary level. The Teacher's Specific Affective Behaviors and the Process Scales appeared more frequently as predictors than either Student Behavior or Teacher's Cognitive Behaviors. However, Student Behavior measures were frequent predictors of gain in Achievement. The percentage of predictive appearances of Student Behavior in Achievement regressions was almost the same for the elementary and the secondary levels although comparing the two levels reveals discrepant percentages for Student Behavior in Absence and Self-Concept Regressions.

Average Level vs. Stability of Functioning as Predictor

Tables 58 and 59 deal with total appearances of a variable regardless of whether it appeared as a Mean (**average level** of teacher's functioning on that variable) or as a Standard Deviation (**stability** of teacher's functioning on that variable). Tables 60 and 61 deal with the predictive appearances of the two kinds of measures for the variables.

In Table 60, the process used to produce Table 3 was repeated, except that for Table 60 **only** the appearances of **standard deviations** of the variables were counted for each cluster and divided by the total number of all (both $\overline{X}$ and 0^-) appearances. This provided a picture of the percentage of Predictive Appearances in Category that is accounted for by the stability of teacher functioning.

In Table 61, the **relative predictive power** of the two kinds of measures for the independent variables (**average level** of functioning and **stability** of functioning) is emphasized. It displays the ratio (proportion) of appearances of the stability measures to the total appearances of the variables. By examining this table, it was apparent that the stability of the teacher's functioning in the Process Levels was more important to secondary school students than to elementary students except in predicting self-concept changes. However, the stability of the Specific Affective Behaviors was more important than average level of functioning in predicting the Absence of elementary students. Compare this with the proportion for prediction of Absence by **stability** of Process levels. With a proportion of .16, it is evident that it is the average level of Interpersonal Process functioning that is more important for the elementary student.

Table 59: Percent of Total Predictive Appearances in Category
by Variable Clusters for School Level

Variable Cluster (Groupings of Independent Variables)	Level and Category Predicted					
	ABSENCE		SELF-CONCEPT		ACHIEVEMENT	
	EL.	SEC.	EL.	SEC.	EL.	SEC.
Specific Affective Behaviors	31%	42%	44%	28%	36%	44%
Teacher Cognitive Behaviors	25%	-0-	15%	28%	11%	11%
Process Scales	37%	29%	19%	28%	21%	12%
Student Behaviors	7%	29%	20%	16%	32%	33%

Specific Affective Behaviors:

F-1: Accepts Feelings
F-2: Uses Praise
F-3: Accepts &/or Uses
      Student Ideas
F-6: Gives Instructions
F-7: Justifies Authority

Process Scales:

Meaning, Genuineness, Respect
for Student, Success Promotion,
Student Involvement

EL: Elementary (1-6)
SEC: Secondary (7-12)

Teacher Cognitive Behaviors:

C-1: Teacher Recalls Facts
C-2: Teacher Asks for Facts
C-3: Teacher Thinks
C-4: Teacher Asks for Thinking

Student Behaviors:

F-9: Student Initiates
C-5: Student Recalls Facts
C-6: Student Asks for Facts
C-7: Student Thinks
C-8: Student Asks for Thinking

Table 60. Percent of Predictive Appearances in Category (by Variable Cluster per Level) that is Accounted for by Stability of Teacher Functioning Factors

Variable Cluster (Groupings of Independent Variables)	Level and Category Predicted					
	ABSENCE		SELF-CONCEPT		ACHIEVEMENT	
	EL.	SEC.	EL.	SEC.	EL.	SEC.
Specific Affective Behaviors	25%	14%	11%	14%	16%	22%
Teacher Cognitive Behaviors	12%	-0-	6%	14%	2%	-0-
Process Scales	6%	29%	11%	7%	13%	12%
Student Behaviors	-0-*	-0-	-0-	-0-	-0-	-0-

Specific Affective Behaviors:

F-1: Accepts Feelings
F-2: Uses Praise
F-3: Accepts &/or Uses Student Ideas
F-6: Gives Instructions
F-7: Justifies Authority

Process Scales:

Meaning, Genuineness, Respect for Student, Success Promotion, Student Involvement

EL: Elementary (1-6)
SEC: Secondary (7-12)

Teacher Cognitive Behaviors:

C-1: Teacher Recalls Facts
C-2: Teacher Asks for Facts
C-3: Teacher Thinks
C-4: Teacher Asks for Thinking

Student Behaviors:

F-9: Student Initiates
C-5: Student Recalls Facts
C-6: Student Asks for Facts
C-7: Student Thinks
C-8: Student Asks for Thinking

*No Stability Measures of Student Behavior Variables were included in the Analysis.

General Relationships

In all but four of the 64 multi-linear regression analyses conducted in this study, the Classroom Functioning variables were related to the student outcome measures at levels of significance less than .05. R-squares achieved in the significant regressions ranged from .14 to .88.

The relationships reported in this study are somewhat stronger than those reported for similar studies by previous investigators. Factors related to the added strength of the relationships reported here include the following:

1. The independent variables were measures of the actual processes occurring in the learning situation rather than presage characteristics of the teacher, the students, the curriculum, or the learning context.

2. The independent variables were generated from **repeated** measures of the processes occurring in the learning situation, thus providing (1) an average level of functioning for the year and (2) an estimate of **stability** of functioning for the year.

3. The dependent variables were **not** change for individual students but were **mean** change for all the students taught by the teacher.

4. The R-squares reported are for a **component** of the total variance; i.e., the variance **remaining** after the variance due to pre-test standing has been adjusted for.

Although the specific relationships between the Classroom Functioning variables and the Change measures varied considerably from grade to grade and from test to test, the data presented here seems to indicate that the teacher's level of functioning is an important contributor to student change as it accounted for one-quarter to nine-tenths of the variance for all but eight of the relationships tested. (See Table 57). The generally low R-squares for the fourth grade (in comparison to the other grades) are interesting and it is hypothesized that these may be related to the "fourth grade slump" in creativity and achievement reported by other researchers.

Specific Patterns

Of particular interest to the researchers were the relationships between the Classroom Functioning variables and student absenteeism. As indicated in Table 59, the Specific Affective Behaviors and the Process Scales were the most frequent predictors of absence at both the elementary and the secondary levels with Student Behavior variables having an equal importance at the secondary level. Examination of the regression equations indicate that student absenteeism increases when process levels, number of questions asked by the teacher, praise, acceptance of student ideas, and acceptance of student feelings are lowered or when criticism is high. Similarly, there is an inverse relationship between absenteeism and student initiation and students asking for facts. Put simply, this means that when the teacher is functioning at high levels of acceptance and responsiveness to students, they miss fewer days of school during the year.

The second interesting pattern or relationships displayed in Table 57 is the systematically higher R-squares for skills tests compared to measures of more abstract kinds of learning for grades 1, 4, 5, and 7-12. In terms of this data, it would seem that, at the upper grade levels, the teacher has a more direct effect on students' attainment of specific skills than on their attainment of concepts or more abstract processes. That this pattern is also reflected in grade 1 reading but not in grades 2 and 3 may be an effect of the nature of first grade reading instruction.

The researchers had hypothesized that the Classroom Functioning variables would have stronger relationships with the Self-Concept Factors than with achievement tests. However, this hypothesis had to be rejected as the average of the R-square for all Self-Concept regressions was .55 while the average for the Achievement regressions was .62. In effect, the Classroom Functioning variables were equally effective predictors for change on **both** the Self-Concept Factors and the Achievement tests.

Relative Predictive Power of Variable Clusters

Table 59 presents the relative predictive power of the different kinds of Classroom Functioning variables. For elementary students (grades 1-6) the Specific Affective Behaviors are most important, followed by Student Behaviors and Process Scales with the Teacher's Cognitive Behaviors contributing less to the variation of both Self-Concept and Achievement measures. Of the Student Behaviors, the most predictive were F-9 (Student Initiates) and C-8 (Student Asks for Thinking) indicating the importance of student participation and student direction setting in learning. Examination of the regression equations indicate that the relationships are in similar directions to those for Absenteeism; i.e., positive gain is positively related to the Classroom Functioning variables except F-6, F-7, and C-1. When F-7 and C-1 appear as predictors, they are usually negatively correlated. F-6 is positively correlated with elementary student gain and negatively correlated with secondary student gain.

The data presented in Table 61 as to the proportion of predictive appearances of the variables which were contributed by the stability of functioning factors indicates that both **stability** (the teacher offers relatively the same levels of functioning; i.e., has a small standard deviation around his own mean) and **average level** of functioning were of equal importance for about half of the relationships. However, the stability of the Specific Affective Behaviors were more frequent predictors of elementary Absenteeism than the average level of functioning while for the secondary students the stability factors were

Table 61: Proportion of Predictive Appearances in Category by Variable Cluster Per Level that is Accounted for by Stability of Teacher Functioning Factors

Variable Cluster (Groupings of Independent Variables)	Level and Category Predicted					
	ABSENCE		SELF-CONCEPT		ACHIEVEMENT	
	EL.	SEC.	EL.	SEC.	EL.	SEC.
Specific Affective Behaviors	.80	.33	.25	.50	.46	.50
Teacher Cognitive Behaviors	.50	-0-	.40	.50	.21	-0-
Process Scales	.16	1.00	.57	.25	.68	1.00

Specific Affective Behaviors:

F-1: Accepts Feelings
F-2: Uses Praise
F-3: Accepts &/or Uses Student Ideas
F-6: Gives Instructions
F-7: Justifies Authority

Process Scales:

Meaning, Genuineness, Respect for Student, Success Promotion, Student Involvement

Teacher Cognitive Behaviors:

C-1: Teacher Recalls Facts
C-2: Teacher Asks for Facts
C-3: Teacher Thinks
C-4: Teacher Asks for Thinking

EL: Elementary (1-6)
SEC: Secondary (7-12)

the **only** Interpersonal Process factors which predicted either Absenteeism or Achievement. Stability factors did not account for a large proportion of the appearances of Teacher Cognitive Behaviors as predictors of change in student outcomes.

SUMMARY

In conclusion, the findings from this study were:

1. *The Classroom Functioning variables are good predictors of student change when raw change is adjusted for pre-test standing.*
2. *When the teacher is functioning at high levels of acceptance and responsiveness to students, students miss fewer days of school during the year.*
3. *At the upper grade levels, the teacher has a more direct effect on students' attainment of specific skills than on attainment of concepts or more abstract processes.*
4. *The Classroom Functioning variables were equally effective predictors for change on both Self-Concept factors and Achievement tests.*
5. *Both the* **stability** *of the teacher's functioning and the* **average** *level of functioning on Specific Affective Behaviors and Process Scales are important predictors of change but the relative importance of the two kinds of measures of teacher functioning vary with the kind of gain predicted and the grade level of the student.*
6. *The* **stability** *of the teacher's functioning in the Cognitive Behaviors was not an important predictor of change, but* **average** *level of functioning was.*
7. *Student gain (positive change) was positively related to the Classroom Functioning variables except F-7 and C-1 which were inversely related while F-6 was positively related for elementary students and inversely related for secondary students.*

The conclusion of the researchers from this study was that higher functioning teachers produce more gain in student measures of Self-Concept and Achievement and their students are absent fewer days.

DOES INTERPERSONAL SKILLS TRAINING OF TEACHERS TRANSLATE TO STUDENT OUTCOMES ON INDICES OF MENTAL HEALTH AND COGNITION?

PURPOSE OF STUDY

To determine if the treatment (Interpersonal Skills Training for Teachers) would translate to differences in student outcomes on mental health and cognitive indices, this study posed the following question:

Can significant differences be detected between Change Means of grade-level groups of control and experimental students on indexes of mental health and cognition when raw change is adjusted for pre-test standing and student IQ?

DESIGN

Sample

The three samples for this study consisted of the students in each year 01, 02, and 03 who (1) had been taught by participating teachers and (2) had taken pre- and post-tests of student outcome measures. For secondary students, "taught by participating teachers" was defined as having received instruction in two or more of their courses by teachers who met the inclusion criteria for Study 10. (Cf. ante.) For elementary students, "taught by participating teachers" meant that their classroom teacher was a teacher who met the inclusion criteria for Study 10.

In Year 02, the study was limited to those students who had been taught by participating teachers for **both** Years 01 and 02. Thus, no 1st grade students were included in the Year 02 analyses. The N for the Control 10th grade was severely reduced in Year 02 as only part of its 10th grade originated in the Control Junior High. The bottom two lines of Tables 62, 63, and 64 display the N by grade level within treatment groups for each year.

Data Collection

For Years 01 and 02, the dependent variables were change from pre- to post-test measures* on Metropolitan Achievement Tests (for students in grades 1-6), California Achievement Tests (for students in grades 7-12), How I See Myself Tests (for students in grades 3-12), and total days absent for the year (for all students). For Year 03, the dependent variables were change from pre- to post-test measures on Metropolitan Achievement Tests (for students in grades 1-12) and How

---

*Except for (1) 1st grade where absolute post-test scores were used as no pre-test data was available and (2) for absenteeism where Total Days Absent for one year was the dependent variable.

Table 62: Significance Levels Less Than .05 Detected Between
Treatment Means of Adjusted Change
on 12 Outcome Measures for Year 01 Students

Dependent Variable	Elementary						Sr. Hi.		
	1	2	3	4	5	6	10	11	12
HISM: Teacher-School	X	X	--	--	--	--	--	--	--
HISM: Physical Appearance	X	X	--	--	--	--	--	--	--
HISM: Interpersonal Adequacy	X	X	--	--	.017*	--	--	--	--
HISM: Autonomy	X	X	--	--	--	--	--	--	--
HISM: Academic Adequacy	X	X	.039*	--	.017*	--	--	--	.024
Total Days Absent	--	--	--	--	--	.001	.005*	--	--
Reading Vocabulary	--	--	--	--	--	X	.039	--	--
Reading Comprehension	--	--	--	--	--	X	.002	--	--
Language Usage	X	X	--	--	--	X	.001	--	--
Language Mechanics	X	X	X	X	--	X	.001	.002*	.018*
Math Computation	X	X	--	--	--	X	--	--	--
Math Concepts	X	X	--	--	--	X	.011	--	--
Experimental N[+]	231	242	209	232	258	257	299	264	207
Control N[+]	211	246	242	260	274	228	263	196	196

*Experimental group (students of NCHE trained teachers) achieved largest gain.
X = No data available at this level for this test.

[+]Study also included 1,481 Junior High students (872 Control and 609
Experimental) for whom data is not reported. See discussion.

Table 63: Significance Levels Less Than .05 Detected Between
Treatment Means of Adjusted Change
on 12 Outcome Measures for Year 02 Students

Dependent Variable	Elementary						Sr. Hi.		
	1	2	3	4	5	6	10	11	12
HISM: Teacher-School	NT	X	--	.046*	.014	.001*	--	--	--
HISM: Physical Appearance	NT	X	--	--	.026*	.005*	--	--	--
HISM: Interpersonal Adequacy	NT	X	--	--	.022	.001*	--	--	--
HISM: Autonomy	NT	X	--	--	.035*	--	--	--	.001
HISM: Academic Adequacy	NT	X	--	--	--	.001*	--	.047*	--
Total Days Absent	NT	.048*	--	--	.043*	.003*	--	.032*	--
Reading Vocabulary		.003*	--	.038	--	--	--	--	.048*
Reading Comprehension	NT	.001*	--	.016	--	--	--	--	--
Language Usage	NT	X	--	--	--	.002*	--	--	.039*
Language Mechanics	NT	X	X	--	.001*	--	.010	.003	--
Math Computation	NT	X	--	--	.001*	.047*	.001	--	--
Math Concepts	NT	X	--	.039*	.030*	.002	.001	.007	--
Experimental N	0	102	129	106	150	119	99	232	198
Control N	0	207	373	183	141	218	251	200	147

NT - No test run as no first grade student had been in program during previous
year.

* Experimental group (students of NCHE trained teachers) achieved largest gain.
X No data available at this level for this test.

Table 64: Significance Levels Less Than .05 Detected Between Treatment Means of Adjusted Change on 11 Outcome Measures for Year 03 Students

Dependent Variable	Elementary						Jr. Hi.		Senior High			
	1	2	3	4	5	6	7	8	9	10	11	12
HISM: Teacher-School	X	X	--	--	--	--	--	--	--	--	--	--
HISM: Physical Appearance	X	X	--	.034*	--	--	.042*	.016*	--	--	--	--
HISM: Interpersonal Adequacy	X	X	--	--	--	--	--	.015*	--	--	--	--
HISM: Autonomy	X	X	.021*	.003*	--	--	--	.035*	--	.042*	--	--
HISM: Academic Adequacy	X	X	.017	--	--	--	.049	.018*	--	--	--	--
Reading Vocabulary	.045*	.049*	--	--	--	--	.044*	--	--	--	--	--
Reading Comprehension	.039*	--	--	--	.046*	--	--	--	--	--	.031	.022
Language Usage	X	X	X	--	.046*	--	.001*	--	0.011*	--	--	--
Language Mechanics	X	X	X	X	--	--	--	.031*	--	--	--	--
Math Computation	X	X	--	.049	.046*	--	.007	--	0.015*	--	.004*	--
Math Concepts	X	X	--	--	.003*	--	--	--	--	.038*	--	.016
Experimental N	119	71	114	132	157	179	121	151	22	32	33	30
Control N	132	102	46	77	70	65	74	116	73	86	70	66

*Experimental group (students of NCHE trained teachers) achieved largest gain.

X - No data available at this level for this test.

I See Myself Tests (for students in grades 3-12). The tests were administered by the students' regular classroom teachers according to the schedule in Table 7 and were scored by the test publishers. Absence data was not collected in Year 03 as the replication site school system did not have a central data processing unit so the data would have had to be manually processed from individual teacher's attendance registers for each month by individual student name for the 2,138 students.

ANALYSIS

The procedure used in this study was Analysis of Co-variance of treatment means with pre-test score and student I.Q. score as the concomitant variables. The analyses were conducted separately for each appropriate variable for each grade-level 1-12. There were two treatment conditions: Experimental (students of teachers who had received Interpersonal Skills training) and Control (students of teachers who had **not** received Interpersonal Skills training). In Year 02, the analysis was restricted to students of teachers who had remained in the same treatment group for both Year 01 and Year 02.

RESULTS

Tables 62, 63, and 64 display the results of the analyses for Years 01, 02, and 03, respectively. They are discussed separately below.

From Year 01

Of the 82 Analyses of Co-variance whose results are displayed in Table 62 for Year 01, only 13 analyses yielded significant differences between the treatment means. Of these 13 significant analyses, 7 were in favor of the control group and 6 were in favor of the experimental group.** Of the four significant differences in grades 1-6, three were in favor of the Experimental group. Six of the 9 significant differences in grades 10-12 were in favor of the Control group.

In addition to the 82 analyses for grades 1-6 and grades 10-12 whose results are displayed in Table 62, 33 analyses were conducted for grades 7-9. The data from these analyses is not reported because:

1. Thirteen of seventeen significant analyses were in favor of the experimental group — a pattern which is widely discrepant from that in the other grades.
2. The researchers had knowledge of matters internal to the Control school which made it seem highly probable that the results yielded in the analyses were an effect of that school and not of the training.
3. The results could not be validated in Year 02 because the Control School withdrew from the study as **one** of the

---

"In favor of" signifies that the group indicated had the **greatest amount of gain on Cognitive or Self-Concept tests or the **fewest** days absent.

consequences of the matters internal to the school mentioned in 2 above.

From Year 02

Of the 88 Analyses of Co-variance whose results are reported in Table 63 for Year 02, thirty-two analyses yielded significant differences between treatment means. Of these 32 analyses, 22 were in favor of the experimental group. Of the 23 significant analyses in grades 1-6, the Experimental group had the mean associated with desired change for 18 variables. At the secondary level, only four of the 10 significant analyses were in favor of the experimental group.

When these totals are broken down by kind of index, the Experimental grades 1-6 had means associated with desired change for 7 of 9 significant analyses on Self-Concept factors, 3 of 3 significant analyses for Total Days Absent and 8 of 11 significant analyses for Achievement Tests. In grades 10-12, on the other hand, the Experimental groups had analyses in their favor for 1 out of 1 significant analyses on Total Days Absent, and 2 of 7 significant analyses on Achievement Tests.

Breaking the significant analyses down by grade levels, the experimental group achieved 3 of 3 at second grade, none of none at third grade, 2 of 4 for fourth grade, 6 of 8 for fifth grade, 7 of 8 for sixth grade, 0 of 3 for tenth grade, 2 of 4 for eleventh grade, and 2 of 3 for twelfth grade groups. Among the elementary grades (2-6), grades three and four seem to be atypical.

From Year 03

Of the 111 Analyses of Co-variance whose results are reported in Table 64 for Year 03, 30 analyses yielded significant differences between treatment means. Of these 30 analyses, 23 were in favor of the Experimental group. Of the 12 significant analyses in grades 1-6, Experimental groups had the mean associated with desired change for 10 variables. For grades 7-9, 10 of the 12 significant analyses were in favor of the experimental groups. For grades 10-12, three of 6 significant analyses were in favor of the Experimental groups.

When these totals are broken down by kind of index, Experimental grades 1-6 had means associated with desired change for 3 of 4 significant analyses on Self-Concept factors, and 7 of 8 significant analyses for Achievement Tests. For grades 7-9, the Experimental groups had means associated with desired change for 5 out of 6 significant analyses for Achievement Tests. For grades 10-12, the Experimental groups had analyses in their favor for 1 of 1 significant analyses on Self-Concept Factors, and 2 of 5 significant analyses on Achievement Tests.

Breaking the significant analyses down by grade levels, the Experimental group achieved 2 of 2 first grade level, 1 of 1 at second grade level, 1 of 2 at third grade level, 2 of 3 at fourth grade level, 4 of

4 at fifth grade level, none of none at sixth grade level, 3 of 5 for seventh grades, 5 of 5 for eighth grades, 2 of 2 for ninth grades, 2 of 2 for tenth grades, 1 of 2 for eleventh grades, and none of 2 for twelfth grades. The sixth grade seemed to be atypical.

DISCUSSION

The results displayed in Tables 62, 63, and 64 are summarized in Table 65. As evident in this summary table, the effect of the Interpersonal Skills Training for teachers was not translated to student benefits in Year 01 but was so translated for Years 02 and 03.

The data concerning significant analyses summarized in Table 65 is converted into percentages in Table 66. The percentages for Year 01 represent only 13 significant analyses out of 82 analyses conducted.

The pattern presented is one of growing effectiveness in translating the benefits from Teacher Training to Student Outcomes. The differences seem to be cumulative — that is, the Year 02 Experimental students whose teachers had been in the program for both years did much better than they did in Year 01 as compared to the Control students. This is especially interesting when compared to the training the teachers received in the two years.

In Year 01, training focused on Interpersonal Skills **per se** while in Year 02 training focused on helping teachers apply their increased levels of Interpersonal Skills to "learning" interactions in the classroom rather than just to the more "personal" interchange. (See Study 10, cf. ante.) Since the "personal" interchanges in the classroom setting are (for most classes) a minor proportion of the interactions occurring, it may well be that few benefits were derived by the Experimental students from the Year 01 training of their teachers simply because the skills were only infrequently exercised in the classroom. When the teachers learned to apply their interpersonal skills to "learning" contexts, the students began to derive benefits from them. This hypothesis is somewhat supported by the results from Year 03 in which the training was combined into a one-year program incorporating **both** interpersonal skills training and training in applying those skills in the learning contexts.

Further support for this hypothesis is supplied by comparing the percentages of significant analyses in the experimental groups favor by kind of Index for the two years. (See Table 66). Thus in Year 01, most of the few significances that occurred were in the Mental Health Indices (Self-Concept and Total Days Absent) which are more "personal" than are the Achievement Indices. (However, it must be kept in mind that these percentages only represent 13 significant analyses). In Year 02, the significant analyses are more evenly split between Mental Health and Cognitive Indices.

In Year 03, when the two kinds of training were combined into a one-year program (with sixteen hours of training as opposed to 12

Table 65: Summary of Tables 62, 63, and 64

Tests	Grades	Class	Year 01	Year 02	Year 03
All Indices	All Grades	Total Number of Analyses	82		111
		Number of Significant Analyses	13	33	30
		N of Sig. Analyses in Favor Exp.	6	22	23
	Grades 1-6	Total Number of Analyses	46	50	45
		Number of Significant Analyses	4	23	12
		N of Sig. Analyses in Favor Exp.	3	18	10
	Grades 7-9	Total Number of Analyses	--	--	33
		Number of Significant Analyses	--	--	12
		N of Sig. Analyses in Favor Exp.	--	--	10
	Grades 10-12	Total Number of Analyses	36	36	33
		Number of Significant Analyses	9	10	6
		N of Sig. Analyses in Favor Exp.	3	4	3
Self-Concept	Grades 1-6	Total Number of Analyses	20	20	20
		Number of Significant Analyses	3	9	4
		N of Sig. Analyses in Favor Exp.	3	7	3
	Grades 7-9	Total Number of Analyses	--	--	15
		Number of Significant Analyses	--	--	6
		N of Sig. Analyses in Favor Exp.	--	--	5
	Grades 10-12	Total Number of Analyses	15	15	15
		Number of Significant Analyses	1	2	1
		N of Sig. Analyses in Favor Exp.	0	1	1
Total Days Absent	Grades 1-6	Total Number of Analyses	6	5	--
		Number of Significant Analyses	1	3	--
		N of Sig. Analyses in Favor Exp.	0	3	--
	Grades 7-9	Total Number of Analyses	--	--	--
		Number of Significant Analyses	--	--	--
		N of Sig. Analyses in Favor Exp.	--	--	--
	Grades 10-12	Total Number of Analyses	3	3	--
		Number of Significant Analyses	1	1	--
		N of Sig. Analyses in Favor Exp.	1	1	--
Achievement Tests	Grades 1-6	Total Number of Analyses	20	25	25
		Number of Significant Analyses	0	11	8
		N of Sig. Analyses in Favor Exp.	0	8	7
	Grades 7-9	Total Number of Analyses	--	--	18
		Number of Significant Analyses	--	--	6
		N of Sig. Analyses in Favor Exp.	--	--	5
	Grades 10-12	Total Number of Analyses	18	18	18
		Number of Significant Analyses	7	7	5
		N of Sig. Analyses in Favor Exp.	2	2	2

-- No data available for this level on this index.

Index	Group	Year 01	Year 02	Year 03
All Indices	All Grades	46%	66%	76%
	Grades 1-6	75	78	83
	Grades 7-9	--	--	83
	Grades 10-12	33	40	50
Self-Concept Tests	All Grades	75%	72%	71%
	Grades 1-6	100	77	75
	Grades 7-9	--	--	83
	Grades 10-12	0	50	100
Total Days Absent	All Grades	50%	100%	--
	Grades 1-6	0	100	--
	Grades 7-9	--	--	--
	Grades 10-12	100	100	--
Achievement Tests	All Grades	28%	55%	73%
	Grades 1-6	X	72	87
	Grades 7-9	--	--	83
	Grades 10-12	28	28	40

X = No analysis at this level for this index
reached .05 significance.

-- No data available for this level on this index.
hours for Year 02 and 15 hours for Year 01) the significant differences
are again divided between Self-Concept and Achievement Test indices.
Further, the cumulative nature of the effects on students seem to be
further supported by the fact that while Year 03 had proportionately
fewer significant analyses than did Year 02, the percentage of these
significant analyses which were in favor of Experimental groups was
higher than in Year 02. Thus, if the students were to be followed for a
second year in the replication site, it would be anticipated that the
incidence of significant differences detected would be increased.

The distribution among the different school levels of the significant
differences reflected the differences detected in response to training of
teachers at the different levels.*** Thus elementary Experimental

***See Study No. 10 (cf. ante.) in which Elementary Teachers made greater
gains in Interpersonal Skills than did Secondary Teachers.

students (grades 1-6) did better (compared to the Control students) than did the secondary students (grades 10-12) for all three years. Data for only one year was available for grades 7–9 but for that year, they did as well as the elementary students.

The few significant differences (split between control and experimental groups) at the third and fourth grades reflect the lower R-squares in those grades for prediction of student achievement (from teacher behavior) which were registered in the analyses conducted in Study No. 14. (Cf. ante.) Patterns of significant differences at other grade levels in this study also reflect other results of Study No. 14 but not in a one-to-one correspondence.

The data for Total Days Absent was most interesting to the researchers. Of the six significant differences detected between the treatment groups for absenteeism in Years 01 and 02, five of them were in favor of Experimental groups. (The one that was not was for the sixth grade in Year 01 and was the only difference detected between the sixth grade treatment groups in that year). This would seem to support the finding of Study No. 14 that when the teachers are using higher levels of interpersonal skills, students miss fewer days of school during the year.

Tables 67 and 68 display the Adjusted Treatment Means for the analyses in Year 02 and Year 03 in which significant differences were detected. Examination of these tables supports the conclusion that not only are the differences detected statistically significant but they are also meaningful in the "real-world"; i.e., they are not trivial. For example, differences between treatment means for grade-level groups of two to four days additional absence a year is a significant proportion of the 176-day school year. A further indication of the meaningful nature of these detected differences is that in the 25 significant analyses for Self-Concept factors, 11 of the favorable gains registered by the Experimental groups were reversals of **negative** change (as indicated by the **sign** of the change on the Control group mean). For the 37 analyses in which significant differences were detected among Achievement test variables, 16 of the favorable gains registered by the Experimental groups were reversals or mitigations of **negative** change (as indicated by the **sign** of the change on the Control group mean).

SUMMARY

In conclusion, findings from this study were:

1. *The effects of Interpersonal Skills Training for teachers were translated to student benefits in Years 02 and 03.*

2. *The student benefits seem to be cumulative; that is, students did better in the second year of the program than in the first year.*

3. *The differences between the treatment means (change on*

Table 67: Adjusted Treatment Means for Variables and Grade Levels in which Significant Differences (p < .05) were Detected in Year 02 Student Data

Dependent Variables	Grade 1 Exp.	Grade 1 Con.	Grade 2 Exp.	Grade 2 Con.	Grade 3 Exp.	Grade 3 Con.
Total Days Absent	NT	NT	8.04	10.24	NS	NS
Reading Vocabulary	NT	NT	8.42	7.89	NS	NS
Reading Comprehension	NT	NT	13.15	9.66	NS	NS

Dependent Variables	Grade 4 Exp.	Grade 4 Con.	Grade 5 Exp.	Grade 5 Con.	Grade 6 Exp.	Grade 6 Con.
HISM: Teacher-School	0.21	-0.71	-0.94	2.84	2.39	-0.32
HISM: Physical Appearance	NS	NS	0.88	-2.63	1.12	0.04
HISM: Interpersonal Adequacy	NS	NS	0.54	3.88	4.20	0.52
HISM: Autonomy	NS	NS	0.40	-2.00	NS	NS
HISM: Academic Adequacy	NS	NS	NS	NS	0.04	-0.82
Total Days Absent	NS	NS	4.72	8.01	8.29	4.61
Reading Vocabulary	3.32	5.08	NS	NS	NS	NS
Reading Comprehension	-5.54	-8.21	NS	NS	12.96	6.93
Language Usage	NS	NS	4.84	-4.38	NS	NS
Language Mechanics	NS	NS	-5.70	-10.48	6.47	3.78
Math Computation	NS	NS	-4.16	-7.50	3.71	7.93
Math Concepts	-1.39	-4.16	NS	NS	NS	NS

Dependent Variables	Grade 10 Exp.	Grade 10 Con.	Grade 11 Exp.	Grade 11 Con.	Grade 12 Exp.	Grade 12 Con.
HISM: Autonomy	NS	NS	NS	NS	-0.19	1.16
HISM: Academic Adequacy	NS	NS	0.91	0.21	NS	NS
Total Days Absent	NS	NS	9.11	12.64	NS	NS
Reading Vocabulary	NS	NS	NS	NS	8.92	4.22
Language Usage	NS	NS	NS	NS	1.96	0.78
Language Mechanics	4.45	6.58	0.90	3.79	NS	NS
Math Computation	-4.22	-2.76	NS	NS	NS	NS
Math Concepts	-6.35	-3.79	0.15	1.51	NS	NS

NT = No Test.

NS = Not Significant.

Table 68: Adjusted Treatment Means for Variables and Grade Levels in which Significant Differences (p < .05) were Detected in Year 03 Student Data

Dependent Variables	Grade 1 Exp.	Grade 1 Con.	Grade 2 Exp.	Grade 2 Con.	Grade 3 Exp.	Grade 3 Con.
HISM: Autonomy	NT	NT	NT	NT	0.99	-1.97
HISM: Academic Adequacy	NT	NT	NT	NT	-0.19	0.94
Reading Vocabulary	4.46	2.28	5.50	2.46	NS	NS
Reading Comprehension	3.70	1.96	NS	NS	NS	NS

Dependent Variables	Grade 4 Exp.	Grade 4 Con.	Grade 5 Exp.	Grade 5 Con.	Grade 6 Exp.	Grade 6 Con.
HISM: Physical Appearance	1.75	0.04	NS	NS	NS	NS
HISM: Autonomy	0.91	-0.22	NS	NS	NS	NS
Reading Comprehension	NS	NS	4.83	2.13	NS	NS
Language Usage	5.69	7.19	-17.04	-23.40	NS	NS
Math Computation	NS	NS	-10.01	-13.52	NS	NS
Math Concepts	NS	NS	-5.78	-9.30	NS	NS

Dependent Variables	Grade 7 Exp.	Grade 7 Con.	Grade 8 Exp.	Grade 8 Con.	Grade 9 Exp.	Grade 9 Con.
HISM: Physical Appearance	1.21	-0.14	1.41	0.14	NS	NS
HISM: Interpersonal Adequacy	NS	NS	1.98	-0.18	NS	NS
HISM: Autonomy	NS	NS	1.97	0.26	NS	NS
HISM: Academic Adequacy	0.48	0.95	0.56	-0.20	NS	NS
Reading Vocabulary	-6.44	-8.40	NS	NS	NS	NS
Language Usage	1.61	-6.22	NS	NS	0.24	-3.46
Language Mechanics	NS	NS	1.89	0.71	NS	NS
Math Computation	-4.89	-7.62	NS	NS	-11.69	-13.02

Dependent Variables	Grade 10 Exp.	Grade 10 Con.	Grade 11 Exp.	Grade 11 Con.	Grade 12 Exp.	Grade 12 Con.
HISM: Autonomy	1.78	-0.31	NS	NS	NS	NS
Reading Comprehension	NS	NS	-2.15	0.12	-0.74	1.36
Math Computation	NS	NS	2.45	0.18	NS	NS
Math Concepts	1.94	0.24	NS	NS	-2.32	1.11

NT = No Test   NS = Not Significant

student outcome indices) reflected the differences in the skills
training which their teachers received.

4. *The distribution among grade levels of significant differences in favor of Experimental groups reflected the differential response to Interpersonal Skills Training of elementary and secondary teachers.*

5. *The significant differences detected between the treatment groups on the Absenteeism variable support the finding of Study 14 that when teachers are using higher levels of interpersonal skills, students miss fewer days of school during the year.*

6. *The differences detected between Treatment means in Years 02 and 03 were not only statistically significant but were also meaningful in the real world.*

Over a period of three years, the National Consortium for Humanizing Education worked with teachers and students in two states to test hypotheses drawn from a model in which student outcomes (including good mental health) are seen as the results of a learning **process** occurring between individuals rather than as the **product** of an institutionalized situation. In this model, mental health is assumed to be learned in much the same way that other capabilities are learned; that is, as the result of an interdependent interpersonal interactive process. Although the learning context of concern in the present study was that within the institution of the school, neither the teachers nor the students leave their emotions and their awareness of themselves as individuals at the door when they enter the schoolroom; therefore the learning process taking place inside the room can not divorce "human interaction" from "knowing" or "growing."

Model Tested

The specific elements of the model to be considered in these studies were drawn from the definition of learning as an "interdependent interpersonal interactive process." The elements of the model included (1) presage characteristics of the teachers and students, (2) contexts of the learning interaction, (3) teacher and student behavior within the learning interaction process, and (4) student outcomes from the process. The major hypothesis to be tested was that intervention (Interpersonal Skills Training) to change the quality of the teacher's input to learning interactions would result in benefits to students.

Illustration 2 displays the complete model for the studies. The number beside each of the listed variables are the numbers of the individual studies (as presented in Parts II and III of this report) in which the variable was considered as a major item in the analysis. The results from the 15 individual studies will be presented below and discussed as they are related to the elements of the model. As the results are presented, the number of the study from which the findings resulted will be referenced.

Illustration 2: Model Tested with Individual Study Numbers Indicated for Variables Considered

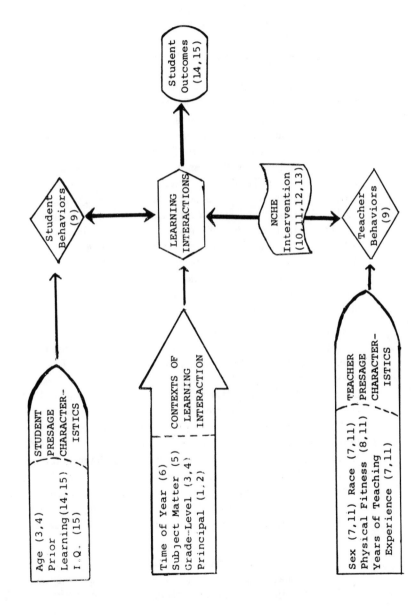

Student Presage Characteristics

Age: Age was only considered indirectly under the rubric of grade-level, since there is an almost one-to-one correspondence between age and grade-level when large numbers of students in all grades 1 - 12 are considered. For findings related to age, see the discussion of grade-level below.

I. Q. and Prior Learning: I. Q. and Prior Learning (pre-test scores) of students were considered as concomitant variables in study 15, in which they were used to adjust the dependent variables of change on student outcomes for entering levels of differences. In Study 15, the regression coefficient for I. Q. was significant at levels less than .05 for 21% of the analyses in which change on a How-I-See-Myself factor was the dependent variable, for 95% of the analyses in which change on an Achievement Test was the dependent variable, and for 70% of the analyses in which Total Days Absent for the year was the dependent variable. The regression coefficient for Pre-test was significant in 94% of the HISM analyses, and 86% of the Achievement Test Analyses.

The most interesting of these findings is the negative correlation between I. Q. and Total Days Absent for the year. It stimulates a question which was not answered by these analyses; that is, "Do students with higher I. Q. come to school more often because it is a more pleasant place for them than for students with lower learning abilities and/or achievement?"

Teacher Presage Characteristics

Studies 7 and 8 considered the relationships between (1) sex, (2) race, (3) years of teaching experience, and (4) physical fitness (level of physical functioning as measured on the Harvard Step Test) and the Classroom Functioning variables (teacher and student behaviors within the learning interaction process.) Sex of the teacher was found to be the most important contributor to the variation of Classroom Functioning with Years of Teaching Experience also having a slight effect. Race of the teacher did not seem to be an important contributor to the variation of classroom processes. (Study 7). A small but non-chance relationship was discovered between the teacher's level of physical functioning and the Classroom Functioning variables. (Study 8). Additional specific findings from Study Number 7 included:

1. Sex contributions to the variation of G (Genuineness of the teacher), SP (Success Promotion), and C-8, Student Asks for Thinking) seemed to be clear-cut, with male teachers functioning at higher levels than female teachers.

2. Sex contributions to the variation of F-5, F-8, F-9, C-1, C-5,

and C-6 may have been contaminated by grade-level differences. However, the significant differences detected for these variables in the present study indicated that male teachers lectured more (F-5), allowed or elicited more student initiated responses (F-9), were asked more fact questions (C-6) by their students, and spent less time presenting facts (C-1) to their students, while female teachers elicited more directed student response (F-8) and more use of facts by students (C-5).

3. Teaching experience showed as a significant factor in four variables; as a main effect for variables F-3 and F-6 and in interactions for variables C-8 and G. The information provided by these analyses seemed to be that teachers beginning their first year of teaching were different from other teachers in that they gave more directions (F-6) and accepted more student ideas (F-3).

All four of these variables were again considered in Study Number 11 in which the effects of teacher characteristics on response to training were analyzed. The teacher's level of physical functioning was used as a co-variate to adjust for individual differences. In the 25 analyses conducted, the regression coefficient of physical functioning was not significant at the .05 level for any analysis. There was no systematic differential response to Interpersonal Skills Training by sub-groups of teachers differentiated according to teacher characteristics of race, sex, or years of teaching experience. (Study Number 11).

Although there were some slight differences (by teacher characteristics of sex, years of teaching experience, and physical functioning) on entering training, the training seemed to be equally received by all sub-groups and the slight entering differences were "washed out" during training.

Context of Learning Interaction

The context variables of (1) Time of Year, (2) Subject Matter, (3) Grade-Level on which the teacher instructs, and (4) the Principal's levels of functioning were considered separately in Studies 1 - 6 to determine their relationships with the Classroom Functioning variables (teacher and student behavior within learning interactions). Of the four variables, only Subject Matter was **not** found to have an important effect on the Classroom Functioning variables. The findings related to each of the context variables are presented separately below.

Subject Matter: The subject matter presented by the teacher was a significant source of variation for only two variables (C-3: Teacher Thinks and C-6: Student Asks for Facts) out of 25 variables analyzed. For both variables, Math teachers attained the highest mean. For C-6, Science teachers scored a mean slightly lower than, but not different from, that of the Math teachers. (Study Number 5).

Grade Level: The grade-level at which the teacher instructs was found to have a significant effect on the variation of both the Flanders' Categories and the Cognitive Functioning Categories but not on the Process Scales. Significant differences among the grade level means of Flanders' and Cognitive Categories were detected for all categories except F-1 (Teacher Accepts Feelings); C-4 (Teacher Asks for Thinking), C-7 (Student Thinks), and C-9 (Non-Cognitive Behavior in the classroom). The sources of these grade-level differences were primarily a result of differences between the means of (1) one or more of the elementary grades and (2) one or more of the levels of the secondary schools. Few significant sources of variation were found **between** the two levels of secondary schools (7 - 9 and 10 - 12) or **among** the elementary grades 1 - 6. (Studies 3 and 4). The pattern of predictive inter-relationships of all Classroom Functioning variables, as well as the relative quantity of each variable, was also different at the elementary and secondary levels. (Study 6).

The question stimulated by these studies has to do with the causative origin of the grade-level differences detected. Are they a function of students' ages, differential school curriculum and organization at the elementary and secondary levels, differential expectation of teachers, or an interaction of two or more of these factors?

Time of Year: Significant trends across time were found in the Control Group data. These trends were consistent with the interpretation that there is a **deterioration** across the year from September till May in the levels of facilitative conditions offered students by their teachers. These trends were also present in the Experimental Group data but were mitigated by the effects of the training in Interpersonal Skills which the experimental teachers had received. (Study Number 6).

Principal's Level of Functioning: Both Studies 1 and 2 dealt with the effect of the principal on learning interactions. In Study Number 2, teachers were grouped according to their principal's level of interpersonal functioning. Then their reports of working environment and instructional tasks (on the Semantic Differential instrument displayed in the Appendix) were analyzed for significant differences. Significant differences were found among the groups of teachers with the teachers of high functioning principals tending to find their working environment and instructional tasks more attractive than the teachers of low functioning principals.

In Study Number 1, the principal's functioning in Teacher/Principal interactions (analogous to the Student/Teacher interactions measured on the Classroom Functioning variables) were analyzed for relationships **with** the Classroom Functioning variables. Specific findings from this study were:

1. Significant ($p < .05$) predictive relationships between the principal's interpersonal behavior and the teacher's classroom behavior were detected for 19 of 25 dependent variables.

2. Five of the 19 significant models accounted for meaningful amounts of variation with RSQ $> .20$ in each case.

3. The best predictors of the teacher's behavior were identified as the principal's (a) level of Respect for the teacher, (b) use of Praise, (c) Acceptance of Ideas, and (d) Asking of Fact Questions.

In conclusion, it seemed that as a principal used higher levels of interpersonal and interactional skills with his/her teachers, they used higher levels of these skills with their students.

The findings relative to each of the four context variables are important in and of themselves. But, together, they have strong implications for the planning of educational research. They pretty well rule out the validity of cross-sectional, one-slice-of-the-research-pie studies unless those studies are **carefully** planned and **controlled** for the effects of the context variables operative on the dependent variables of concern in the research to be undertaken.

Inter-relationships of Teacher and Student Behavior within Learning Interactions

Study Number 9 generated 300 Response Surfaces through a backward elimination multilinear regression analysis technique using quadratic terms. These Response Surfaces specified the inter-relationships of teacher and student behavior within learning inter-actions. Specific findings from this study included:

1. **Replicable, predictable,** and **significant** relationships were detected among variables of teacher and student classroom functioning.

2. These **relationships were different** at the secondary and elementary levels.

3. **Specific recurring predictors** for each of the study variables were identified.

4. Some of the classroom functioning variables **co-varied significantly** and **frequently** with a large number of the other study variables, and these predictors were few enough in number to suggest that efficient programs for changing overall classroom functioning could be developed by focusing training efforts on these few highly predictive variables.

5. The **individual response surfaces** generated for each study variable **provided specific suggestions** for focusing training efforts aimed at changing selected aspects of teacher or student behavior.

6. Two of the 4 most **frequently recurring predictors** (and 3 of

the top 10) were variables which had been postulated by Rogers as being positively related to effective learning environments.

7. Most of the **frequently recurring predictors** were related to the kinds of behavior classified by Flanders as "Indirect."

8. The kinds of behavior hypothesized by the National Consortium for Humanizing Education as characterizing a humane classroom were also the kinds of behavior which were **frequently recurring predictors** of the other study variables.

9. The **curvilinear relationships** detected were strong enough and constant enough to suggest that educational researchers need to emphasize the building and testing of **at least** quadratic models.

The general picture presented was that of increased student participation and higher levels of student thinking when teacher behaviors were characterized as (1) indirect, (2) offering high levels of facilitative conditions to students, and (3) expecting students to perform at high levels.

NCHE Intervention

The intervention (treatment applied) by the National Consortium for Humanizing Education was Interpersonal Skills Training for Teachers. Studies Number 10, 11, 12, and 13 tested the efficacy of the training and Study Number 6 provided additional information as to the nature of the process occurring as a result of training.

Over-all Effectiveness: Findings related to the over-all effectiveness of the training included:

1. Significant differences were detected between control and experimental groups for all three years of the study. (Study Number 10).

2. Elementary teachers responded better to the training than Secondary teachers. (Study Number 10).

3. The changes achieved by Experimental groups (teachers receiving Interpersonal Skills Training) were of magnitudes large enough to be both statistically significant and not trivial; i.e., they were meaningful in the real-world. (Study Number 10).

4. The 97 significant trends across time detected in the Experimental teacher data was compatible with the interpretation that treatment benefits were in directions opposed to the direction of "normal" **deteriorative** processes evidenced across the school year in the Control group data. (Study Number 6).

5. The variables on which movement occurred were directly and positively related to the specific content of the training

program and varied when the content varied. (Studies 10 and 12).

6. The major effect of the training was a change in the quality of the interactions between student and teacher with a smaller but supporting change in the proportions of teacher/student participation in classroom verbal interchanges. (Study Number 10).

7. The training was equally effective with sub-groups of teachers differentiated according to teacher characteristics of race, sex, or years of teaching experience. (Study Number 11).

Table 51 ("Magnitude of Change in Experimental Teacher Behavior") in Study 10 compared the gains made by the Experimental teachers with their pre-test (entering training) levels of functioning. Another way to examine the meaningfulness of the gains made by the Experimental teachers is to compare their **exiting** levels with the normative data derived from the Control groups over the three-year period as displayed in Table 69. (Exiting level can be computed from Table 51 by adding the Change means to the Pre-test means).

Comparing the exiting levels of the Experimental teachers to the data in Table 69 for Flanders' Interaction Analysis Categories shows that (on exit from training) the Experimental elementary teachers (grades 1 - 6) were using almost 4 times as much acceptance of student feelings as the norm for the Control teachers, two and a half times as much praise and encouragement, almost three times as much acceptance of student ideas, asked about a tenth more questions, and lectured about a tenth less. Their students spent about 15% more time in the Student Responds Category and almost twice as much time in the Student Initiates Category as the students of the Control teachers and there was only half as much silence or confusion in the classrooms of the Experimental teachers. However, the Experimental teachers gave about the same amount of directions or commands as the Control teachers and used slightly more than twice as much criticism or justification of authority.

For Experimental secondary teachers, (grades 7 - 12) the picture was much the same. They used about three- fourths more praise or encouragement than the Control secondary teachers did, almost five times as much acceptance of student ideas, asked about three times as many questions, lectured about a twentieth less, used about a third more directions or commands and criticism or justification of authority. Their students spent about 25% more time in the Student Responds Category and about a tenth more time in the Student Initiates Category than the students of the Control Teachers and there was about 60% less silence or confusion in Experimental classrooms.

Table 69: Normative Data for Classroom Functioning Variables -- Means
from 1,951 One-hour Audio Tape Recordings of Instruction
Submitted by Control Teachers in Texas from May, 1971 to
May, 1973 and in Louisiana from September, 1973 to April, 1974

Classroom Functioning Variable	Elementary Teachers $\bar{X}$	Secondary Teachers $\bar{X}$
F-1: Teacher Accepts Feelings of Student	0.04	0.06
F-2: Teacher Praises or Encourages Student	1.46	0.71
F-3: Teacher Accepts Ideas of Student	0.74	0.41
F-4: Teacher Asks Questions	21.77	6.94
F-5 Teacher Lectures	82 83	113.33
F-6: Teacher Gives Directions or Commands	8 49	3.49
F-7: Teacher Criticizes or Justifies Authority	1.24	0.53
F-8: Student Responds	74.65	60.13
F-9: Student Initiates	11.69	14.07
F-10: Silence or Confusion	36.91	31.48
C-1: Teacher Recalls Facts	92.10	115.66
C-2: Teacher Asks for Facts	21.31	14.26
C-3: Teacher Thinks	0.10	0.50
C-4: Teacher Asks for Thinking	1.21	1.37
C-5: Student Recalls Facts	81.23	68.10
C-6: Student Asks for Facts	1 01	2.43
C-7: Student Thinks	2 51	3.62
C-8 Student Asks for Thinking	0.12	0.38
C-9 Non-Cognitive Behavior	2 91	2.08
C-10: Silence or Chaos	37.15	31 54
M: Meaning	2.65	2.65
G: Genuineness	2.65	2.66
SP: Success Promotion	2.66	2.30
R: Respect	2.70	2.71
SI Student Involvement	2.84	2.82
N of Teachers	153	91
N of Tapes	1,258	693

For Flanders' and Cognitive variables, data is reported as the total number
of 3-second intervals coded in category during 12 minutes selected at random
in four 3-minute segments from a 1-hour tape. For Process Scales, data is
reported as mean level of functioning maintained during the four 3 minute
segments

For the Cognitive Functioning Categories, the Experimental
elementary teachers spent about a tenth less time recalling facts and
asking students for facts and about three times as long in thinking and in
asking students to think than did the Control Teachers. Experimental
students spent about 20% more time recalling facts, about a fourth
more time asking for facts, about a third more time thinking and about
15% less time asking for thinking than the students of the Control
teachers. The Experimental teachers had about three times as much
Non-Cognitive Behavior (primarily affect-related behaviors) in their
classrooms as was registered in the classrooms of the Control teachers.

The Experimental secondary teachers spent about 5% less time
recalling facts, about a fourth more time asking for facts, about half as
much time thinking, and about a fourth more time asking for thinking
from their students than was the norm for the Control teachers. The
students of the Experimental secondary teachers spent about a fifth
more time recalling facts, about a fifth **less** time asking for facts, about
two and a half more time thinking, and about one and a half as much
time asking for thinking as did the students of the Control teachers.
The Experimental secondary teachers had about half again as much
Non-Cognitive Behavior in their classrooms as did the Control teachers.

The Process Scales are characterized by the general effect on
students of teachers operating at each level as:

1.0   Crippling
2.0   Hurting
3.0   Minimally Effective
4.0   Adding Significantly
5.0   Adding, Encouraging, Exploring

The data displayed in Table 69 shows that the Control teachers had
means in the upper half of level two. The exiting levels for the
Experimental elementary teachers were 3.15 on Meaning, 3.12 on
Genuineness, 3.10 on Success Promotion, 3.29 on Respect, and 3.40 on
Student Involvement. For secondary Experimental teachers, the exiting
levels were 3.03 for Meaning, 2.98 for Genuineness, 3.01 for Success
Promotion, 3.03 for Respect, and 3.12 for Student Involvement. In
every case except that of Genuineness for secondary teachers, the
Experimental teachers made large enough gains to put them across the
Minimally Effective threshold.

Relative Effectiveness of Different Versions of Training Program

The final Training Program was the product of two research and
development cycles. Analyses comparing the different versions yielded
the following results:

1.   The greatest gains were made by teachers who received two
     years of training (totaling 27 hours) with the first year focused
     on increasing levels of interpersonal skills and the second year

focused on applying interpersonal skills to learning interactions as well as more personal exchanges. (Study Number 10).

2. The second largest gains were made by teachers who had one year of training (totaling 16 hours) which combined (in the **one** year program) training focused on increasing levels of interpersonal skills with training focused on applying these skills to learning interactions. These gains were not as large as the gains made over the **total** two years by the teachers who received the two-year program but were greater than the gains made by those teachers in any **single** year. The one year combined program was more **efficient** than the two-year program when gains are considered in terms of the total number of hours involved in the training. The training was applied by teams of Peer/Professional trainers with racial intermixes. (Study Number 10).

3. A pilot of the one-year **combined** program (described in 2 above) was compared with two versions of the one-year program which focused on increasing levels of interpersonal skills. The two versions with which the **combined** program was compared were (1) the program applied in Year 01 of the two year program (described in 1 above) and (2) with revision of that Year 01 program which was applied to new experimental teachers in the second research year. No conclusion was drawn as to the relative effectiveness of the original and the revised version of the Year 01 program although there was some indication in the data that the revised version was slightly more effective. However, it was concluded that the **combined** program was more effective than either version of the Year 01 program. (Study Number 12).

4. A small N study was conducted to compare the relative effectiveness of the training when the principal of the school had received **prior** training in Interpersonal Skills and when he had not. The null hypothesis was rejected and the conclusion was that prior training of the principal enhances teacher response to Interpersonal Skills Training. (Study Number 13).

Student Outcomes

Two studies were concerned with the evaluation of Student Outcomes. Study Number 14 examined the predictive relationships between the Classroom Functioning variables and Student Outcomes to see whether or not the process variables were good predictors of student change (gain). Study Number 15 compared the change made by students of Experimental teachers with that made by students of Control teachers.

Specific findings from Study Number 14 included:

1.   The Classroom Functioning variables are good predictors of
     student change when raw change is adjusted for pre-test
     standing.

2.   When the teacher is functioning at high levels of acceptance
     and responsiveness to students, the students miss fewer days of
     school during the year.

3.   At the upper grade levels, the teacher has a more direct effect
     on students' attainment of specific skills than on attainment of
     concepts or more abstract processes.

4.   The Classroom Functioning variables were equally effective
     predictors for change on both Self-Concept factors and
     Achievement tests.

5.   Both the **stability** of the teacher's functioning and the **average**
     level of functioning on Specific Affective Behaviors and
     Process Scales were important predictors of change but the
     relative importance of the two kinds of measures of teacher
     functioning varied with the kind of gain predicted and the
     grade level of the student.

6.   The **stability** of the teacher's functioning in the Cognitive
     Behaviors was not an important predictor of change, but
     average level of functioning was.

7.   Student gain (positive change) was positively related to the
     Classroom Functioning variables except F-7 and C-1 which
     were inversely related while F-6 was positively related for
     elementary students and inversely related for secondary
     students.

Specific findings from Study Number 15 included:

1.   The effects of the Interpersonal Skills training for teachers was
     translated to student benefits in Years 02 and 03, but not in
     Year 01.

2.   The student benefits seemed to be cumulative; that is, students
     did better in the second year of the two-year program than in
     the first year.

3.   The differences between the treatment means on student
     outcome indices reflected the differences in the skills training
     which their teachers received.

4.   The distribution among grade levels of significant differences
     in favor of Experimental groups reflected the differential
     response to Interpersonal Skills Training of elementary and
     secondary teachers.

5.   The significant differences detected between the treatment
     groups on the Absenteeism variable support the findings of

Study 14 that when teachers are using higher levels of interpersonal skills, students miss fewer days of school during the year.

6. The differences detected between the treatment means in Years 02 and 03 were not only statistically significant but were also meaningful in the real world.

The conclusion of the researchers from these two studies was that higher functioning teachers produce more gain in student measures of Self-Concept and Achievement and their students are absent fewer days. In fact, then, benefits do accrue to students when their teachers receive Interpersonal Skills Training.

Results Related to Model

Of the presage characteristics hypothesized as having an effect on learning interacitons and/or student outcomes, only one was **not** supported. That is, the Race of the teacher did not seem to be an important contributor to the variation of Classroom Functioning. Both Prior Learning (as represented by pre-test scores) of the student and his I. Q. were important contributors to the variation of student outcomes; however, I. Q. was not as highly related to outcomes on Self-Concept tests as was pre-test score.

Subject Matter was the only one of the Contexts of Learning Interaction variables which did not have a significant effect on the variation of teacher and student behavior in learning interactions (Classroom Functioning variables). Among the context variables, grade-level (as an organizational factor and/or as an effect of student age) was the greatest contributor to the variance **within each time period** but Time of Year was also an important contributor. The principal's contribution to the variation seemed to have much of the effect of a constant in a regression equation; i.e., she/he moved the mean of the school up or down on the vertical axis.

Learning Interaction (at least, as measured in these studies) was demonstrated to be both a dynamic and a curvilinearly inter-related process; i.e., teacher and student behaviors within the classroom were both interdependent and interactive. Further, it was demonstrated that student outcomes could be predicted from the Classroom Functioning variables.

Student Outcomes were demonstrated to be related directly to both student presage characteristics and to student and teacher behaviors in learning interactions (as measured by the Classroom Functioning variables). Further, it was demonstrated that manipulating the quality of the teacher's input to learning interactions affected both the student behaviors in the interactions and student outcomes.

Statistical Treatment

Before discussing the implications of these findings for practice and

further research, it is perhaps worth noting that the results presented
above represent a synthesis of the following analyses:

500	Sixth-Degree orthogonal polynomial multilinear regression analyses across time
150	Backward elimination multilinear regression analyses with quadratic terms yielding 150 two-variable and 150 three-variable response surfaces
89	Stepwise multilinear regression analyses
250	Analyses of co-variance (two-way)
311	Analyses of co-variance (one-way)
50	Analyses of variance (two-way)
20	Analyses of variance (one-way)
5	Chi-Square Analyses
19	Kruskal-Wallis one-way analyses of variance by ranks

IMPLICATIONS FOR PRACTICE

The research results presented here strongly support several conclusions about educational practice:

1. It is worthwhile making sure that teachers use high levels of interpersonal skills in interaction with their students because (a) benefits accrue to the students in terms of increases on both mental health and cognitive indices and (2) the higher attendance rates of students whose teachers are functioning at higher levels mean increased financial support for the school in those states where state aid is based on ADA statistics.

2. It is worthwhile incorporating interpersonal skills as an important evaluative criteria for selecting principals and other local instructional leaders because of the effect their level of functioning has on the interpersonal skills used by teachers with their students.

3. Large numbers of teachers can be trained to increase their interpersonal skills.

4. The methodology used in this research can be adapted for use in personnel selection.

Items 1 and 2 above are self-evident on the basis of the research presented previously. Items 3 and 4 are amplified below.

Teacher Training

The project successfully demonstrated a training program to increase the interpersonal skills utilized by teachers. The program involved three elements (1) self-diagnosis of needed skills on the basis of training in measurement skills, (2) periodic feedback from professional coders using the instruments which the teachers had learned, and (3) training in Interpersonal Skills and their application within classroom learning interactions. The program went through several cycles of application and research. The most effective program (as finally developed) is described below.

Diagnosis: The teachers were taught the use of Flanders' Interaction Analysis Categories, the Cognitive Functioning Categories, and the Process Scales. They evaluated audio tape recordings of their instructional interactions and determined areas in which they needed skills improvement. Their self-diagnoses were supplemented with diagnoses by the NCHE trainers from the recordings coded by professional raters. On the basis of this diagnostic process, skills training modules were co-operatively (trainer with teachers) selected from the list of available modules for small groups of teachers. (When the teachers expressed a need for training in a skills area in which no module had yet been developed, the trainers either developed a module applying Interpersonal Skills to the area of need or brought in a supplementary consultant to supply the need. Thus, the modules "Planning for Learning" and "Working with Small Groups" and the series of modules, "Organizing for Learning, Parts I, II, III, and IV" were developed in direct response to trainees' expressed needs).

Feedback: The teachers were periodically supplied with feedback from professional raters as to their classroom functioning. (Individual ID number procedures were used to assure anonymity for the teacher's protection). Each teacher received (1) his/her individual scores, (2) the month's mean for his/her school, and (3) the month's mean for the school system for each of the Flanders' and Cognitive Categories and the Process Scales and (4) his/her individual Flanders' Matrix.

The trainer was supplied with group norms (for the teachers with whom he/she was working) as a guide to continuing training needs. A portion of each training session was set aside for discussing individual feedback with teachers who felt the need of such a conference.

The NCHE was gathering tape data on a monthly basis for research purposes so each Experimental teacher was supplied with feedback for each tape submitted. However, this is a relatively expensive process — averaging about $5.00 per tape rated, including computer processing and feedback return. Subjective evaluations of trainer and trainees was that monthly feedback was not necessary. Their suggested schedule for feedback was (1) before entering training for diagnostic purposes, (2) about midway through training, and (3) at the end of training for evaluative purposes.

Skills Training: Skills training was standardized for purposes of analysis and replication through the use of standard training modules. The most effective format included the elements of (1) use of pre- and post-testing, (2) a high proportion of experiential to didactic material, and (3) provision of "take-home" programs for application of skills in the trainees' classroom settings. The first portion of each training session was always a general discussion to share results of the "Practical Application" exercises from the last training session.

Although the trainees determined which modules they would receive, the trainer determined the sequence of modules based on an "Ideal Sequence" which incorporated all available modules. This sequence for the elementary school was:

Theoretical Overview
Flanders' Interaction Analysis
Developing Skills in Accepting Feelings
Scales for the Measurement of Interpersonal Processes
Cognitive Functioning Categories
Increasing Praise
Accepting Student Ideas
Questioning Skills, Parts I and II
Program for Increasing Student Involvement
Problem Solving Module
Program Development Skills
Planning for Learning
Organizing for Learning I: Teacher-Pupil Interaction
Organizing for Learning II: Responsive Physical Environment
Organizing for Learning III: Curriculum-Student Interaction
Organizing for Learning IV: Pupil-Task Interaction
Working with Small Groups
Consumatory Experience

The sequence for the secondary schools was similar. However, for the secondary schools the more directly Affective- related modules were delayed in presentation. Hence, the "Problem-Solving" and "Program Development Skills" were presented directly after the Flanders' Interaction Analysis and the Scales for the Measurement of Interpersonal Processes was not presented until after "Questioning Skills, Parts I and II".

The 18 modules represent about 30 hours total training time. However, no group of teachers ever received all 18 modules. The teachers who were in the program for two years received a total of 27 hours training and had the greatest gains. The Year 03 teachers (who had the second greatest gains) received about 16 hours training. All teachers, however, received a common nucleus of modules. This common nucleus consisted of the first nine modules listed in the Elementary sequence (above) plus the "Program Development Skills" module.

Enhancing Training Effectiveness: Subsequent to the results of Study Number 13 in which the teachers whose principal had had prior training in Interpersonal Skills were demonstrated to have made greater gains than the other experimental teachers in Year 03, the principal concerned was asked to recollect his activities related to the program. He stated that primarily they consisted of (1) using his own Interpersonal Skills with his teachers — a statement supported by the available tape data in which he was one of the top functioning principals from the three years of the study, (2) expressing his own enthusiasm for the program, and (3) setting aside time in faculty meetings for talking with his teachers about the training, their feelings about the NCHE program, and the results of the training as they used the skills in their classrooms.

A second source of subjective evaluation which offers clues to enhancing the program is that of the trainers who compared their perceptions of the program during the first two years and the third year regarding the training schedule. In the first two years, the bulk of the training had been administered in the summer immediately prior to school opening and the rest of the training was scheduled at intervals of a month and a half or two months. (In year 01, the first training session following the pre-school training had been delayed until December because of start-up problems* with the project.) In Year 03, the pre-school workshop was shorter and the bulk of the training occurred during the school year at approximately one-month intervals (varied slightly according to the activity schedules of the individual schools).

The trainers felt that the shorter interval between training sessions was much better. In fact, they felt that even shorter intervals (of about two weeks) would probably be even better. They also stated that placing the bulk of the training within the school year was better as it allowed the trainees to use the "Practical Applications" in their classrooms after each session and bring the results of their skills practice with them to the next training session. Although the Peer Trainers who administered much of the training in Year 03 had not observed the Year 01 and 02 training, they, too, felt the shorter interval might be even better.

Suggested Program for Interpersonal Skills Training: On the basis of both the statistical analysis of the training conducted by the NCHE and the subjective evaluations of that program discussed above, the following procedures are suggested as the most effective program of Interpersonal Skills Training for large groups of teachers:

---

*Funding was delayed. The cost of the pre-school training had been assumed by the researchers (and the school system had paid the participants' stipends) in order to get the project off the ground, but follow-up training could not be held until funds for teacher stipends were available.

Step 1: Provide Interpersonal Skills training for the principals (or other instructional leaders) of the schools to be involved. The training should include making and evaluating tape recordings of their functioning in their professional situations.

Step 2: At the same time, provide initial Interpersonal Skills Training for selected teachers from whom a core of Peer Trainers will be drawn.

Step 3: On the basis of training results and evaluation of post-training tapes of instructional activities of the teachers trained in Step #2, select teachers to be trained as Peer Trainers.

Step 4: Train the Peer Trainers in administering the program.

Step 5: Orient teachers to the training program and explain what will be involved. The Principal of each school should be involved in this orientation procedure.

Step 6: Have the teachers who will receive the training make a tape of their classroom interaction to be used for diagnostic purposes.

Step 7: Train teachers in the initial measurement modules and have them (1) evaluate their own tapes and (2) diagnose skill needs. Combine this with professional rating of their tapes, if possible, and if this is not too threatening to the teachers. (The degree of threat will depend on initial orientation to the program, on the arrangements for the professional rating – who, where, what kind of identification procedures, etc. – and on local trust relationships).

Step 8: Plan the skills training co-operatively with the teachers, selecting the skills modules to be used on the basis of their needs. One module that must always be selected is "Developing Skills in Accepting Feelings" as it is a pre-requisite to most of the other skills modules.

Step 9: Administer training modules at regular intervals of not longer than a month. In between the training sessions, the principal or other local instructional leader (trained in Interpersonal Skills) should provide time for discussing the program and its effects and for sharing results.

Step 10: Provide tape-data feedback about half-way through the program. (If professional rating is not available, teachers can rate their own tapes).

Step 11: Provide tape-data feedback at the end of the program for teacher self-evaluation.

Adapting the Methodology to Personnel Selection: The methodology for rating Interpersonal Skills was demonstrated to be a reliable measure of the functioning of both teachers and principals and the ratings obtained were shown to have significant relationships with selected outcome measures. It could be adapted to personnel selection very simply by requiring persons applying for positions within the school system to submit a one-hour tape of their professional functioning. This tape could then be coded and the data used in the selection procedure.

IMPLICATIONS FOR FURTHER RESEARCH

NCHE demonstrated (1) that Interpersonal Skills in the education setting are amenable to measurement and research, (2) that the selected technology works, and (3) that working within the specified model yielded significant and replicable results. The project also stimulated many questions for further research:

1. The version of Interpersonal Skills Training for Teachers used in the research project works. It might be possible to enhance it even further with careful study. Comparisons need to be made of gains with the enhanced program suggested above versus gains made under the previous versions of the program and in still other variations of intensity and sequence of training.

2. This research studied only the effects of training teachers in Interpersonal Skills applied to learning interactions. The gains demonstrated in student mental health indexes with this kind of program need to be compared with those of students under programs in which:

   a. *Teachers are trained in a "Promotion of Mental Health Curriculum"* which they teach to their students,

   b. *Teachers are trained in* **both** *Interpersonal Skills and a PMH Curriculum which they teach to their students,*

   c. *Interpersonal Skills are taught directly to students but* **not** *to their teachers,*

*For example, the **Teacher Education Program in Social Causality** developed from Dr. Ojemann's work with **Education in Human Behavior and Potential** and **One to Grow On** (NIMH).

    d.   *The PMH Curriculum is taught to students by teachers* **not** *trained in Interpersonal Skills, and, in addition, the Interpersonal Skills are taught directly to students (by other than their classroom teacher),*

    e.   *The PMH Curriculum is taught to students by teachers trained in Interpersonal Skills and, in addition, the students are directly taught Interpersonal Skills.*

The hypothesis of the researchers is that the greatest amount of gain on Student Mental Health Indices would be achieved by students in condition "e".

3.   This research was carried out with **in-service** teachers. The training program needs to be carried out **in toto** with **pre-service** teachers in a longitudinal study which will follow-up the trainees when they become in-service teachers and compare their functioning against the classroom functioning of 1st year teachers from traditional teacher education programs. It is the hypothesis of the researchers that such a program would result (1) in eventual levels of Interpersonal Skills functioning at or above the 4.0 level on the Process Scales and (2) reduce the rate of drop-out from the profession of the new, young teacher.

This hypothesis is based on a serendipitous bit of anecdotal data: Three of the NCHE student raters (who knew the measurement devices) did their practice teaching in the spring of 1974. Within the first two weeks of practice teaching, each of them, individually, came to the researchers for help "in reaching the students." The researchers gave them a crash course in Interpersonal Skills applied to teaching and requested tapes of their classroom functioning. During the final week of their student teaching, they were averaging about 3.6 on the Process Scales with comparable functioning in the Flanders' and Cognitive categories.

4.   One important project that needs to be undertaken is an investigation of the causative origins of the **deteriorative trend** across time from September till May that was detected in the Control Group Data. The current researchers hypothesize that it is related to physical functioning of the teachers. The problem could be approached through gathering periodic (1) physiological and physical functioning data and (2) classroom functioning data.

5.   The causative origins of the grade-level differences detected in the data need to be investigated.

6.   The study involving the effects of prior training of instructional leaders needs to be replicated with a larger sample.

7. Student response to the Classroom Functioning variables needs to be analyzed by student presage characteristics of age, I. Q., prior learning, race, and sex.

8. The relationship of Classroom Functioning variables with Student Outcomes (particularly Absenteeism) needs to be investigated using clinical research procedures to follow individuals through "chain of effect" relationships.

IMPLICATIONS BEYOND THE EDUCATIONAL CONTEXT

Because of the size and the nature of the sample involved in the research, it is possible to draw some implications to contexts in addition to that of education. These implications have to do with wider applications of Interpersonal Skills Training to the population in general and to leadership personnel in particular. They are presented below in syllogistic form.

Syllogism I:

IF (1) *a sample of 10,000 students comprising members from 3 ethnic groups can be considered an adequate sample of the general run of the child population,*

AND (2) *it has been demonstrated that raising the levels of interpersonal skills of the adults (teachers) with whom they interact causes mental health and cognitive benefits to accrue to those students,*

THEN (3) *it can be concluded that it would be worthwhile to raise levels of interpersonal skills on a widespread basis among the general population with whom children have frequent contacts, particularly the parent population.**

Syllogism II:

IF (1) *a sample of 500 teachers from two races can be considered an adequate sample of the general run of the population,*

AND (2) *it has been demonstrated that that sample can be trained to increase their levels of Interpersonal Functioning,*

THEN (3) *it can be concluded that properly conducted Interpersonal Skills Training can effectively increase the level of functioning of the population in general.*

---

*In line with Syllogism I, the current researchers have developed and are pilot testing Interpersonal Skills Training for Parents.

The qualifier "properly conducted" is inserted to ensure that consideration is given to the need to adapt the application modules when
Interpersonal Skills Training is transferred from context to context.

The three studies which dealt with the effects of the principal on
the functioning of the teachers in his/her school stimulated some
conclusions about leadership and/or managerial functioning in relation
to Interpersonal Skills Training. These conclusions are embodied in
Syllogisms III, IV, and V.

Syllogism III:

IF   *(1)*   *the principal/teacher relationship can be considered a status-leader/follower or manager/
employee relationship,*

AND   *(2)*   *it has been demonstrated that, in a largely self-
contained work situation (one adult and some young
people in a single room), the teacher can be strongly
enough affected by the principal's Interpersonal
Functioning that (a) his own work behavior can be
predicted by the level of the principal's and (b) his
reports of the attractiveness of his working environment and professional tasks can be significantly
differentiated according to who his principal is,*

AND   *(3)*   *the process of influence is a person-to-person interaction,*

THEN   *(4)*   *one should anticipate even stronger effects of the
leader's functioning in the more common situations
where contact between the leader/manager and his
follower/employees is more interactive and more
continuous.*

Syllogism IV:

IF   *(1)*   *the effect of training the principal/leader/
manager in Interpersonal Skills is to en-
hance the response of his teachers/followers/
employees to similar training,*

AND   *(2)*   *it is desirable to raise the levels of Interpersonal Skills for large numbers of the
population,*

THEN   *(3)*   *the place to begin is with Interpersonal
Skills Training at the status-leader/
managerial level.*

Syllogism V:

IF   *(1)*   *it is desirable that the population in
general utilize high levels of Interpersonal*

*Skills in their daily person-to-person
functioning on a widespread basis,*

AND   *(2)*   *it has been demonstrated that the
teacher/follower/worker with a high
functioning principal/status-leader/manager
uses increased levels of these skills,*

THEN   *(3)*   *the principal/status-leader/manager
should (a) be selected for leadership
position on the basis of his levels of
Interpersonal Functioning as well as
on other job-related criteria and (b)
should be held accountable for exercising
those skills in his day-to-day functioning.*

The above syllogisms are far-reaching in their effect and a few years ago would have been purely pie-in-the-sky dreaming, but not today. The technology for putting the pie on the table is now available. Both training and accountability tools have been developed in the last few years. The "Open Society" is a **possibility**, today. Tomorrow, it could be made a **reality**.

OVERVIEW

This section was included to provide the reader with the kinds of "tools" we used at the NCHE. Each of them is presented in two forms — a research scale and a teaching module.

The Carkhuff Model is represented by the most recent version of the scale for assessing level of interpersonal skills and a teaching module that can be delivered in approximately 60 to 90 minutes. The module can best be used to acquaint an audience with the skills involved or prepare them for more extensive training in these skills.

Bloom's Taxonomy is represented by a simplified scale for assessing the level of cognitive functioning in the classroom and a module for teaching the use of this scale.

Flanders' Interaction Analysis categories are presented along with a module appropriate for introducing these categories to teachers to let them analyze their own classroom interactions.

Carkhuff Interpersonal Skills Scale[1,2,3]

by Robert R. Carkhuff, Ph.D.
Carkhuff Institute of Human Technology
Amherst, Massachusetts

[1]**The Art of Helping III.** Amherst, Mass.: Human Resource Development Press, 1977.

[2]**The Skills of Teaching: Interpersonal Skills.** Amherst, Mass.: Human Resource Development Press, 1977.

[3]**Teacher-Student Interpersonal Skills Assessment Audiotape.** Amherst, Mass.: Human Resource Development Press, 1976.

CARKHUFF INTERPERSONAL SKILLS SCALE

Rating Levels	Functions Does teacher or helper response serve this function?	Format Does teacher or helper response serve this format?
1.0	No expression or expression unrelated to content	"I _____ " or "What _____ ?"
1.5	Expression related to content (usually as guidance or advice)	"I think you should _____ ."
2.0	Responding to content	"You're saying _____ ."
2.5	Responding to feeling	"You feel _____ ."
3.0	Responding to feeling and meaning	"You feel _____ because _____ ."
3.5	Personalizing problems	"You feel _____ because you cannot _____ ."
4.0	Personalizing goals	"You feel _____ because you cannot _____ and you want to _____ ."
4.5	Operationalizing goal	"Your goal is _____ ."
5.0	Developing steps	"Your steps are _____ ."

THE INTERPERSONAL SKILLS TEACHING MODULE
Contents

The purpose of this interpersonal skills teaching module will be to introduce you to some of the interpersonal skills which you need in order to help or teach someone to grow or develop constructively. The goal will be to increase your understanding of effective interpersonal skills.

Specifically, the objectives will be two-fold:

1) To increase the level of accuracy of your discriminations of interpersonal skills in teaching situations; and

2) To increase the level of effectiveness of your communication of interpersonal skills in teaching situations.

Before we begin, however, it will be helpful for you to get an index of where you are functioning now in your interpersonal skills. That way, you will know how much you have gained from the teaching module.

A   Communication Index
1.   Read the following:
a.   Background:

"Assume that you know a young child in the 12- to 14-year-old range, whether in your class or a friend or a neighbor. We will call her a learner. After having interacted with the learner over a period of time, she presents you with a problem."

b.   Instructions:

"Please formulate the most helpful response that you might make to the learner under the circumstance. Be as helpful as you can in communicating your understanding and a helpful, new direction for her. Formulate the response directly, just as you would if you were talking with her."

2.   Learner stimulus expression:

12-year-old girl: (Sadly)

"I really want to play in their games. But they never pick me. The only time I get to play with the boys is when they decide that they want to play our games."

B   Discrimination Index
1.   Rate responses.
a.   Background:

"Again, assume that the teachers involved have been interacting with the learner over a period of time and, after hearing the child's problems, respond in the most helpful manner that they can."

b.   Instructions:

"Rate each of the responses to the learner stimulus expressions using the following scale:

Level 1 – Very Ineffective: No understanding or direction.
Level 2 – Ineffective: No understanding, some direction.
Level 3 – Minimally Effective: Understanding with no direction.
Level 4 – Effective: Understanding and direction.
Level 5 – Very Effective: Understanding plus specific direction.

c.   Show the scale to the group.

2.   Learner stimulus expression:

12-year-old girl: (Sadly)

"I really want to play in their games. But they never pick me. The only time I get to play with the boys is when they decide that they want to play our games."

Teacher Responses:

1)   "I can understand that a girl would feel that way at your age, but later on, when you're older, you'll feel different."

2) "You're really going to have to work hard to assert yourself – to make them give you a chance."

3) "You feel sad because the boys never pick you."

4) "You feel disappointed in yourself because you haven't been able to get the boys to give you a chance and you want to be able to do that."

5) "You feel disappointed because you haven't stood up for yourself and you want to. Maybe we could practice some assertive behavior to help you stand up for yourself in these situations."

   3. Provide discrimination feedback.
      a. Display discrimination feedback figure.
         1) Review rating system.

a) **Level 1** – Responds to nothing (usually inane responses or stupid questions.)

b) **Level 2** – Initiates general direction for where learner wants or needs to be (usually an attempt at guidance or advice).

c) **Level 3** – Responds to where learner is (interchangeable response with the feeling and the reason for the feeling as expressed by the learner).

d) **Level 4** – Personalizes understanding of where learner is in relation to where learner wants to be (personalizes the learner's expression of experience of problems and goals).

e) **Level 5** – Initiates action programs to get from where learner is to where learner wants to be (develops goal and steps to goal which learner must take).

         2) Review all responses in regard to rating system.

a) Explain how each is rated.

b) Make sure teachers understand feedback.

      b. Calculate discrimination scores.

1) Obtain absolute deviations (independent of direction) of personal ratings from trained raters' ratings.

2) Add absolute deviations (independent of values of + or –).

3) Divide by number of items (in this case: 5).

4) The dividend is your average deviation or **discrimination score.**

Discrimination Feedback Figure

Personal Ratings		Trained Raters' Ratings	Deviation
2.0	–	1.0	1.0
4.0	–	2.0	2.0
3.0	–	3.0	0
2.0	–	4.0	2.0
3.0	–	5.0	2.0

$$\text{TOTAL:} \quad \frac{7.0}{5} = 1.4$$

Discrimination
Score

    c.   Your communication responses will be scored after post-test.

III. Presentation: Interpersonal Skills Teaching

A   **Display learning model** (Figure 1)

B   **Explain learner activities.**
1. **Exploring** where he or she is.

2. **Understanding** where he or she is in relation to where he or she wants to be.

3. **Acting** to get from where he or she is to where he or she wants to be.

C   **Explain teacher interpersonal skills**
1. Attending in order to involve learner in learning process.
    a. Explain attending briefly.
       1) Attending physically
          a) Squaring
          b) Leaning
          c) Eye Contact
       2) Observing
       3) Listening

    b. Illustrate attending
2. Responding to facilitate learner exploration.
3. Personalizing to facilitate learner understanding.
4. Initiating to facilitate learner acting.

D Introduce Tell-Show-Do teaching

1. Tell teachers what it is you want them to do and how to do it.

2. Show teachers what it is you want them to do and how to do it.

3. Provide teachers an opportunity to do it.

4. Follow training steps as follows: **Tell** Step 1 — **Show** Step 1 — **Do** Step 1; **Tell** Step 2 — **Show** Step 2 — **Do** Step 2; etc.

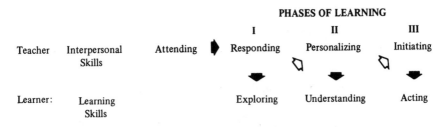

Figure 1. Learning Model

IV. Teaching Steps

A Responding Skills

1. **Tell**: Repeat the learner's expression verbatim.

    Show: Read the following, emphasizing that it is part of a continuous interaction.

John, a **13-year-old boy**: (Frustrated) "I try to do my homework and all. But all kinds of stuff comes up. You know, the guys come over and all. And sometimes it never gets done. Besides, that stuff is just too hard. Man, I'm probably going to go into the service anyway."

    Do: Read the following, and have the teachers repeat the content verbatim.

Paul, a **14-year-old boy**: (Angry) "I mean, I try not to be against them or anything. I really try to be friends. But if they don't want me, the heck with them. I can be mean, too."

2. **Tell**: Next, ask yourself, "How would I feel if I said that?"

    Show: Re-read John's statement. "I would feel upset."

    Do: Re-read Paul's statement. They ask themselves how they would feel. ("I feel angry.")

3. **Tell**: Respond to feeling. "You feel _____ "

    Show: Re-read John's statement. "You feel upset."

Do: Re-read Paul's statement. Let them respond to the feeling. ("You feel angry.")

4. **Tell**: Respond to the feeling and meaning. "You feel because _____."

Show: Re-read John's statement. "You feel upset because the stuff is so hard."

Do: Re-read Paul's statement. Ask them to respond to the feeling and meaning ("You feel angry because they don't want anything to do with you.")

B Personalizing Skills

1. **Tell**: Personalize the meaning: "You feel _____ because you _____ ."

Show: Re-read John's statement. "You feel upset because you are going to be left behind."

Do: Ask your teachers to personalize the meaning of Paul's statement. ("You feel angry because you are closed out.")

2. **Tell**: Personalize the problem: "You feel _____ because you can't _____ ."

Show: Re-read John's statement. "You feel upset because you can't handle that stuff."

Do: Ask your teachers to personalize the problem of Paul's statement. ("You feel angry because you can't handle the situation to make friends with them.")

3. **Tell**: Personalize the feeling based upon the personalized problem: "You feel _____ because you can't _____ ."

Show: Re-read John's statement. "You feel disappointed (down) because you can't handle that stuff."

Do: Ask your teachers to personalize the feeling based upon the problem in Paul's statement. ("You feel hurt (disappointed) because you can't make friends with them.")

4. **Tell**: Personalize the goal: "You feel _____ because you can't _____ and you want to _____ ."

Show: Re-read John's statement. "You feel disappointed (down) because you can't handle that stuff and you really want to."

Do: Ask your teachers to personalize the goal in Paul's statement. ("You feel hurt (disappointed) because you can't make friends and you really want to.")

1. **Tell**: Define the goal and its functions. "Your goal is
    so that _____ ."

    Show: For John's statement: "Your goal is handling your
    homework so that you won't feel so disappointed in yourself
    because you can't handle that stuff."

    Do: Ask your teachers to define the goal in Paul's statement
    ("Your goal is making friends so that you won't feel so hurt.")

2. **Tell**: Develop the first step: "Your first step is _____ ."

    Show: For John's statement: "Your first step is listening for
    the assignment."

    Do: Ask your teachers to develop the first step for Paul's goal.
    ("Your first step is greeting others.")

3. **Tell**: Develop the intermediary steps. "Your next steps are
    _____ ."

    Show: For John's statement: "Your intermediary steps are
    checking out the assignment, getting ready to do it and doing
    it."

    Do: Ask your teachers to develop the intermediary step to
    Paul's goal. ("Your intermediary steps are attending,
    responding and initiating.").

4. **Tell**: Develop the sub-steps by treating each previous step as a
    goal: "Your sub-steps are _____ . Your first sub-step is
    _____ ."

    Show: For John's goal.

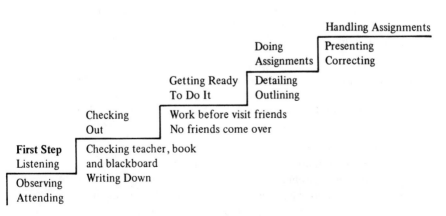

GOAL

Handling Assignments

Doing Assignments | Presenting Correcting

Getting Ready To Do It | Detailing Outlining

Checking Out | Work before visit friends
No friends come over

First Step Listening | Checking teacher, book and blackboard
Writing Down

Observing Attending

Do: Ask your teachers to develop the sub-steps for each step of Paul's program.

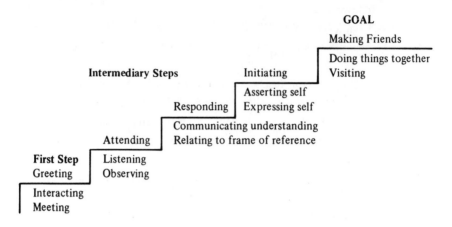

GOAL

Making Friends

Doing things together
Visiting

Intermediary Steps · Initiating

Asserting self
Expressing self

Responding

Communicating understanding
Relating to frame of reference

Attending

First Step
Greeting

Listening
Observing

Interacting
Meeting

V. Post-Test

A Communication Index

    1. **Formulate responses.**

        a. Background:

"Assume that you know a young child in the 12- to 14-year-old range, whether in your class or a friend or a neighbor. We will call her a learner. After having interacted with the learner over a period of time, she presents you with a problem."

        b. Instructions:

"Please formulate the most helpful response that you might make to the learner under the circumstances. Be as helpful as you can in communicating your understanding and a helpful, new direction for her. Formulate the response directly, just as you would if you were talking with her."

    2. **Learner stimulus expression**:

14-year-old girl: (Distressed)

"There's really no place for me. If I come on too strong, the guys don't want anything to do with me. And if I don't come on strong, I'm nobody."

B Discrimination Index

    1. **Rate responses.**

        a. Background:

"Again, assume that the teachers involved have been interacting with the learner over a period of time and, after hearing the learner's problems, respond in the most helpful manner that they can."

b.   Instructions:
"Rate each of the responses to the learner stimulus expressions using the following scale:
Level 1 – Very Ineffective: No understanding or direction.
Level 2 – Ineffective: No understanding, some direction.
Level 3 – Minimally Effective: Understanding with no direction.
Level 4 – Effective: Understanding and direction.
Level 5 – Very Effective: Understanding plus specific direction.

c.   Show the scale to the group.

2.   Learner stimulus expression:
14-year-old girl: (Distressed)
"There's really no place for me. If I come on too strong, the guys don't want anything to do with me. And if I don't come on strong, I'm nobody."

Teacher Responses:
1)   "You feel confused because there doesn't seem to be a real place for you."

2)   "You're really going to have to work on the guys so that they will accept you better."

3)   "You feel disillusioned because you haven't been able to be yourself and relate to the guys, too, and you really want to."

4)   "This is a most difficult age, especially for a girl in today's world."

5)   "You feel cheated because you can't be yourself and still relate and you want both. A first step might be to spend some time exploring who you are in relation to them and then trying to understand where you want to be."

C   Discrimination Feedback

1.

Stimulus Expressions	Helper Response	Where She Is	Where She Wants To Be	How To Get There	Trained Rater's Ratings
1	1	X			3.0
	2		X		2.0
	3	X	X		4.0
	4				1.0
	5	X	X	X	5.0

2.   **Calculate discrimination scores.**

D   Communication Feedback
1.   Rate Post-Communication.

2.   Rate Pre-Communication.

E   Review
1.   **Communication:**
a.   Use steps:

1) Respond to where she or he is.
2) Personalize where she or he wants to be.
3) Initiate programs for how to get there.

      b. Use format.

  2. **Discrimination**:
     a. Rate as follows:

	Where She Is	Where She Wants To Be	How To Get There
Level 1.0			
Level 2.0		X	
Level 3.0	X		
Level 4.0	X	X	
Level 5.0	X	X	X

VI. Summary

A   **Review Phases of Learning – Simple** (Figure 2)

B   **Review Phases of Learning – Complex** (Figure 3)
    1. **Show how communication skills operationalize helping skills:**
      a. Responding
      b. Personalizing
      c. Initiating

    2. **Show how communication skills facilitate learner activities:**
      a. Exploring
      b. Understanding
      c. Acting

C   **Emphasize applications in learning**

Figure 2. Phases of Learning – Simple

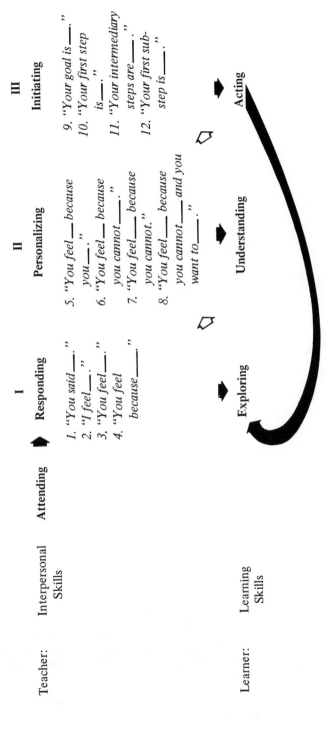

Figure 3. Phases of Learning - Complex

248

Cognitive Functioning Categories [1,2]

adaptation of Bloom's Taxonomy[3]

by

David N. Aspy and Flora N. Roebuck

[1] Interpersonal Skills Training for Teachers. Interim Report Number 2 of the National Consortium for Humanizing Education, Monroe, Louisiana, 1974.

[2] Metfessel, N.S., Michael, W. B. and Kirsner, D. A. Instrumentation of Bloom and Krathwohl's taxonomies for writing of educational objectives. **Psychology in the Schools,** 1969, 7(3), 227-231.

[3] Bloom, B. S., Englehart, M.D., Furst, E. J., Hill, W. H. and Krathwohl, D. R. **A taxonomy of educational objectives: Handbook I, The cognitive domain.** New York: Longmons, Green, 1956.

Instrumentation of the Taxonomy of Educational Objectives:
Cognitive Domain

Taxonomy Classification	Key Words	
	Examples of Infinitives	Examples of Direct Objects
1.00 Knowledge		
1.10 Knowledge of Specifics		
1.11 Knowledge of Terminology	to define, to distinguish, to acquire, to identify, to recall, to recognize	vocabulary terms, terminology, meaning(s), definitions, referents, elements
1.12 Knowledge of Specific Facts	to recall, to recognize, to acquire, to identify	facts, factual information (sources, names, dates, events, persons, places, time periods), properties, examples, phenomena
1.20 Knowledge of Ways and Means of Dealing with Specifics		
1.21 Knowledge of Conventions	to recall, to identify, to recognize, to acquire	form(s), conventions, uses, usage, rules, ways, devices, symbols, representations, style(s), format(s)
1.22 Knowledge of Trends, Sequences	to recall, to recognize, to acquire, to identify	action(s), processes, movements, continuity, development(s), trend(s), sequence(s), causes, relationship(s), forces, influences
1.23 Knowledge of Classifications and Categories	to recall, to recognize, to acquire, to identify	area(s), type(s), feature(s), class(es), set(s), division(s), arrangement(s), classification(s), category/categories
1.24 Knowledge of Criteria	to recall, to recognize, to acquire, to identify	criteria, basics, elements
1.25 Knowledge of Methodology	to recall, to recognize, to acquire, to identify	methods, techniques, approaches, uses, procedures, treatments
1.30 Knowledge of the Universals and Abstractions in a Field		

Taxonomy Classification	Key Words	
	Examples of Infinitives	Examples of Direct Objects
1.31 Knowledge of Principles, Generalizations	to recall, to recognize, to acquire, to identify	principle(s), generalization(s), proposition(s), fundamental(s), laws, principal elements, implication(s)
1.32 Knowledge of Theories and Structures	to recall, to recognize, to acquire, to identify	theories, bases, interrelations, structure(s), organization(s), formulation(s)
2.00 Comprehension		
2.10 Translation	to translate, to transform, to give in own words, to illustrate, to prepare, to read, to represent, to change, to rephrase, to restate	meaning(s), sample(s), definitions, abstractions, representations, words, phrases
2.20 Interpretation	to interpret, to reorder, to rearrange, to differentiate, to distinguish, to make, to draw, to explain, to demonstrate	relevancies, relationships, essentials, aspects, new view(s), qualifications, conclusions, methods, theories, abstractions
2.30 Extrapolation	to estimate, to infer, to conclude, to predict, to differentiate, to determine, to extend, to interpolate, to extrapolate, to restructure	consequences, implications, conclusions, factors, ramifications, meanings, corollaries, effects, probabilities
3.00 Application	to apply, to generalize, to relate, to choose, to develop, to organize, to use, to employ, to transfer, to restructure, to classify	principles, laws, conclusions, effects, methods, theories, abstractions, situations, generalizations, processes, phenomena, procedures
4.00 Analysis		
4.10 Analysis of Elements	to distinguish, to detect, to identify, to classify, to discriminate, to recognize, to categorize, to deduce	elements, hypothesis/ hypotheses, conclusions, assumptions, statements (of fact), statements (of intent), arguments, particulars

Taxonomy Classification	Examples of Infinitives	Examples of Direct Objects
4.20 Analysis of Relationships	to analyze, to contrast, to compare, to distinguish, to deduce	relationships, inter-relationships, relevance, relevancies, themes, evidence, fallacies, arguments, cause-effect(s), consistency/consistencies, parts, ideas, assumptions
4.30 Analysis of Organizational Principles	to analyze, to distinguish, to detect, to deduce	form(s), pattern(s), purpose(s), point(s) of view(s), techniques, bias(es), structure(s), theme(s), arrangement(s), organization(s)
5.00 Synthesis		
5.10 Production of a Unique Communication	to write, to tell, to relate, to produce, to constitute, to transmit, to originate, to modify, to document	structure(s), pattern(s), product(s), perform-ance(s), design(s), work(s), communica-tion(s), effort(s), specifics, composition(s)
5.20 Production of a Plan, or Proposed Set of Operations	to propose, to plan, to produce, to design, to modify, to specify	plan(s), objectives, specifications(s), schematic(s), opera-tions, ways, solu-tion(s), means
5.30 Derivation of a Set of Abstract Relations	to produce, to derive, to develop, to combine, to organize, to synthe-size, to classify, to deduce, to develop, to formulate, to modify	phenomena, taxonomies, concept(s), scheme(s), theories, relationships, abstractions, general-izations, hypothesis/hypotheses, percep-tions, ways, discoveries
6.00 Evaluation		
6.10 Judgments in Terms of Internal Evidence	to judge, to argue, to validate, to assess, to decide	accuracy/accuracies, consistency/con-sistencies, fallacies, reliability, flaws, errors, precision, exactness
6.20 Judgments in Terms of External Criteria	to judge, to argue, to consider, to compare, to contrast, to standardize, to appraise	ends, means, efficiency, economy/economies, utility, alternatives, courses of action, standards, theories, generalizations

252

Cognitive Functioning Categories
Training Module[1]
by
David N. Aspy and Flora N. Roebuck

[1]Interpersonal Skills Training for Teachers. Interim Report Number 2 of the
National Consortium for Humanizing Education, Monroe, Louisiana, 1974.

OBJECTIVES

1. To establish a trust relationship between the instructor and the trainees so that each trainee participates in discussion and contributes his own ideas.
2. To present the Cognitive Functioning Categories so that each trainee can distinguish the memory-recall categories from the thinking categories of given teacher-student verbal interchanges.
3. To develop proficiency in the use of the Cognitive Categories so that each trainee can identify the appropriate Cognitive category of a given teacher-student verbal interchange.
4. To provide skills practice in using the Cognitive Functioning Categories so that each trainee can model thinking and elicit thinking from students.

MATERIALS

1. Cognitive Functioning Categories (1 copy for each trainee)
2. Flanders' and Cognitive training tape (See Appendix C)
3. Master ratings for training tape (See Appendix B)
4. Metronome
5. Cassette recorder
6. Chalkboard and chalk
7. Copies of Worksheets for each trainee
8. Pencils
9. Transparencies, CT-1, CT-2
10. Illustration of Categories #1 (1 copy for each trainee – See Appendix A)
11. Copy of Practical Applications sheet for each trainee

PROCEDURES

Overview:

There are lots of things happening in the classroom. When you are trying to assess what's going on, you must pay attention to some things and ignore others. In order to avoid the "Noise" (i.e. what you don't want to listen to) you use a device to focus in on what you **do** want to listen to. The Cognitive Functioning Categories is such a device. Today you are going to learn how to listen for and to assess the Cognitive processes occurring in your classroom.

Cognition = act of knowing. The Cognitive instrument is concerned with the thinking or learning that is taking place. The Cognitive categories **describe the intellectual processes** occurring during the verbal interaction of the class. Emotions or affect are not of major concern. In fact, all primarily emotional-type exchanges are lumped together and put into one category to get rid of them.

There are three major divisions on the instrument.

1. Teacher Talk
2. Student Talk
3. Other: Affective Talk and Silence or Chaos

Training:

I. Learning takes place in many ways. Bloom's Taxonomy of Cognitive Processes has 6 descriptive levels of intellectual functioning. However, research has shown 85% of the intellectual processes in the classroom occur at the Memory-Recall level. Of the 15% that occur at the Thinking level, the teacher accounts for 10%. That means students generally spend only 5% of the class time in thinking activities. The Cognitive instrument, therefore, breaks the Teacher Talk and the Student Talk into only two process levels, RECALL and THINKING. USE TRANSPARENCY CT–#1: COGNITIVE MAJOR CONCEPTS.

A. **Memory** is recalling. That is, you learned it once before and now you are asked to remember it. Relating or telling experiences that happened to you falls into this category. In general, when the process covers familiar territory, it is put into the recall or memory category.

ASK TRAINEES: What are some examples of this? Possible answers: lecturing; reporting; reading when using skills that are already learned (learning a new word is not recall); singing; talking from experience (show and tell); giving proof of having studied or listened; and questions such as What? When? Where?

B. **Thinking** is the other kind of cognitive functioning to look at. Thinking is taking place when you:
1. Put separate bits of knowledge together and come up with something new that you didn't know before. For example, a second grader reading a word he had never seen before . . . He knows the letters, he knows the letter sounds, but he must integrate them to be able to say the word.
2. Apply knowledge from one place to another kind of situation. For example, solving a problem in math. The student knows the mathematical rules, but must determine which to apply in the problem context.

The thinking level of cognition frequently involves creativity and imagination. In general, when the process covers **new material** for the person doing it, it is called thinking. It is an **expansion** of the existing knowledge base. USE TRANSPARENCY CT-2: BREAKDOWN OF MENTAL PROCESSES.

II. Look at your copy of the Cognitive Functioning Categories. Numbers 1, 2, 3, and 4 are the teacher behavior categories. Numbers 1 and 2 are teacher memory talk – numbers 3 and 4 are thinking talk.

A. Look at Category 1. (ALLOW TIME TO READ). DISCUSS. THEN TELL TRAINEES. Look at number one on your worksheet. Write 3 statements you might make at this level in your classroom. ALLOW TIME FOR TRAINEES TO WRITE THEIR STATEMENTS, THEN ASK: What are some of the things you wrote? – DISCUSS.

> (Examples of the **kinds** of statements that might be suggested: Lecture, giving directions, acknowledging correctness of student's response, reading to students.)

B. Look at Category 2. (ALLOW TIME TO READ). DISCUSS. THEN TELL TRAINEES. In this category, the teacher is asking questions calling for recall or memory. On number 2 of your worksheet write 3 questions on this level that you might ask in your classroom. ALLOW TIME FOR THE TRAINEES TO WRITE THEIR QUESTIONS, THEN ASK: What are some of the questions you asked? DISCUSS AND EVALUATE LEVEL OF RESPONSES.

C. Look at Category 3. (ALLOW TIME TO READ). DISCUSS. THEN TELL TRAINEES. In this category, the teacher would be modeling how to analyze and how to solve. Most teachers do this **before** class, when they do their planning. It is very important, however, to plan to model analyzing and thinking **in** class as well. On number 3 of your worksheet, use the same topics or subjects as you used for your statements in number 1, but now write statements on those topics which analyze or solve instead of recall from memory.
Examples:

1) Columbus needed money to finance his trip, and since the King of Spain controlled that nation's money, he went to the king to ask him to pay for the voyage to find a short way to Asia.

2) From our oral practice today, I can see that you need practice on using the correct pronoun. On page 68 there is a good practice that will only take a few minutes.
ALLOW TIME FOR TRAINEES TO WRITE THEIR STATEMENTS. THEN ASK, What were some of the statements you wrote? DISCUSS. REQUIRE SUPPORT FOR CONSIDERING THE RESPONSE AS "THINKING" LEVEL.

D. Look at Category 4. (ALLOW TIME TO READ). DISCUSS. THEN TELL TRAINEES: The teacher is asking the student to analyze and think. Generally these are questions of How? Why? What if? and, What do you think? In the spaces of number 4 on your worksheet, use the **same topics** you used in number 2, but write questions asking the student to analyze or solve – to think.
Examples:

1) Why do you think Columbus wanted to go to China — or Asia?

2) When might it be helpful **to you** to know how to find the common denominator of a set of fractions? ALLOW TIME FOR TRAINEES TO WRITE THEIR QUESTIONS, THEN ASK TRAINEES: What are some of the questions you wrote? DISCUSS.

E. Look at Categories 5 and 6. (ALLOW TIME TO READ). DISCUSS. THEN TELL TRAINEES: These are like 1 and 2 except they refer to **student** talk instead of teacher talk. You can expect the student to function on levels 5 and 6 (memory) if the teacher functions on levels 1 and 2. In fact, it is very rare for a student to function on a level 7 (thinking statement) if the teacher has asked a level 2 (memory) question. On number 5 of your worksheet write 4 examples of student responses that would be classified as level 5 and 6. ALLOW TIME FOR TRAINEES TO WRITE THEIR EXAMPLES, THEN ASK, What did you list? DISCUSS.

Examples: Reading, specific answers, singing familiar songs, show and tell, questions about homework assignments, what to do, permission to go somewhere or do something.

F. Look at Categories 7 and 8. (ALLOW TIME TO READ). DISCUSS. THEN TELL TRAINEES: These are like categories 3 and 4 except they refer to **student** talk instead of teacher talk. Why do you think a student would function on a level 7 instead of a level 5? GIVE TIME FOR TRAINEES TO RESPOND. (Possible answers: Because teacher asked a level 4 or thinking question — or — He was an interested student who was excited about the subject — or — Class discussion stimulated it). ASK TRAINEES: Would these also be the reasons for a student to ask a level 8 — or thinking question? (Answers — most probably, there could be exceptions). What might be additional reasons?

G. As was noted at the beginning of this module, Categories 9 (affective talk) and 10 (silence or chaos) are not of major concern, and are lumped together. In Category 9 put laughter, argument (other than about intellectual matters), praise, and emotional statements. Category 10 would include time at the chalkboard, doing work in notebooks, watching a movie, group work, or actual chaos.

H. In using this instrument, coding should be done at regular intervals such as 3 or 5 seconds, with the descriptive category number recorded once for each interval. This produces a series of numbers which show not only what intellectual levels the teacher

and students are functioning on, but the sequence of functioning.
You can see what followed what.

III. **PRACTICE USING CATEGORIES WITH CONTROLLED MATE-RIALS**

A. DIVIDE THE TRAINING GROUPS INTO SUB-GROUPS OF SIX. TELL TRAINEES: Look at the paper titled **Illustration of Categories #1**. This is to give you practice in coding with the **Cognitive Functioning Categories**. It is a transcript of a continuous classroom interaction which has been divided into segments. TELL TRAINEES. In your small groups, you are to discuss this transcript and determine into which of the Cognitive categories each segment falls, then place the appropriate category number in the column to the right of the segment. You must have **one** category number for each segment and not more than two. In 10 minutes we will re-assemble the whole group and discuss the different ways each segment was classified.

ALLOW TIME FOR WORKING. THEN RE-ASSEMBLE AND DISCUSS DISCREPANT ANSWERS. REMEMBER, EVERYBODY IS RIGHT!

B. The important thing to look for is **patterns**.
PATTERNS. For example, on number 6 of your worksheet you will see 3 columns of numbers with a line under each column. Each column represents a sequence of class talk. Under each column write what that pattern describes.

DISCUSS EACH COLUMN SEQUENCE. POINTS TO BE MADE:

1)		2)		3)	
	1		2		4
	1		5		4
	1		2		7
	1		5		7
	1		2		7
	1		5		7
	1				7
Teacher Memory Statements		Teacher Question and Student Answer on Memory Levels		Teacher Question and Student Answers on Thinking Levels	

On number 7 of your worksheet, write 3 examples of cognitive patterns you would like to have in your classes. ALLOW TIME, THEN SHARE RESPONSES.

IV. **PRACTICE CODING CATEGORIES WITH SPONTANEOUS STIMULI: SUB-DIVIDE TRAINEES INTO GROUPS OF SIX.**

A. PAIR OFF TRAINEES AS TEACHER/STUDENT PAIRS. TELL TRAINEES: One pair at a time is to try to demonstrate higher levels of cognition while the remainder of the group act as observer/evaluators.

B. Each "teacher" of a teacher/student pair is to devise and ask a thinking question. The "student" is to answer it.

C. The other group members decide whether the question was a category 2 or 4 (Cognitive Scale), and whether the student's answer was a category 5 or 7. Whenever a question is evaluated as being a level 2, the group members each say how they could have rephrased the same question so that it would be a category 4.

D. Repeat these steps ("B" and "C") with the other teacher/student pairs until every member of your small group has been both a teacher and a student.

E. Repeat the exercise, but extend the interaction to two inter-changes. That is (1) the teacher asks a question, (2) the student answers, (3) the teacher responds to the student's answer, and (4) the student responds again. The teacher's response to the student may be either a question or a statement but her goal is to keep the interaction going at a high level of cognition.

F. The other group members code each of the four parts of the interchange. Then they discuss it and seek ways in which it could have been improved.

G. Repeat the exercise, but extend the interaction to as many interchanges as possible, providing that each response must be at a thinking level. (That is, the teacher can use only categories 3, 4, and 9; the student only categories 7, 8, & 9). The other members of the group code the responses. The interaction stops when either the teacher or student falls below a thinking level. Then another pair tries it.

NOTE: Step ("G") can be made into a game with the teacher/student pairs competing for high score. Scoring is 1 point for each two-part interchange (teacher/student) **completed**. The teacher/student pair "on deck" do not stop if they goof and get below the thinking level . . . instead they bluff and try to complete as many interchanges as possible before being "called." The other teacher/student pairs categorize each response and "call" when the interaction falls below the thinking level. The first pair to correctly "call" the on-deck pair get to be on deck next. If the "on-deck" pair does not agree with the call (that is, they do not agree that they have made a factual response) they can **challenge** the call. This means that the teacher/student pair who did not make the "call" act as judges and decide whether it was a correct call. If a challenge is made and the "call" is judged to be correct, (that is, the "on-deck" pair **had** made a factual response), the on-deck pair lose **two** points and the "calling" pair become "on-deck" pair. Scoring, then, is like this:

a.   1 point for each two-part interchange completed.

b.   "Call" ends turn of on-deck pair and gives turn to the calling pair.

c.   "Challenge" results in:

1)   on-deck pair loses two points and their turn if "call" was correctly made.

2)   "calling" pair loses one point and on-deck pair continues if "call" was made in error.

V.   **PRACTICE CODING TAPED CLASSROOM INTERACTIONS**

A.   Listen to one segment of the Cognitive training tape (See Appendix C). Turn the metronome to a slow speed and code the segment once every beat. Write code numbers in sequence on a sheet of paper. Remember that inside of one interval several categories may occur. The coder should code the category which is most significant for that interval. This could be the category which lasts the longest or the category which does not occur often, such as 3, 4, 7, and 8. DISCUSS AND COMPARE CODING BY COUNTING CATEGORIES, PLACEMENT, AND PATTERNS.

B.   REPEAT THIS PROCEDURE ON VARIOUS TRAINING TAPE SEGMENTS UNTIL THE DESIRED PROFICIENCY IS OBTAINED.

VI.   Now you have skills in measuring the levels of thinking that go on in your classroom. What you do with your skills is up to you. If you want to use your skills, here are some suggestions. CALL ATTENTION TO SHEET "PRACTICAL APPLICATIONS OF COGNITIVE CATE-GORIES." GO OVER ASSIGNMENTS WITH PARTICIPANTS.

OUTCOME INDICES

For objective 1:
Each individual is physically attentive, alert, and participates in the small group work.

For objective 2 and 3:
Each trainee codes teacher/student interchanges.

For objective 2 and 4:
Each trainee writes: a) teacher statements on both memory and thinking levels, and b) teacher questions which can elicit thinking from the student.

COGNITIVE FUNCTIONING CATEGORIES

PERSON		CATEGORY OF BEHAVIOR
TEACHER	**Memory**	1. Demonstrates knowledge of a fact (Memory or recall and recognition). 2. Solicits student to demonstrate knowledge of a fact.
	Thinking	3. Uses a fact (thinking) Examples: (a) to solve a problem or propose an attack on problem (b) to analyze a situation 4. Solicits student to use a fact (thinking) Examples: (a) to solve a problem (b) to analyze a situation
STUDENT	**Memory**	5. Demonstrates knowledge of a fact (memory or recall). 6. Solicits someone else to demonstrate knowledge of a fact.
	Thinking	7. Uses a fact (thinking) Examples: (a) to solve a problem (b) to analyze a situation 8. Solicits someone else to use a fact Examples: (a) to solve a problem (b) to analyze a situation
		9. Affective behavior 10. Silence or confusion

1   2   4
1   5   4
1   2   7
1   5   7
1   2   7
1   5   7
1   7

1. Tape Record one hour of your classroom interaction and play it over to yourself. Whenever you come to a section that you particularly **like**, stop and code it on Cognitive categories. See what it was that you or the students were doing which makes that a section which **you feel** was a **worthwhile learning** experience. Then, try to repeat the same kinds of patterns again. You might even plan a lesson just to get at that kind of Cognitive functioning. Tape it for yourself to listen to. CHALLENGE: See if you can reach a particular cognitive pattern whenever you wish.

2. Another thing to do with your tape is to look for a section that you **did not like**. Code it on Cognitive categories. See what it was that you or the students were doing that made you feel that was **not** a **worthwhile learning experience**. What could you have done to have changed the nature of the interaction?

3. Make a column in your lesson plan book called "Cognitive Pattern." When you plan each lesson, also plan the levels of cognition you want to use. Write it down as a Cognitive # pattern . . . for example, 2-5-2-5 or 1-2-5-1 or 4-7-3-4 or 3-4-7-8 or 4-7-8-3 or 4-7-8-7 or 2-5-6-4-7-8.

4. Once a week, plan a CHALLENGE lesson in which you will try to increase the number of responses in the thinking categories of Cognitive Functioning; that is, categories 3, 4, 7, and 8. For each week, pick **one** category you want to emphasize and then pick one of the lessons you will be teaching that week and set a goal for yourself for that lesson. Set the goal in terms of numbers of responses in that category per units of time. For example, you might say: During this lesson, I will make two Category 4 responses every five minutes. TAPE RECORD YOUR CHALLENGE LESSON. Listen to it later and code it for Cognitive categories. Did you make your goal? **If not**, try the same goal on another lesson. **If you did make it**, you might try for a higher frequency on this category in the next week's CHALLENGE lesson or you might pick another Cognitive category to work on.

5. Listen for student interaction on your recording of the CHALLENGE LESSON. What kind of student responses followed your use of a Cognitive category 3 or 4? Were the student responses near the end of the lesson (after you had used several category 3's or 4's) different than near the beginning? Did the students respond more frequently? Did the students do more thinking? Did the students do more initiating?

(a) Cognitive = act of knowing.

(b) Instrument focuses on intellectual activity — the **mental processes**. All emotional things — category 9.

(c) Learning processes categorized — **memory** and **thinking**.

(d) Memory — recalling. Identification, relating experiences.

(e) **Thinking** — involves creativity, imagination; covers new material; and expansion of existing knowledge base. Thinking: 1) combines separate bits of knowledge into something new, or 2) applies knowledge from one place to another.

CT-2: BREAKDOWN OF MENTAL PROCESS

MEMORY

1. Receives information

2. Repeats it back — checks comprehension

3. Puts two received informations together

THINKING

4. Creates something new for him. Solves a problem correctly.

Flanders' Interaction Analysis Training Module[1]
by
David N. Aspy and Flora N. Roebuck

[1]Interpersonal Skills Training for Teachers. Interim Report Number 2 of the
National Consortium for Humanizing Education, Monroe, Louisiana, 1974.

OBJECTIVES

1. To establish a trust relationship between the instructor and the trainees so that each trainee will feel secure enough to examine teaching behavior.
2. To present Flanders' Interaction Analysis so that each trainee comes to see it as one tool with which he can examine teaching behavior.
3. To present Flanders' Interaction Analysis so that each trainee can identify the category and/or categories of a given teacher-student interchange.
4. To develop proficiency in the use of Flanders' Interaction Analysis so that each trainee can identify the categories of verbal interaction at regular intervals.

MATERIALS

1. Flanders' Interaction Analysis (1 copy for each trainee)
2. Flanders' and Cognitive Training Tape (See Appendix C)
3. Master ratings for training tape (See Appendix B)
4. Metronome
5. Cassette recorder
6. Chalkboard and chalk
7. Paper
8. Pencils
9. Transparencies FT-1, FT-2
10. Overhead projector
11. Illustration of Categories 1, 2, and 3 (See Appendix A)
12. Copies of "Practical Applications of Flanders'" (1 copy for each trainee)

PROCEDURES

Overview

A great deal of research has been focused on devising some way of describing the things that are happening in the classroom. Dr. Ned Flanders developed an instrument with ten categories that tells: 1) who is talking, 2) what kind of talk it is, and 3) the sequence of the talk. This module is designed to show you how to use Flanders' Categories to examine your own teaching behaviors.

Training:

1. AS INTRODUCTION, ASK QUESTIONS ABOUT CLASSROOM INTERACTIONS AND ACTIVITIES. QUESTIONING COULD BE PHRASED IN THIS WAY: "What goes on in a classroom?" "Could we say upon examination that most of the activities are verbal? — that verbally we indicate each activity that is going on?" "What are

the different types of verbal exchange?" LIST RESPONSES ON BOARD. ACCEPT ALL ANSWERS.

2. THIS DISCUSSION IS FOLLOWED WITH AN EXPLANATION BY THE INSTRUCTOR OF FLANDERS' CATEGORIES. USE THE TRANSPARENCIES AT THIS POINT.* General points to be made:

   a. Categories are descriptive, not evaluative.
   b. 97% of everything that goes on in the classroom can be determined by verbal behavior, thus Flanders' instrument is effective for use in research.

   Apply Flanders' category numbers to different types of verbal behavior listed on board. If some need to be broken down, break them down through questioning a sample sequence; such as discussion brought on by asking a question, which initiated response, which in turn motivated someone else to respond. Three categories (4, 8, 9) are thus brought forth through closer examination.

3. SHOW TRANSPARENCY: FT-1; Function of Flanders' Categories. This transparency shows the functions of Flanders' categories. They describe — who is talking, the type of talk going on (refer back to listing of types on board), and what follows what in the type of talk (question followed by answer, followed by praise, etc.).

4. Examine individual copies of Flanders' Interaction Analysis.
   Point out these major divisions of Flanders' Interaction Analysis.

   a. The instrument is broken down as to who is talking — teacher, student, or no identifiable person (silence and chaos).
   b. Teacher talk is broken down as to whether the teacher is using indirect teaching methods (accepts feelings, praises, uses student ideas, asks questions) or whether she is using direct teaching methods (lectures, gives directions, justifies authority).

5. HAVE A TRAINEE TAKE EACH CATEGORY, READ, EXPLAIN, AND GIVE EXAMPLES. In the discussion of each category these points should be made:

   a. There is a distinction between categories 1 and 3. Category 1 is accepting **feelings**: Category 3 is accepting or using student **ideas**.
   b. Distinction between categories 8 and 9 — Category 8 is a teacher elicited response — called for directly by teacher. Category 9 is a student initiated response — the student wants to respond or to add something to class.

---

*Masters for the transparencies to be used with the module follow the module.

c. Emphasize that no category is "bad". The good teacher uses
whatever category is appropriate to the needs of the situation
and to the immediate instructional goals. Flexibility is
important – the ability to hit whatever category is needed by
the class.

d. Distinguish verbal tics from genuine praise as coded in
Category 2. Verbal tic – a "praise" type word used so
frequently that it becomes meaningless, such as "good",
"right", "O.K.", etc. Frequently these words are used as "let's
move along" signals.

6. DIVIDE INTO SMALL GROUPS AND DO ILLUSTRATION OF
CATEGORIES #1. (SEE APPENDIX A). RETURN TO LARGE
GROUP AND DISCUSS. Each group should be able to give reasons
for choosing the category that they did. No one is wrong. The
instructor simply gives his way of "hearing" the different responses
on the worksheet. Explain that the basic purpose is for the group
to "hear" it alike.

7. At this time it should be brought out that within one three-second
interval several exchanges may occur, or one person can use several
categories in an interval. The coder should code the category which
is most significant for that interval. This could be the category
which lasts the longest or the category which does not occur often,
such as 2 or 1. The important overall view is the pattern that the
sequence of numbers form. This pattern should be representative
of the verbal behavior.

8. PROVIDE BRIEF SUCCESS EXPERIENCE WITH CATEGORIES.
The trainees can relate their classroom experiences to Flanders'
categories by translating category numbers into familiar patterns of
interaction. Show the transparency of Flanders' Patterns: FT-2.
Indicate a pattern and ask the trainees to tell what is going on.

PATTERNS

a	b	c	d	e	f	g	h	i
4	4	4	5	5	5	5	4	4
8	10	10	5	5	5	5	8	8
4	4	8	4	6	6	5	2	9
8	8	9	4	8	10	9	9	2
4	4	9	8	8	7	5	9	3

Points to be made for each pattern:

a. Question and answer. More likely to be a drill than a
discussion.

b. Teacher asked question; student unable to answer, teacher
rephrased question; student answered.

    c.   Teacher asked question; pause for thinking; students answered question. Presence of 9 indicates the question stimulated thinking. The 10 can be indicative of thinking time or of confusion.

    d.   Lecture; question; answer. Question probably required recall of item in lecture.

    e.   Lecture; directions; student compliance with directions.

    f.   Lecture; directions; student failed to comply; teacher criticized students' failure.

    g.   Lecture interrupted by student question; reply to question.

    h.   Question; answer; praise; unsolicited participation.

    i.   Question; answer; unsolicited response; praise; clarifying and building on idea presented.

9. DIVIDE AGAIN INTO SMALL GROUPS AND HAVE EACH PARTICIPANT PLAN A 3-MINUTE LESSON USING AS MANY OF FLANDERS' CATEGORIES AS HE CAN. The lesson should be for the subject and grade level that he normally teaches. (ALLOW 5 MINUTES FOR PREPARATION) Then, as each presents his lesson, the other members of the small group role-play students. Tape record each presentation. After each member has taught his lesson, the small group will code the taped interaction at regular intervals of 5, 4, or 3 seconds.

10. The trainees should now listen to one segment of Flanders' training tape. Turn the metronome to a slow speed and code the segment once every beat. Write code numbers in sequence on a sheet of paper. Discuss and compare codings by counting categories, placement, and patterns. This should be repeated on various segments until desired proficiency is attained.

11. **TELL TRAINEES**:

Now you have the skills for measuring the interaction — the "What goes on" — in your classroom. What you do with them depends on you. If you want to use your skills, here are some suggestions.

READ AND DISCUSS "PRACTICAL APPLICATIONS OF FLANDERS' INTERACTION ANALYSIS."

OUTCOME INDICES

For objective 1:

Each trainee maintains an alert attentive physical posture and participates in the activities of the group.

For objective 2:

Each trainee identifies patterns in a verbal classroom interaction.

For objective 3:

Each trainee codes a written classroom teacher-pupil interaction.

For objective 4:

Each trainee codes a given tape segment at regular intervals.

Flanders' Interaction Analysis[1]
by
Dr. N. A. Flanders

---

[1]Flanders, N. A. **Analyzing Teaching Behavior.** Reading, Mass. Addison-Wesley, 1970.

TEACHER TALK	**Indirect Influence**	1.	**Accepts Feelings:** Accepts and clarifies the feeling tone of the students in a non-threatening manner. Feelings may be positive or negative. Predicting or recalling feelings are included.
		2.	**Praises or Encourages:** Praises or encourages student action or behavior. Jokes that release tension, not at the expense of another individual, nodding head or saying, "um hm?" or "go on" are included.
		3.	**Accepts or Uses Ideas of Student:** Clarifying, building, or developing ideas suggested by a student. As teacher brings more of his own ideas into play, shift to Category 5.
		4.	**Asks Questions:** Asking a question about content or procedure with the intent that a student answer.
	Direct Influence	5.	**Lecturing:** Giving facts or opinions about content or procedure; expressing his own ideas; asking rhetorical questions.
		6.	**Giving Directions:** Directions, commands, or orders to which a student is expected to comply.
		7.	**Criticizing or Justifying Authority:** Statements intended to change student behavior from non-acceptable to acceptable pattern; bawling someone out; stating why the teacher is doing what he is doing; extreme self-reference.
STUDENT TALK		8.	**Student Talk:** Response; talk by students in response to teacher. Teacher initiates the contact or solicits student statement.
		9.	**Student Talk:** Initiation; talk by students which they initiate. If "calling on" student is only to indicate who may talk next, observer must decide whether student wanted to talk. If he did, use this category.
		10.	**Silence or Confusion:** Pauses, short periods of silence and periods of confusion in which communication cannot be understood by the observer.

1. Tape record one hour of your classroom interaction and play it over to yourself. Whenever you come to a section that you **particularly** like, stop and code in on Flanders' Categories. See what it was that you or the students were doing which makes that a section which **you feel** was a **worthwhile** learning experience. Then, try to repeat the same kinds of patterns again. You might even plan a lesson just to get at the kind of interaction and tape it for yourself to listen to. CHALLENGE: See if you can reach a particular interaction pattern whenever you wish.

2. Another thing to do with your tape is to look for a section that **you did not like.** Code in on Flanders' Categories. See what it was that you or the students were doing that made you feel this was **not** a worthwhile learning experience. What could you have done to have changed the nature of the interaction?

3. Make a column in your lesson plan book called "Flanders' Patterns." When you plan each lesson, also plan the kind of interaction you want to have. Write it down as a Flanders' # pattern . . . for example:
   4-8-2-4 or 4-9-3-4 or 4-9-1-9 or 5-6-8-9

4. Once a week, plan a CHALLENGE lesson in which you will try to increase the number of responses you make in the indirect areas of Flanders', particularly categories 1, 2, and 3. For each week, pick **one** category you want to emphasize and then pick one of the lessons you will be teaching that week and set a goal for yourself for that lesson. **Set the goal in terms of the number of responses in that category per units of time.** For example, you might say: During this lesson, I will make two category 3 responses every five minutes. TAPE RECORD YOUR CHALLENGE LESSON. Listen to it later and code it for Flanders' categories. Did you make your goal? **If not,** try the same goal on another lesson. **If you did make it,** you might try for a higher frequency on this category in the next week's CHALLENGE lesson or you might pick **another** Flanders' category to work on.

5. Listen for student interaction on your recording of the CHALLENGE LESSON. What kind of student responses followed your use of a category 1, 2, or 3? Were the student responses near the end of the lesson (after you had used several category 1, 2, or 3's) different from those near the beginning? Did the students respond more frequently? Did the students do more thinking? Did the students do more initiation?

FT-1: FUNCTION OF FLANDERS' CATEGORIES

1. DESCRIPTIVE (non-evaluative)
   (a.) WHO IS TALKING?
   (b.) TYPE OF TALK
   (c.) SEQUENCE OF TALK (what follows what)

FT-2: FLANDERS' PATTERNS

A	B	C	D	E	F	G	H	I
4	4	4	5	5	5	5	4	4
8	10	10	5	5	5	5	8	8
4	4	8	4	6	6	5	2	9
8	8	9	4	8	10	9	9	2
4	4	9	8	8	7	5	9	3

APPENDICES

Segment		Illustration of Categories #1 High School English Class	Flanders' Category	Cognitive Category
A	**Teacher:**	I think you were very perceptive in writing your essays . . .	2	1
B	**Teacher:**	. . . and I think that from the essays you have written we can develop in the classroom a fine scale that would really be meaningful, one that would mean something to students who were trying to evaluate their teacher's performance and mean something to the teacher who is using the evaluation system.	3–5*	1
C	**Teacher:**	Now, the first thing we do, some of you said your best-liked teacher and your best teacher were not the same person. Would you clarify that? Someone?	4	4
D	**Student: A:**	Sometimes we have a real good time in class but we don't learn anything.	8–9	7
E	**Student: B:**	Sometimes we have a bad time but we learn a great deal.	9	7
F	**Teacher:**	Is it possible to have a good time and still learn something, though?	4	4
G	**Student: C:**	We should.	8	7
H	**Teacher:**	Does that happen often?	4	2
I	**Student: D:**	We feel like we are wasting our time if we don't learn anything.	9	7
J	**Teacher:**	I think that is a very important statement. It's nice to have fun but you are here to learn. Right?	2–3	3
K	**Student: B:**	If I want to have fun, I go out and drink beer.	9	5
L	**Class:**	(LOUD, LONG LAUGH)	10	10
M	**Student: C:**	Go to the swimming hole or someplace.	9	5

*Moves from category 3 to category 5.

Segment		(Cont'd) Illustration of Categories #1 High School English Class	Flanders' Category	Cognitive Category
N	Teacher:	Shouldn't learning be fun?	4	4
O	Student: B:	It should be fun but not funny.	8	7
P	Teacher:	I think you have a valid point in that it shouldn't be a party; that learning should take place.	3	1–3
Q	Student: A:	If we go home and it has been fun in class, but then we can't work the problems and we don't know what to do and make bad grades, then it's not so funny.	9	7
R	Student: C:	Sometimes I worry about next year. I'm having fun this year, but I bet next year it is going to be hard.	9	7
S	Teacher:	You are afraid you won't be prepared for next year.	1	9
T	Student:	Yes, and I want my teacher now to teach the things I need to know then.	9	7
U	Teacher:	O.K., you all indicated on your papers that you think that the teacher should be evaluated on the knowledge of the subject matter even though most of you think to yourself that most of your teachers were well prepared in this area.	3–5	1
V	Teacher:	Are there any disagreements with that statement?	4	4
W	Student: C:	Some teachers may think they are well prepared but they aren't planning on our reading the book because the book may say one thing and then they may say something else completely different and then if you point it out to them they get angry.	8–9	7
X	Teacher:	That is a **good** observation and it . . .	2	9
Y	Teacher:	. . . brings up another quality that we will be talking about further down the line, the fact that some teachers resent ever being wrong.	3–5	1

Segment		(Cont'd) Illustration of Categories #1 High School English Class	Flanders' Category	Cognitive Category
Z	**Student: A:**	I think sometimes some of my teachers act like they are condemning some of my other teachers for something my other teachers are doing.	9	7
AA	**Student: C:**	I don't understand.	9	8
BB	**Teacher:**	I do, I think he means that sometimes the teacher criticizes one of his other colleagues in front of his class.	3	3
CC	**Student: D:**	Right, some of my teachers do that.	9	7
DD	**Teacher:**	You think that is not good?	4	4
EE	**Student: D:**	Yeah, 'cause it makes us think well there's a teacher talking about other teachers.	8–9	7
FF	**Student: C:**	And if they talk about other teachers, what do they say about us behind our backs?	9	7
GG	**Teacher:**	Among teachers, they can call that professionalism. Their relationship within the profession itself. Would you like to add a category, professionalism to the scale we are developing?	3–4	1–2
HH	**Student: A:**	They don't act like teachers.	9	7
II	**Teacher:**	You mean, they don't act as you think teachers should.	3	1–3
JJ	**Student: D:**	I had teachers who never learned all the students' names during the year.	9	5
KK	**Teacher:**	You resent their lack of interest in you as an individual.	1	9
LL	**Teacher:**	I'm afraid I'm pretty bad about that in my classes, too.	3–5	1
MM	**Student: A:**	Old lady Adams has pets and I don't think that's fair.	9	9
NN	**Teacher:**	We must keep this on an anonymous scale because we are not dealing in specific personalities.	7	9

Segment		Illustration of Categories #2 High School Speech Class	Flanders' Category	Cognitive Category
A	**Teacher:**	Good morning class. I want to remind you that your speech communication models are due Friday. Please do not wait until Thursday night to start them. Put them on my desk the first thing Friday.	6	1
B		(Three Second Pause)	10	10
C	**Teacher:**	We were talking about the elements of persuasion yesterday when the bell rang. We noted that there were three components.	5	1
D	**Teacher:**	Who remembers what they are?	4	2
E	**Student: A:**	Ethical proof, emotional proof, and logical proof.	8	5
F	**Teacher:**	Good, now which of these do you think is the most important?	4	4
G	**Student: A:**	Ethical proof is the most important because if the speaker doesn't have a good personality, or image, or reputation, you won't listen to him.	8–9	7
H	**Student: B:**	I would think that the emotional aspect would be more important, because after all, he's trying to get the audience to accept what he's saying. H could do it better if he appealed directly to them.	9	7
I	**Teacher:**	In other words, you think that the most powerful tool is in the audience and not in the speaker himself.	3	3
J	**Student: B:**	Well, yeah, if he can get the audience "with" him, emotions can sweep people along and be a strong persuasive power.	9	7
K	**Student: C:**	But you're looking at it wrong. We want to know what the speaker does, not what the audience does.	9	5
L	**Student: B:**	It is the speaker using the audience's emotions, Dummy!	9	5
M	**Student: C:**	Dummy yourself! I can think what I want!	9	9

Segment			(Cont'd) Illustration of Categories #2 High School Speech Class	Flanders' Category	Cognitive Category
N	Teacher:		It makes you mad to be labeled, especially when you are reasoning the facts as you see them, and you both are exploring the same problem from different angles.	1	9–3
O	Student: C:		Ya know, I guess I just did what an audience would do if a speaker called them a name.	9	7
P	Teacher:		That is a very perceptive statement. Since you react in anger to being labeled, you can understand how an audience would react if a speaker called them a name.	2–3	3
Q	Student: B:		Well, now I can see what happens if the speaker resorts to name-calling.	9	7
R	Teacher:		This brings up a good point. Let's list speaker actions that arouse audience emotions. We can begin with what just happened here . . .	3	3
S	Teacher:		"Antagonizing audience by labeling them." Any other ideas about what arouses audience emotion?	5–4	1–4
T	(Three Second Pause) Teacher writes on board.			10	10
U	Student: D:		I think a speaker would want to make the audience feel he is "one of them," you can trust me because we're alike type of thing.	9	7
V	Teacher:		Great. We sometimes call that "Plain folks Appeal."	2–3	1
W	(Three Second Pause) Teacher writes on board.			10	10
X	Student: E:		How about when the speaker makes everything seem bad on one side and good on the other, and we're good, so naturally we all fight the bad.	9	7
Y	Teacher:		Do you mean like saying Communism is bad, so we have to hate the Russians?	3–4	3

Z	**Student:** Yeah, somethin' like that. **C:**	8	5
AA	**Teacher:** Since everybody else feels this way, you ought to feel this way, too. Sort of "you, too . . ."	3	1
BB	(Three Second Pause) Teacher writes on board.	10	10

Segment		Illustration of Categories #3 College Educational Psychology Class	Flanders' Category	Cognitive Category
A	**Teacher:**	Good morning. Today I want to continue with our discussion of learning theory, so I'd like for you to get some paper and take notes. I'll collect the notebooks at the end of the week and grade them for completeness and order.	6	1
B	(Pause)		10	10
C	**Teacher:**	Yesterday we discussed the idea that there are several different explanations for human learning, and yes, it is possible to divide them into two general groups. This is something like the biological classification of animals and plants.	5	1
D	**Teacher:**	Now, who can name the two major families of learning theory?	4	2
E	**Student: A:**	The two major families are behavioristic and field theory?	8	5
F	**Teacher:**	Right. Now, which one of the families deals primarily with precise factors and which considers more general components of learning? Maybe it would be clearer to ask which of the two families is more scientifically rigorous?	4	2
G	**Student: B:**	The behavioristic family tends to be more scientifically rigorous, and tends to deal with very precise factors of human learning.	8	5
H	**Teacher:**	Right. What are some reasons why there are different kinds of learning theories? That is, if we're talking about the way people learn, why have we come to different conclusions?	4	4
I	**Student: A:**	Well, people don't see things the same way. It's like the expression, "Beauty is in the eye of the beholder."	8	7

Segment			(Cont'd) Illustration of Categories #3 College Educational Psychology Class	Flanders' Category	Cognitive Category
J	Student: C:		You know I think the real problem is that we're not scientific enough in our study of learning. What I'd like to see is for someone to try all the learning theories on the same group of students and find which one explains their learning.	9	7
K	Teacher:		If I hear you right, what you'd like to do is to test the theories in a "real" situation so you could decide which one you think is the right explanation.	3	3
L	Student: C:		Yeah, surely one of the theories is better than the others, or at least we should have some clues after all the researching we've been doing.	9	7
M	Student: B:		Hey, it seems to me you're hung up on the notion that knowledge must be either right or wrong. You seem to like categories rather than dealing in shades of gray.	9	7
N	Teacher:		You must see his thinking about learning theory as only a part of his more general thought processes which you feel are focused around categories.	3	3
O	Student: C:		Maybe I do deal in "Black and White" thinking but putting a label on me is not dealing with the problem of how people learn.	9	7
P	Teacher:		If I'm not mistaken you feel a little upset because he avoided your question and tried to make your thought processes the problem. I certainly can understand your feelings and want you to . . .	1	9
Q	Teacher:		. . . know that I found your questions very stimulating. In fact, the class's enthusiasm has been very refreshing to me. I really like your active minds. Let's keep it going.	2	9

Segment			(Cont'd) Illustration of Categories #3 College Educational Psychology Class	Flanders' Category	Cognitive Category
R	Student:	C:	Great! I did feel defensive, but I'd like to suggest seriously that we conduct studies of learning theories in this class. I want to try them under controlled conditions. I really want to know about them!	9	9
S	Teacher:		Wonderful! You make me feel excited about that approach.	2	9
T	Teacher:		Does anyone have specific suggestions about how we could do this study?	4	4
U	Student:		I do, but I'm not sure of all the details. We could be "Guinea Pigs" for each other and each of us could conduct his own experiment and see for himself.	8–9	7
V	Teacher:		Good suggestion! We could each take one theory and apply it to a learning situation.	2–3	3

Master ratings for the three basic training tapes are displayed on the following pages. The master ratings on each sheet are arranged sequentially by number as they occur on **that** tape.

Some of the segments are repeated on the different training tapes. This is to demonstrate behavior correspondence among ratings on the seven instruments. Frequently, a behavior that is a high or low example on one scale is also a high or low example on another. The chart below shows the various locations of repeated segments.

On Flanders' and Cognitive Tape	On Meaning Tape	On Student Involvement
Segment 1	Segment 5	Segment 7
Segment 2	Segment 9	–
Segment 3	Segment 17	Segment 4
Segment 4	Segment 2	–
Segment 5	Segment 11	–
Segment 6	–	Segment 8
Segment 7	Segment 16	–
Segment 9	Segment 6	Segment 5
Segment 10	–	Segment 9
Segment 12	Segment 3	–
Segment 13	–	Segment 11
Segment 14	Segment 14	–
–	Segment 7	Segment 1
–	Segment 8	Segment 2
–	Segment 15	Segment 10

MASTER RATINGS FOR FLANDERS' AND COGNITIVE TRAINING TAPE

Segment	Approximate Time	Level-Subject	Comments	Flanders' Category	Cognitive Category	Meaning	Genuineness	Success Promotion	Respect	Student Involvement
1	3 min.	Secondary History	Low energy level. Tone of voice monotonous; rate of speaking slow. Good example of low Success Promotion. Teacher fills up time with his own low level usage of time. Student resistance shown in questions: "What page?" "Explain in simple terms."	5, 9, 10	1, 6, 10	1.3	1.3	1.7	1.5	2.3
2	2 min.	Elementary English	Low energy level. Teacher's tone and rate of speaking have repeated pattern which detracts. Uses no praise.	4, 5, 8	1, 2, 5, 10	2.3	2.5	2.5	2.5	2.7
3	3 min.	Elementary Reading (Word analysis)	Low on all process scales. Teacher punishes. Tone quality of students: monotone, subdued.	4, 5, 6, 7, 8	1, 2, 5, 9	1.5	1.7	1.5	1.5	2.3

MASTER RATINGS FOR FLANDERS' AND COGNITIVE TRAINING TAPE (Cont'd)

Segment	Approximate Time	Level-Subject	Comments	Flanders' Category	Cognitive Category	Meaning	Genuineness	Success Promotion	Respect	Student Involvement
4	4 min. 30 sec.	Elementary Science	Very structured class. Very low on all process scales. Teacher makes same errors she corrects students for making. Good example of clues to "faked" or "rehearsed" interaction.	4, 5, 6, 7, 8, 9	1, 2, 5, 6, 9	1.7	1.7	1.5	1.7	2.5
5	2 min.	Elementary Reading (Film Discussion)	This teacher uses Flanders' 1, although not frequently. She interrupts the feeling response with her own feelings. High on all process scales.	1, 3, 4, 5, 8, 9	1, 2, 5, 6, 7, 9	4.0	3.5	3.5	3.7	3.7
6	3 min.	Secondary Social Studies	Some praise. Some involvement elicited. One confrontation (Flanders' 7) on segment with no proper base laid for it.	2, 4, 5, 7, 8, 9	1, 2, 4, 5, 7, 9	3.0	3.0	2.7	3.0	3.0

MASTER RATINGS FOR FLANDERS' AND COGNITIVE TRAINING TAPE (Cont'd)

Segment	Time Approximate	Level-Subject	Comments	Flanders' Category	Cognitive Category	Meaning	Genuineness	Success Promotion	Respect	Student Involvement
7	4 min.	Elementary Special Education Science (Animals)	Teacher uses good praise; it's specific. He understands his students and has great patience. Flanders' 7 occurs when child answers out of turn. He exhibits good level of Respect and waits for students to think.	2, 3, 4, 5, 6, 7, 8, 9	1, 2, 4, 5, 7, 9	3.3	3.5	3.3	3.5	3.5
8	3 min.	Secondary Biology	Praise is mainly in vocal tone. Very genuine. Uses no feeling words. Applies new concepts to familiar situations. Flanders' 6 is "calling on" students.	3, 4, 5, 6, 8, 9, 10	1, 2, 3, 4, 5, 6, 7, 8, 9, 10	3.0	3.5	3.5	3.5	3.7
9	4 min.	Elementary Science	Class is completely student oriented. Teacher relates this lesson to his students at a very high cognitive level. Excellent example of Respect: "No, I believe you . . ."	2, 3, 4, 5, 8, 9	1, 2, 4, 5, 6, 7, 8, 9	4.5	4.5	4.5	5.0	5.0

MASTER RATINGS FOR FLANDERS' AND COGNITIVE TRAINING TAPE (Cont'd)

Segment	Approximate Time	Level-Subject	Comments	Flanders' Category	Cognitive Category	Meaning	Genuineness	Success Promotion	Respect	Student Involvement
10	2 min.	Elementary Science (Communication)	Teacher accepts all answers. Allows students to discuss. Students are eager to participate, exploring new ideas within subject area.	2, 4, 5, 8, 9	1, 2, 4, 5, 7, 9	3.3	3.7	3.7	3.7	3.7
11	4 min.	Secondary English (Crossword) Puzzle	Praise not specific, "Someone knows their geography." Students are allowed to participate. Teacher talks "over" students if she does not recognize them. Thinking-applying words, analyzing puzzle.	2, 3, 4, 5, 6, 8, 9	1, 2, 3, 4, 5, 7, 9	2.7	2.7	2.7	3.0	3.3
12	3 min.	Elementary English	Very person-to-person teaching. Accepts student ideas, works to expand them. Some feeling responses but without feeling words. On this level "making up sentences" is a thinking activity.	2, 3, 4, 5, 6, 8, 9	1, 2, 4, 5, 7, 9	3.7	3.7	3.5	3.5	3.5

MASTER RATINGS FOR FLANDERS' AND COGNITIVE TRAINING TAPE (Cont'd)

Segment	Approximate Time	Level-Subject	Comments	Flanders' Category	Cognitive Category	Meaning	Genuineness	Success Promotion	Respect	Student Involvement
13	3 min.	Secondary Science (Sound Vibration)	Excellent thinking stimulated. Teacher occasionally uses mild words to convey feelings. Responds to all of his students' questions. Students ask good questions.	2, 3, 4, 5, 8, 9	1, 2, 3, 4, 5, 6, 7, 8, 9	3.5	3.5	3.7	3.5	3.7
14	2 min.	Elementary Reading	Low Respect and Genuineness. Teacher answers own question; talks "down" to her students; role-plays "teacher" with tone and words.	4, 5, 6, 8	1, 2, 5	2.0	2.0	2.0	2.0	2.7

MASTER RATINGS FOR MEANING TRAINING TAPE

Segment	Time Approximate	Level-Subject	Comments	Flanders' Category	Cognitive Category	Meaning	Genuineness	Success Promotion	Respect	Student Involvement
1	3 min.	Secondary Science (Sound Vibration)	High Respect & Student Involvement. Good encouragement. Praises with vocal warmth. Ability to question excellent – stimulates thinking.	2, 3, 4, 5, 8, 9	1, 2, 4, 5, 6, 7 9	3.5	3.5	3.5	3.5	3.5
2	4 min.	Elementary Science (Birds)	Very structured class. Very low on all affective scales. Teacher makes same errors she corrects students for making. Good example of clues to "faked" or "rehearsed" interaction.	4, 5, 6, 7 8, 9	1, 2, 5, 6 9	1.7	1.7	1.5	1.7	2.5
3	3 min.	Elementary English	Very person-to-person teaching. Accepts student ideas, works to expand them. Some feeling responses but without specific feeling words. On this level "making up sentences" is thinking.	2, 3,	1, 2,	3.7	3.7	3.5	3.5	3.5

MASTER RATINGS FOR MEANING TRAINING TAPE (Cont'd)

Segment	Time Approximate	Level-Subject	Comments	Flanders' Category	Cognitive Category	Meaning	Genuineness	Success Promotion	Respect	Student Involvement
4	3 min.	Secondary English	Teacher's tone quality subtracts-monotone, singsongy. Uses little praise. She is mechanical.	2, 4, 5, 6, 8	1, 2, 5. 9	2.7	2.7	2.5	3.0	3.0
5	3 min.	Secondary History	Low energy level: tone of voice monotonous, rate of speaking slow. Little attention to student cues. Teacher fills up time with his low level usage of time. Student resistance shown in questions: "What page?" "Explain in simple terms."	5, 9, 10	1, 6, 10	1.3	1.3	1.7	1.5	2.3
6	4 min.	Elementary Science	Class is completely student oriented. Teacher relates this lesson to his students at a very high cognitive level. Excellent example of Respect: "No I believe you . . . ."	2, 3, 4, 5, 8, 9	1, 2, 4, 5, 6, 7, 8, 9	4.5	4.5	4.5	5.0	5.0

MASTER RATINGS FOR MEANING TRAINING TAPE (Cont'd)

Segment	Approximate Time	Level-Subject	Comments	Flanders' Category	Cognitive Category	Meaning	Genuineness	Success Promotion	Respect	Student Involvement
7	2 min. 30 sec.	Elementary Music	Low energy level for teacher. Vocal monotone, subdued. Little affect. Students meet requirements of teacher but nothing more.	4, 5, 6, 8	1, 2, 5	2.5	2.5	2.3	2.5	3.0
8	3 min. 30 sec.	Secondary Math	Teacher has low reserves of energy. Teacher's "good" is not praise, it is used sarcastically. Low Respect: "Are you sick today?" Student's response forced, hostile.	4, 5, 6, 7, 8	1, 2, 5, 9	1.3	1.3	1.5	1.0	2.0
9	2 min.	Elementary English	Low energy level. Teacher's tone and rate have repetitious pattern which detracts. Uses no praise or feeling words.	4, 5, 8	1, 2, 5, 10	2.3	2.5	2.5	2.5	2.7
10	2 min. 30 sec.	Elementary Reading	Low energy. Complete disregard for student. Every teacher response is punishing, almost a Flanders' 7.	5, 6, 7, 8	1, 5, 9	1.0	1.0	1.0	1.0	2.0

MASTER RATINGS FOR MEANING TRAINING TAPE (Cont'd.)

Segment	Approximate Time	Level-Subject	Comments	Flanders' Category	Cognitive Category	Meaning	Genuineness	Success Promotion	Respect	Student Involvement
11	2 min.	Elementary Reading (Film Discussion)	Teacher uses Flanders' 1 although not frequently. She interrupts the feeling **response** with her own feelings. High on all process scales.	1, 3, 4, 5, 8, 9	1, 2, 4, 5, 7, 9	4.0	3.5	3.5	3.7	3.7
12	2 min. 30 sec.	Elementary Math (Counting)	Good attention to cues. Allows student to talk about song. Much praise and encouragement.	2, 4, 5, 6, 8	1, 2, 5, 9	3.7	3.5	3.7	3.5	3.5
13	4 min.	Secondary Math	Good examples of Low Success Promotion: "That's all we're going to talk about." "That's irrelevant." Antagonistic tone; voice tends towards monotone, machine-gun.	4, 5, 6, 8, 9	1, 2, 4, 5, 6, 7	2.0	2.3	2.0	2.5	2.5
14	2 min.	Elementary Reading	Low Respect and Genuineness. Teacher answers own questions; talks "down" to her students; role-plays "teacher" with tone and words.	4, 5, 6, 8	1, 2, 5	2.0	2.0	2.0	2.0	2.7

MASTER RATINGS FOR MEANING TRAINING TAPE (Cont'd)

Segment	Time Approximate	Level-Subject	Comments	Flanders' Category	Cognitive Category	Meaning	Genuineness	Success Promotion	Respect	Student Involvement
15	2 min.	Elementary Reading	Good example of low Genuineness. Contrast "teaching" voice throughout segment with last statement on segment.	2, 4, 5, 6, 8	1, 2, 5, 9	2.5	2.5	2.5	2.5	2.7
16	4 min.	Elementary Special Education	Teacher uses good praise; it's specific. He understands his students and has great patience. F-7 (structuring not punishing) occurs when child answers out of turn.	2, 3, 4, 5, 6, 7, 8, 9	1, 2, 4, 5, 7, 9	3.3	3.5	3.3	3.5	3.5
17	3 min.	Elementary Reading	Low on all process scales. Teacher punishes instead of encouraging. Tone quality of students is monotone, subdued.	4, 5, 6, 7, 8	1, 2, 5, 9	1.5	1.7	1.5	1.5	2.3

MASTER RATINGS FOR STUDENT INVOLVEMENT TRAINING TAPE

Segment	Approximate Time	Level-Subject	Comments	Flanders' Category	Cognitive Category	Meaning	Genuineness	Success Promotion	Respect	Student Involvement
1	2 min.	Elementary Music	Low energy level for teacher. Tone monotone, subdued. Little affect. Students meet requirements of teacher but nothing more.	4, 5, 6, 8	1, 2, 5	2.5	2.5	2.3	2.5	3.0
2	3 min. 30 sec.	Secondary Math	Teacher showed low reserves of energy. "Good" is not praise but sarcasm. Low Respect: "Are you sick today?" Student response forced, negative.	4, 5, 6, 7, 8	1, 2, 5, 9	1.3	1.3	1.5	1.0	2.0
3	1 min. 30 sec.	Elementary Health (Breakfast) Foods	Success Promotion and Student Involvement. Teacher accepts answers and praises. She is "with" her students. Directions (Flanders' 6) are "calling on" students to answer.	2, 3, 4, 5, 6, 8, 9	1, 2, 5, 9	3.5	3.5	3.7	3.5	3.7

MASTER RATINGS FOR STUDENT INVOLVEMENT TRAINING TAPE (Cont'd)

Segment	Approximate Time	Level-Subject	Comments	Flanders' Category	Cognitive Category	Meaning	Genuineness	Success Promotion	Respect	Student Involvement
4	3 min.	Elementary Words	Low on all process scales. Teacher punishes verbally. Tone quality of students is monotone, subdued.	4, 5, 6, 7 8	1, 2, 5, 9	1.5	1.7	1.5	1.5	2.0
5	4 min.	Elementary Science	Class is completely student oriented. Teacher relates lesson to students at a very high cognitive level. Excellent example of Respect: "No, I believe you . . . ."	2, 3, 4, 5, 8, 9	1, 2, 4, 5, 6, 7, 8, 9	4.5	4.5	4.5	5.0	5.0
6	2 min.	Secondary Social Studies	Uses praise words. Accepts student ideas. Responds to feelings of students but without using feeling words. Students have high initiative.	2, 3, 4, 5, 8, 9	1, 2, 4, 5, 7, 9	3.3	3.5	3.5	3.5	3.3

MASTER RATINGS FOR STUDENT INVOLVEMENT TRAINING TAPE (Cont'd)

Segment	Time Approximate	Level-Subject	Comments	Flanders' Category	Cognitive Category	Meaning	Genuineness	Success Promotion	Respect	Student Involvement
7	3 min.	Secondary History	Low energy level of teacher. Teacher fills up time with his low level usage of time. Student resistance shown: "What page?" "Explain in simple terms." Good example of little attention to cues.	5, 9, 10	1, 6, 10	1.3	1.3	1.7	1.5	2.0
8	3 min.	Secondary Social Studies	Some praise. Some involvement elicited. One confrontation (Flanders' 7) on segment. No proper base laid for it.	2, 4, 5, 7, 8, 9	1, 2, 4, 5, 7, 9	3.0	3.0	2.7	3.0	3.0
9	2 min.	Elementary Science (Communication)	Teacher accepts all answers. Allows students to discuss. Students are eager to participate, exploring new ideas within subject area.	2, 4, 5, 8, 9	1, 2, 4, 5, 7, 9	3.3	3.7	3.7	3.7	3.7

MASTER RATINGS FOR STUDENT INVOLVEMENT TRAINING TAPE (Cont'd)

Segment	Time Approximate	Level-Subject	Comments	Flanders' Category	Cognitive Category	Meaning	Genuineness	Success Promotion	Respect	Student Involvement
10	2 min.	Elementary Reading	Good example of low Genuineness. Contrast "teaching" voice throughout segment with last statement on segment.	2, 4, 5, 6 8	1, 2, 5, 9	2.5	2.5	2.5	2.5	2.7
11	3 min.	Secondary Science	Excellent thinking stimulated. Teacher uses mild words to demonstrate feelings. Accepts and responds to all of his students' questions. Students ask good questions.	2, 3, 4, 5, 8, 9	1, 2, 3, 4, 5, 6, 7, 8 9	3.5	3.5	3.7	3.5	3.7

The three basic tapes used in the rater training are:

1. Flanders' and Cognitive Training Tape
2. Meaning Training Tape
3. Student Involvement Training Tape

Copies of these training tapes are located at:

Juvenile Problems Research Section
Applied Research Branch
National Institute of Mental Health
5600 Fishers Lane
Rockville, MA 20852

National Consortium for Education
P. O. Box 64952
Dallas, TX 75206
Telephone: (214) 692-9726

Mrs. Martha Willson
Northeast Louisiana University
College of Education
Monroe, LA 71201

SECTION IV REFERENCES

Aspy, D. N. Maslow and teachers in training. **The Journal of Teacher Education,** 1969, **20,** 362-369.

Aspy, D. N. Toward **A technology for humanizing education.** Champaign, Ill.: Research Press, 1972.

Aspy, D. N. The effects of teacher-offered conditions of empathy, positive regard and congruence upon student achievement. **Florida Journal of Educational Research,** 1969, **2,** 39-48.

Aspy, D. N. (Ed.). **The self in school.** New York: Simon & Schuster, 1971.

Aspy, D. N. Reaction to Carkhuff's Articles. **The Counseling Psychologist,** 1972, **3,** 35-41.

Aspy, D. N. **A practical psychology for practical educators.** Dallas, Texas: Dynamic Press, 1973.

Aspy, D. N. The relationship between selected student behavior and the teachers use of Interchangeable Responses. **The Humanist Educator,** 14 (1); September, 1975.

Aspy, D. N. An interpersonal approach to humanizing education. Chapter in **Phi Delta Kappa's** Annual Research Series, In press, 1977.

Aspy, D. N., Black, B. and Roebuck, F. N. The relationship of teacher offered conditions of respect to behaviors discussed by Flanders' Interaction Analysis. **Journal of Negro Education,** 1972, **61,** 370-376.

Aspy, D. N. and Kratochvil, D. (Eds.). **Carkhuff: The HRD Model In Education.** Baton Rouge, La.: Southern University Press, 1973.

Aspy, D. N. and Roebuck, F. N. An investigation of the relationship between student levels of cognitive functioning and the teacher's classroom behavior. **Journal of Educational Research,** 1973, **65,** 365-368.

Aspy, D. N. and Roebuck, F. N. From humane ideas to humane technology. **Education,** 1974, **95,** 163-171.

Aspy, D. N. and Roebuck, F. N. A discussion of the relationship between selected student behavior and the teacher's use of interchangeable responses. **Humanistic Education,** 1975, **14,** 3-10.

Aspy, D. N. and Roebuck, F. N. The relationship of teacher-offered conditions of meaning to behaviors described by Flanders' Interaction Analysis. **Education,** 1975, **95,** 216-222.

Aspy, D. N. and Roebuck, F. N. **Research summary: Effects of training in interpersonal skills.** Washington, D. C.: N.I.H., 1975.

Aspy, D. N., Roebuck, F. N., Willson, M. A. and Adams, O. B. **Interpersonal skills training for teachers.** Washington, D. C.: N.I.H., 1974.

Association for Supervision and Curriculum Development, NEA. **Life Skills in School and Society,** prepared by the ASCD Yearbook Committee. Louis J. Rubin, chairman, and editor. Washington, D. C.: National Education Association, 1969.

Belter, E. K., Weber, W. A. and Amidon, E. J. **Classroom Interaction Newsletter,** December, 1965, p. 9

Berenson, B. G. and Mitchell, K. M. **Confrontation.** Amherst, Mass.: Human Resource Development Press, 1974.

Berenson, B. G. and Carkhuff, R. R. **Sources of gain in counseling and psychotherapy,** New York: Holt, Rinehart & Wilson, 1967.

Berenson, S. R., Carkhuff, R. R., Berenson, D. H. and Pierce, R. M. **The Do's and Don'ts of Teaching.** Amherst, Mass.; Human Resource Development Press, 1977.

Bills, R. E. Helpful people. Mimeographed paper presented to Kentucky ASCD, October, 1964.

Bloom, B. S., (Ed.). Englehart, M. D., Furst, E. J., Hill, W. H. and Krathwohl, D. R. **A taxonomy of educational objectives: Handbook I, The cognitive domain.** New York: Longmans, Green, 1965.

Bowers, N. E. and Soar, R. S. Influence of teacher personality on classroom interaction. **Journal of Experimental Education,** 1962, **30,** 309-311.

Brown, G. I. Which pupil to which classroom climate? **Elementary School Journal,** February, 1960.

Bucheimer, A. Development of ideas about empathy. **Journal of Counseling Psychology,** 1963, **10,** 61-70.

Buhler, J. H. and Aspy, D. N. (Eds.). **Physical Health for Educators.** Denton, Texas: North Texas State University Press, 1975.

Building a classroom climate for learning. **NEA Journal,** December, 1961, **50,** 34-8.

Campbell, Jr. R. Cognitive and affective process development and its relation to a teacher's interaction ratio. Unpublished doctoral thesis, New York University, 1968.

Carkhuff, R. R. Toward explaining success or failure in interpersonal learning experiences. **Personnel and Guidance Journal,** 1966, **44** 723-728.

Carkhuff, R. R. Training in the counseling and therapeutic process: Requiem or reveille? **Journal of Counseling Psychology,** 1966, **13,** 360-367.

Carkhuff, R. R. **Helping and Human Relations.** New York: Holt, Rinehart & Winston, 1969.

Carkhuff, R. R. **The art of Helping III.** Amherst, Mass.: Human Resource Development Press, 1972, Third edition, 1977.

Carkhuff, R. R. **The development of human resources.** New York: Holt, Rinehart & Winston, 1971.

Carkhuff, R. R. and Berenson, B. F. **Teaching as Treatment.** Amherst, Mass.: Human Resource Development Press, 1967.

Carkhuff, R. R., Berenson, D. H. and Pierce, R. M. **The Skills of Teaching: Interpersonal skills.** Amherst, Mass.: Human Resource Development Press, 1977.

Carkhuff, R. R. and Pierce, R. M. **Teacher as person.** Washington, D. C.: National Education Association, 1975.

Christenson, C. M. Relationships between pupil achievement, pupil affect-need, teacher warmth and teacher premissiveness. **Journal of Educational Psychology,** June, 1960, **51,** 169-74.

Clements, M. Research and incantation: A comment. **Phi Delta Kappan,** October, 1968, p. 107.

Cogan, M. L. The behavior of teachers and the productive behavior of their pupils. **Journal of Experimental Psychology,** 1958, **27,** 89-124.

Combs, A. W. (Ed.) **Perceiving, behaving, becoming.** ASCD Yearbook, 1962, Washington, D. C.: Association for Supervision and Curriculum Development, 1962.

Combs, A. W. and Soper, D. L. Helping relationships as described by good and bad teachers. **Journal of Teacher Education,** 1963, **14,** 64-67.

Cooley, W. W. and Lohnes, P. R. **Multivariate procedures for the behavioral sciences.** New York: John Wiley and Sons, 1962.

Cronbach, L. J. **Educational psychology.** New York: Harcourt, Brace and World, 1963.

Crosby, G. and Blatt, B. Attention and mental retardation. **Journal of Education,** February, 1968, **150,** 67-81.

Davidson, R. L. The effects of an interaction analysis system on the development of critical reading in elementary school children. **Classroom Interaction Newsletter,** May, 1968, p. 13.

Della Piana, G. M. and Gage, N. L. Pupils' values and validity of the MEAL. **Journal of Educational Psychology,** 1955, **46,** 167-178.

Dixon, W. R. and Morse, W. C. Prediction of teaching performance: Empathic potential. **Journal of Teacher Education,** 1961, **12,** 322-329.

Editorial introduction to Concept of attention in education. (D. I. Mostofsky). **Journal of Education,** February, 1968, **150,** 3-91.

Fisher, R. A. and Yates, F. **Statistical tables for biological, agricultural and medical research,** 6th Ed. Edinburgh: Oliver and Boyd, Ltd., 1964.

Flanders, N. A. **Interaction analysis in the classroom - A manual for observers.** Michigan: University of Michigan, 1965, p. 7.

Flanders, N. A. **Teacher influence, pupil attitudes and achievement.** U. S. Department of Health, Education and Welfare, Cooperative Research Monograph No. 12. Washington, D. C.: Government Printing Office, 1965.

Furst, N. and Amidon, E. J. Teacher-pupil interaction patterns in the elementary school. **In Interaction analysis: Theory, research, and application.** Massachusetts: Addison-Wesley Publishing Co., 1967, pp. 167-75.

Gage, N. L. **Handbook of research on teaching.** Chicago: Rand-McNally, 1963.

Garrison, J. C., Kingston, A. J. and McDonald, A. S. **Educational Psychology,** New York: Appleton-Century-Crofts, 1964.

Hicks, L. H. A pilot Human Relations Program at Southern University. **Peabody Journal of Education,** 53 (1), October, 1975.

Hicks, L. H. and Buhler, J. H. Schools children like: What do they say about them? **Educational Leadership,** 1977, 34 **5,** 388-397.

Jackson, P. W. **Life in Classrooms.** New York: Holt, Rinehart and Winston, 1958, p. 111.

Jackson, P. W. and Belford, E. Educational objectives and the joys of teaching. **The School Review,** 1965, **73,** 267-291.

Joslin, L. C. Knowledge and counseling competence. **Personnel and Guidance Journal,** 1965, 43, 8, 790-795.

Jourad, S. M. **The transparent self: Self-disclosure and well-being.** Princeton, N. J.: Van Nostrand Co., Inc. 1964.

LeBenne, W. D. and Greene, B. I. **Educational implication of self-concept theory.** Pacific Palisades, California: Goodyear Publishing Co., 1968, p. 29.

Lahaderne, H. M. Attitudinal and intellectual correlates of attention: A study of four sixth-grade classrooms. **Journal of Educational Psychology,** October, 1958, 59, 320-4.

LaShier, W. S. An analysis of certain aspects of the verbal behavior of student teachers of eighth-grade students participating in a SSCS laboratory block. **Dissertation Abstracts,** June, 1966, pp. 7-168.

Lewis, W. A. and Wigel, W. Interpersonal understanding and assumed similarity. **Personnel and Guidance Journal,** 1964, **43,** (2), 155-158.

Marsh, J. E. Development report-systematic observation of instruction behavior. USAF: Personality Training Research Center Development 1956, No. AFPTRC TN 56-52.

McKeachie, W. J. Motivation, teaching methods and college learning. Nebraska Symposium on Motivation, Lincoln: University of Nebraska Press, 1961, p. 111-146.

McKenna, B. H. School staffing patterns and pupil interpersonal behavior: Implications for teacher education. Burlingame: California Teachers Association, 1967, p. 27.

Melton, C. The helping relationship in college reading clinics. **Personnel and Guidance Journal,** 1955, **18,** 925-928.

Menninger, W. C. Mental health in our schools. **Education Leadership,** 1950, 7, 520.

Metfessel, N. S., Michael, W. B. and Kirsner, D. A. Instrumentation of Bloom's and Krathwohl's taxonomies for the writing of educational objectives. **Psychology in the Schools,** 1969, 7 (3), 227-231.

Moore, J. J. Application of an attention theory to retardate work learning. **Teachers College Journal,** Novermber, 1963, **35,** 49-50.

Morgan, H. G. How to facilitate learning. **NEA Journal,** 1960, **49,** 54-55.

Mostofsky, D. I. Concept of attention in education. **Journal of Education,** February, 1968, **150,** 3-91.

Neill, A. S. **Summerhill.** New York: Hart Publishing Co., 1960, p. 29.

Nelson, L. Teacher leadership: An empirical approach to analyzing teaching behavior in the classroom. **Journal of Teacher Education,** Winter, 1966, p. 425.

Olden, C. Adult empathy with children. **Psychoanalytic Study of the Child,** New York: International University Press, 1953, 8, 115.

Patterson, C. H. Note on the construct validity of the concept of empathy. **Personnel and Guidance Journal,** 1962, **40,** 803-806.

Powell, E. V. Teacher behavior and pupil achievement. **Classroom Interaction Newsletter,** May, 1968, p. 24.

Prescott, D. **The child in the educative process.** New York: McGraw-Hill, 1957.

Purkey, W. W. **Self-concept and school achievement,** Englewood Cliffs, N. J.: Prentice-Hall, 1970.

Reed, H. B. Effects of teacher warmth. **Journal of Teacher Education,** September, 1961, **12,** 330-4.

Roebuck, F. N. Human thoughts and humane procedures - effective behavior. **Peabody Journal of Education,** 1975, **53,** 9-14.

Roebuck, F. N. Humanistic education from a human resources development viewpoint. Chapter in **Phi Delta Kappa's** Annual Research Series, In press, 1977.

Roebuck, F. N. and Aspy, D. N. Grade-level contributions to the variance of Flanders' Interaction Categories. **Journal of Experimental Education,** 1974, **42,** 86-92.

Roebuck, F. N., Aspy, D. N., Sadler, L. L. and Willson, M. A. **Maintaining reliability.** Washington, D. C.: N.I.H., 1975.

Roebuck, F. N. and Aspy, D. N. **Response surface analyses.** Washington, D. C.: N.I.H., 1975.

Roebuck, F. N. and Aspy, D. N. The principal's interpersonal skills make a difference. **Elementary School Principal,** In press, 1977.

Rogers, C. R. **Client-Centered Therapy.** Boston: Houghton Mifflin, 1951.

Rogers, C. R. **Freedom to learn.** Columbus, Ohio: Charles E. Merrill Co., 1969.

Rogers, C. R. The interpersonal relationship: The core of guidance. **Harvard Educational Review,** 1962, **32,** 416-429.

Rogers, C. R. The necessary and sufficient conditions of therapeutic personality change. **Journal of Consulting Psychology,** 1957, **22,** 95-110.

Rogers, C. R. **On becoming a person.** Boston: Houghton Mifflin, 1961.

Rogers, C. R., Gendlin, E. T., Kiesler, D. and Truax, C. B. **The Therapeutic relationship and its impact.** Madison, Wisconsin: University of Wisconsin, 1967.

Ryans, D. R. Inventory estimated teacher characteristics as covariants of observer assessed pupil behavior. **Journal of Educational Psychology,** 1961, **52,** 91-97.

Samuels, S. J. Attentional process in reaching: The effect of pictures on the acquisition of reading responses. **Journal of Educational Psychology,** December, 1967, **58,** 337-42.

Siegel, A. W. Variables affecting incidental learning in children. **Child Development,** December, 1967, **39,** 957-68.

Siegel, A. W. and Corsini, J. A. Attentional differences in children's incidental learning. **Journal of Educational Psychology,** February, 1969, **60,** 65-70.

Skinner, B. F. **The technology of teaching.** New York: Appleton-Century-Crofts, 1968, pp. 57-58.

Smith, B. O. Conceptual framework for analysis of classroom social interaction: Comments on four papers. **Journal of Experimental Education,** June, 1962, **30,** 325-6.

Soar, R. S. Effects of teachers' classroom methods and personality on pupil learning. **High School Journal,** May, 1961, **44,** 288-92.

Soar, R. S. Pupil needs and teacher-pupil relationships: Experiences needed for comprehensive reading. **In Interaction analysis: Theory, research, and application.** Massachusetts: Addison-Wesley Publishing Co., 1967, pp. 243-50.

Soar, R. S. The study of presage-process-product relationships: Implications for classroom process measurement. Educational Research Association, Los Angeles, California, February, 1968, p. 8-9.

Spauling, R. L. **Achievement, creativity, and self-concept correlates of teacher-pupil transactions in elementary schools.** U. S. Office of Education, Cooperative Research Report No. 1352. Urbana: University of Illinois, 1963.

Stabler, E. What is this thing called love? **Peabody Journal of Education,** May, 1960, **37,** 338.

Stansfield, R. N. Human side of teaching. **Peabody Journal of Education,** May, 1961, **38,** 345-50.

Stephens, J. M. **The psychology of class-room learning.** New York: Holt, Rinehart and Winston, 1965.

Thelen, A. H. One small head. **Journal of Teacher Education,** 1961, **12,** 401-406.

Thurman, H. Putting yourself in another's place. **Childhood Education,** February, 1962, **38,** 359-60.

Traverse, R. M. **Essentials of learning,** New York: MacMillan, 1963.

Truax, C. B. and Carkhuff, R. R. **Toward effective counseling and psychotherapy.** Chicago: Adline, 1967.

Weber, W. A. Teacher behavior and pupil creativity. **Classroom Interaction News-letter,** May, 1968, p. 34.

Willis, N. **The guinea pigs after 20 years.** Columbus, Ohio: Ohio State University, 1961.